The Busy Person's Guide to British History

By
Jem Duducu

Second edition

This book is sold subject to the condition that it shall not, by way of trade or otherwise be lent, resold, hired out, or otherwise circulated without the prior consent of the author.

First published 2013

Second edition 2014

The Busy Person's Guide to British History

Contents

Introduction

Chapter 1 (14-31)
Well you've got to start somewhere

Chapter 2 (32-58)
Invaders with Attitude

Chapter 3 (59-84)
1066 the tale of 2 brothers

Chapter 4 (85-103)
A man called Henry

Chapter 5 (104- 116)
The Endless War Part I: the Unwinnable Civil War

Chapter 6 (117-136)
The Endless War Part II: England Goes on Crusade

Chapter 7 (137-165)
The Endless War Part III: the Brief Unification of Britain

Chapter 8 (166-186)
The Endless War part IV: Armageddon

Chapter 9 (190-221)
The Endless War Part V: The Problem with Consistency

Chapter 10 (222-232)
The Endless War part VI: It ends! Sort of

Chapter 11 (233-246)
People Power

Chapter 12 (247-263)
The Last Civil War

Chapter 13 (264-282)
Empire

Chapter 14 (283-295)
Britain's First World War also known as the Seven Years War

Chapter 15 (296-313)
Britain's Second World War also known as The Napoleonic Wars

Chapter 16 (314-331)
Britain's Third World War also known as The Great War

Chapter 17 (332-341)
Britain's Fourth World War also known as World War II

Conclusion

Introduction

There are a few problems with history. The first and most important one is that we view it the wrong way round. Think for a moment about tomorrow: it is just 24 hours away and yet it is as unknowable as 100 years from now. Looking the other way however and it's a very different story. We can see the cause and effect of everything from wars to economic decisions made by parliaments. It is said that hindsight is always 20/20 and that's never truer than in bad history.

There was a part of me as a child that thought, "Why did Hitler bother?" He was always going to lose. And I don't think I'm the only one who has thought that while reading history. The stories sit there rarely changing and then can feel predictable. "Oh Napoleon's off to invade Russia, that'll end badly for him." We of course know that now, but in both Hitler and Napoleon's case it was far from obvious at the time; indeed in both cases it took the super human sacrifices of the Russian people (and other Soviet ethnicities in the case of World War 2) to turn back the tide of military aggression.

So this is a plea to do your best not to pre-empt things because just as you have no idea what tomorrow may bring, neither did any of the people who had to make earth shattering decisions in their day.

The second issue is patterns. Psychologists have shown time and time again that humans are very good at finding patterns, even when there isn't one to be found. The reason for this is apparently evolutionary. It's better to put the shadows of a tree together and think you see a tiger and promptly run away from nothing, than never seeing the tiger in the tree and turning into its lunch.

This same issue plagues history. While undeniably some events led to further issues, some things are far vaguer. Take for example the issue of the industrial revolution. Why did it happen in this fairly insignificant country on the edge of Europe, as opposed to France or the Ottoman Empire or imperial China? I have read it was due to the demands of the Royal Navy, or that it was due to the growing freedom of trade and the comparative liberal society of Britain, or that it was pressures on population combined with scientific breakthroughs. There are many theories, some more robust than others, but the ultimate answer has to be "nobody knows for sure". But happen it did and it led to an unhealthy advantage for this small rain- swept island nation for a good century or so.

And yet this search for patterns or perhaps more accurately, purpose, leads to this idea of everything moving in one direction. This is highly inaccurate. History is a series of stories plucked from the maelstrom of the human condition. It was no more inevitable that Britain would break from the Catholic faith anymore than England would win the FIFA World Cup in 1966. It is only with hindsight that these things look preordained and are turned into a summarised narrative. I am amazed at the fractal nature of history in that the deeper you look the more you find. For example you can buy a book on the Seven Years War in the 18th century. However I have read the excellent *1759 by Frank McLynn* which is 392 pages concentrating on one pivotal year of that war. Indeed one of the events he discusses is the capture of Quebec, which in turn can generate books of 300-400 pages just on that one event.

The messiness of history as it unfolds is worth remembering. For example it is singularly unhelpful to refer to the dynastic wars between England and France in the 14th and 15th centuries as The Hundred Years War. No contemporary thought of it as the same war and it went through very different phases. One of the key issues that pops up again and again in British history is the fact that as soon as you have to fight for land that is legally yours, you've ultimately lost already. As unpalatable as it may sound to a French reader, King Henry VI of England was the only man to have a full and correct coronation in England and France and his right to rule both countries was as water tight as it gets in the middle ages but that didn't stop the internecine warfare from continuing. However the issue that it was somehow inevitable that England would lose in France was by no means a done deal at any point between 1066 and 1453, and that is a very long span of human life.

The next key point on the topic of patterns is that some parts of the jigsaw of our past are resurrected more often than others. You want a book on World War 2? How many do you want? Napoleonic Wars? Certainly sir, which angle of the conflict do you want to read about? Roman history? Oh where to start? However go off the beaten track just by a little bit and things get sparse very quickly. Tamerlane was probably the greatest general that ever lived, roughly contemporary with Edward III and Richard II; he never lost a battle in thirty years of campaigning. This is a man who was the only person in history to capture an Ottoman Sultan in battle. He also ventured (and conquered) as far afield as Georgia and Delhi. Most of this was done with him being paralysed down one side of his body. The man deserves to be remembered in the same breath as Alexander the Great or Genghis Khan. There are however very few books on him. Aethelstan, the first king of England and indeed the first ruler of Britain, is a man almost utterly forgotten to all but the mustiest of history lecturers, with a paucity of books about a great man in fascinating times. This book will also help to resurrect some of these forgotten people (sadly not Tamerlane he doesn't enter into British history). Very few people remain well known much beyond their own lifetime while a few others have been remembered in ways that would have surprised them.

This leads onto the point of context. While it is obvious that leaders a thousand years ago could have their heads turned by some busty young blonde just as easily as their modern counterparts, sometimes they acted in ways it is hard for the modern mind to fathom. The danger here is to start using modern standards to judge past actions. A common mistake is to describe an event as an atrocity or war crime.

This is at best unhelpful and at worst, deliberately misreading the situation. I am not saying terrible acts of violence didn't happen. What I am saying is you have to judge these events by the level of outrage at the time. Let's take a very contentious person in British history, Oliver Cromwell. Firstly it must be noted that some acts of violence associated with him are folklore: getting soldiers to strap babies to their chests to stop the locals from firing, is a powerful and mythical image. Think for a moment about the logistics of this. Did the New Model army raid villages for babies; put them on carts and keep feeding them so they could try this tactic in a future battle? On the morning of the battle, how did they strap the babies to themselves? Once the artillery and muskets started up, how distracting is a crying, thrashing baby strapped inches from your face? Babies aren't bullet or blade proof; wouldn't you prefer to wear armour? Also humans generally find it very hard to be cruel to infants. We are all hard-wired to be gentle with them and the idea that the troops were all so psychopathic as to break this basic rule of humanity is hard to swallow. What it does do is underline the bitter feelings that real massacres had on the local population that this myth is still repeated hundreds of years later.

If there's one country the Brits (and it wasn't just the "English") should hang their heads with shame over, it has to be Ireland. It was treated as a play thing for the rich, with scant regard for the indigenous population for the best part of 1,000 years. It wouldn't be inappropriate if everyone with a British passport going into the Republic of Ireland had to apologise before going through passport control- not that detonating bombs in Northern Ireland or mainland England is right either.

The point (and there is one coming) is that Cromwell was no different to any other contemporary general. The Republican period occurred at the tail end of the Thirty Years War in Europe, one of Europe's bloodiest. To put it in context, most Germans would have the gut feel that their country was more damaged by this 17th century conflict than World War 2. There were massacres and counter massacres between Protestants and Catholics, between Swedes, Germans, French and Swiss populations. Putting Cromwell's campaign in Ireland against the backdrop of what was accepted practice at the time, shows that he wasn't especially cruel and indeed, in mainland Europe he may have been despised for heading a regime that had carried out regicide, but he wasn't seen as particularly bloodthirsty. So I will try and judge people on the norms of their times, not ours.

Linked to this, I want to debunk the phrase "History is written by the winners", which is probably one of the most pointless phrases ever devised. It can be but it isn't on a regular basis. Indeed from virtually the start of chronicled historical events we get both sides, be it Babylon at war with Egypt, or the Greeks feuding with Persians. Getting both sides of the story is vital; and at times it is very hard to unpick the truth from two highly biased sources. It can sometimes be seductive to think that your country's writings are bound to be more accurate than some dubious foreign source. Sadly there are fibbers of all nationalities. Defeat lingers longer than any victory, seems to be an important lesson from history and events that are long forgotten in the "winners" country can become national scars to others. This should be remembered, as long-dead warriors who suffered against the odds are given a fresh coat of paint and used for new and usually dubious means. You will get a few examples during this book.

If you want to make the point that the life of the everyday person in Britain is far more affected by farming, or trade deficits or the introduction of certain taxes than almost any battle in history, you are right. It is odd that we tend to learn about many periods of history through royalty and what it was doing. We get almost fond or misty-eyed about long-dead kings who would never have spent a moment thinking about our peasant ancestors. They would have been generally aware of whether it was a good or bad year for harvests or tax returns, and occasionally kings would face revolts by the population at large, but we do tend to get distracted by the exotica of history.

Social history is absolutely more important than military or dynastic history but it has one unavoidable problem: it is dull, really, really dull. As much as I have tried to embrace the corn reform laws or get my head around how the crop rotation system was improved into modern agricultural methods, it was a thankless slog. So I pause here for a moment to say emphatically that the real history of any country is the story of the peasant class. Some of these people would, over many generations rise to the highest stations in the land. The vast majority never did. They were the corpses on the field of Crecy, or the annihilated villages of the Black Death, or the starved masses of the potato famine. That is the real history of Britain and not the one where Kings made daring decisions about war or the acquisition of foreign lands. However as I am hoping not to send my readers off to sleep, I will be avoiding it as much as possible. This book is not a very worthy study of the social history of Britain.

That final point is an important one when assessing the value of a history book. I once read a review of the very readable *The Hundred Years War by Desmond Seward* in the "Brief History" series. The last bit is the clue. It's a nicely manageable 268 page book, and yet one review said that it was a shame it didn't go into more detail. Well seeing the title of the series is "A Brief History", to therefore criticise the brevity is simply unfair. It's a bit like complaining that *Romeo and Juliet* is a poor play because there are no car chases. I ask that you judge this book against the goals of its author.

This is not a heavy and worthy research book; you should have gleaned that from the title. Instead this is a tour of some well known and not-so-well known events and people in British (OK, largely English) history. It's here to demystify a few common misconceptions and as history is ultimately a series of stories, I have tried to find important and interesting ones. Because this is definitely leaning on the light side of the "historyometer", I will not fill the end of this book with endless references to primary, secondary or tertiary source material. Basically if any chapter in this book inspires you to go further, I have sprinkled in a number of books for a more in-depth look at things (I have already mentioned two). I am aware this breaks a cardinal rule for non-fiction, but tough, my book my rules. Realistically how often do you read those last 20 pages of source materials? I mean really, between you and me? Now a days you can do most fact checking on Google or Wikipedia.

Chapter 1

Well you've got to start somewhere

And exactly where to start is hard. Some like to start with 55 BC and Julius Caesar's first invasion; others with the end of Roman Britain, and of course the other watershed date is 1066.

So let's really start at the beginning, in the Oldupai (it was called Olduvai) Gorge in modern day Tanzania. Here about 1.9 million years ago, apes got smarter and started to walk more effectively on two feet. Fast forwarding a considerable length of time to around 480,000 BC and arriving on the scene, is Britain's first evidence of habitation. "Boxgrove Man" from West Sussex was from a species of early humans called Homo heidelbergensis. Later still there are Neanderthal remains, but things go very quiet during the various ice ages and as most of Europe was under tens of meters of ice, it was likely that Britain wasn't permanently settled until the end of the ice age, about 10,000 years ago.

However let us think about the very first Britain. A jawbone of a Homo Sapien was discovered in Kents Cavern in Devon and was dated to the late Palaeolithic between 44-41,000 years ago. Consider that time frame. Most of this book will cover a little over a thousand years and yet this person lived forty millennia ago. If this book is about 300 pages then imagine a 12,000 page book to cover that time frame. He was also the country's first immigrant. Going back to Oldupai Gorge, we are ultimately all African immigrants.

The concepts of nations and borders are false, sometimes reinforced by changes of language, culture or religion, but the reality is that we are all the same and no country has a "special" people. For some rather hysterical British papers it's worth thinking about how we're all immigrants to this once desolate series of rocks. Even in the historical periods there were waves of immigration, sometimes quite violent invasions and nowadays I am glad we are dealing with a few illegal immigrants from Africa rather than having to run from Viking raiders. The name of the country Scotland comes from the Roman name for the Scoti, a generic term for overseas (largely Irish) raiders, so the Scots themselves are foreigners in their own land. If you are looking for the most ethnically pure race in Britain it's probably the Welsh and yet they get gently teased for being Welsh! Even after 1066 and before the Empire, British ports teemed with peoples from all over Europe and art, culture and language were shaped by these outside sources. I am however getting ahead of myself.

I myself was on a dig uncovering microliths and microburins from the Mesolithic era (about 8,000 years ago). These time frames cannot really be absorbed by the human mind. While sites in Eastern Turkey like Chatal Hoyuk and Gobekli Tepe have rewritten the history books showing that humanity did create small settlements and permanent structures as far back as 12,000 years ago (Stonehenge is about 5,000 years old, so is about halfway between us and these other sites), the reality however is that in North Western Europe for tens of thousands of years, the way we survived was as migrant hunter gatherers.

Life was tough; giant elk, cave bears, wolves and large boars were creatures that a small family of migrants would have treated with caution. Life was presumably brutal and short. Without agriculture and settlements you didn't know where your next meal was coming from and pregnancy could be a death sentence. However as we slowly learnt the tricks of civilisation, our achievements were dwarfed by the near east civilisations of the Babylonians and Egyptians. Indeed it is worth remembering that for most of our history, the vast majority of our history, we were a cultural, scientific and educational backwater.

Saying that, there are still many fascinating prehistoric sites in Britain. The Neolithic period is where agriculture and permanent settlements arrive in Britain. Of course one of the issues of putting a name to a stretch of time is again the human preoccupation with patterns. No contemporary sat down and told their son that the good old Mesolithic was over and it was time to face the fact that the Neolithic was here to stay. Indeed, just referring to any of these periods as "stone ages" is a misnomer. As archaeology has become more refined, there is far more evidence of the obvious truth that humans used whatever materials they could to survive and thrive. It is really from our much later perspective that we think our early ancestors were obsessed with stone.

One of my favourite pieces in the British Museum is a flint knife that the craftsman has made to look like it has a leather-stitched handle. This tells us that such genuine combinations once existed, but it can also be considered the world's first "knock off"- an inferior copy of a superior product.

Stonehenge to one side, there are many sites across Britain that show that no geographic area had a technological dominance over the other. Skara Brae in the Orkneys is roughly contemporary with Stonehenge and yet this is not a monument but a group of dwellings with stone houses where you can still see where people cooked and sat all those millennia ago. Grimes Graves on the Norfolk/Suffolk border is a Neolithic mine where there was an ancient industry of mining the flint and turning it into tools.

Some people find this all mysterious and you start getting talk of "ley lines" or "cosmic energies". I find them comforting, they show that humans really haven't changed much, from early jewellery – because everyone likes to look nice- to the aforementioned cheap and cheerful product (in this case a flint knife), rather than the more expensive name brand.

The New Age movement has somewhat hijacked prehistory in many countries and the best example is the robed Druids, who on the summer solstice, go to Stonehenge to worship. There is no evidence the druids either built or were in any way aware of Stonehenge. It is obviously a religious site and the Druids were the religious class of Celtic Briton, but the time separating Stonehenge and the Druids can be described in millennia. Furthermore, after the Romans wiped out the druids at Anglesey (which was their powerbase and nowhere near Stonehenge, which you would have thought would be their place for a last stand if it was the most important site of worship- a bit like the Jews defending the temple in Jerusalem). This means that genuine ancient druid traditions were lost forever and indeed the modern Druidic movement can't push their origins much beyond the 1700s. So while it's a matter of faith, as with a lot of areas of faith, the facts on the ground conflict with people's beliefs. The Druids have no more right to pray at Stonehenge than does an Archbishop.

Similarly we get Danu, the mother goddess and the sacred feminine being used a lot in pseudo history. It is true that there are many statues of the naked female form in prehistory, but what does it mean? We don't know. It is just as legitimate a theory that it could be an abstract statue of a future bride of a long forgotten king who wanted to remind everyone of her fertility, than it is a sign that Europe was awash with female priests who were wiped out by some early Christian misogyny. It could even be the Neolithic equivalent of an "adult" website. Back to the intro: "nobody knows for sure" and it's therefore wrong to ascribe a personal or modern agenda to an ancient artefact that is unlikely to have remained in its intended context.

So while prehistoric/Celtic Britain can sound exotic and mysterious, what we can say is that while literacy and writing have yet to arrive in Britain until the Roman period, it is wrong to think of the Romans as somehow civilising Britain. It had by the 1st century BC become a well-ordered group of societies that we can at least understand. There were kings, forts, priests, trade, craftsman, warriors and art. There was evidence of social and trade connections to the continent, too. Doesn't sound much different to Henry VIII's, times does it?

Tom Holland is one of the best popular historians in the English language. His book on the Roman world called *Rubicon* is a vivid and wonderfully salacious account of Rome's rise, focusing on mainly its change from Republic to Imperial dictatorship. In it he reminds us all that in the ancient world the centre of the world was the Mediterranean. This civilised lake was in turn surrounded by all the lands in the world and then wrapped around that, the outer sea. A bit like a global sandwich- water, a filling of land and then more water. So to have an island in this outer zone of water was a very exciting and slightly terrifying prospect. Tom Holland points out that Caesar landing in Britain, from an ancient point of view, was like man landing on the moon in the modern era.

Britain in 55 BC was "other" or alien to the great civilisations to the South and East. It has already been noted that it had a culture very similar to parts of mainland Europe and it was because of this that the Romans came. Caesar realised that he was going to have difficulty fully subjugating Gaul if leaders could sail off to those mysterious islands just on the horizon.

The Southern tribes of Britain didn't really know what hit them either. To keep the space analogy going, it was as if they were experiencing an alien invasion from some unstoppable military force. But stop it did and strangely it went away. However the next year it came back bigger and badder. Ultimately the reason why Julius Caesar failed to capture Britain was that he had underestimated its size. His supply lines were too long and his resources too meagre to stamp his authority permanently. To his credit he quit while he was ahead and went off to install himself as the dictator of Rome and the rest as they say, is history.

As I described in the introduction, some areas of history have a glut of books. The Roman era is one of them. Want to learn more? Start with *Rubicon* and go from there however I am now going to fast forward through Claudius and co and get us to the other side of the Roman occupation of Britain.

So to the "Dark Ages", which will be the only time I will use that phrase. Groups love to use past events to meet present day needs. There is a politicising of history that is synonymous with history itself. The above phrase is a bit of that politicising, created when British scholars were in love with the classics and were poor at archaeology. Therefore when things went quiet in written history the default position was that everyone was a barbarian scrabbling through the mud, waiting to read Plato again. There can be no denying that the literary sources are meagre. Gildas and Bede are about it for the early Anglo-Saxon period buildings and art changed to what some may consider a cruder style, but the contemporaries did not consider themselves ignorant, nor were they isolated from the outside world.

Archaeology has done much to remedy the situation. Take the two most famous early Anglo-Saxon finds: Sutton Hoo and the Staffordshire

Hoard. Ever since I was a child, I have been bowled over by the helmet from Sutton Hoo, the remains of which can be seen in the Britain Museum. To me it exudes the glamour of the distant past. My mother noticed this fascination early on as every time I went there I would return with a post card or jigsaw with that ghostly face staring back at you. It helps that the fragments have been put on some sort of clay, making it looked like it has just been teased from the soil. Staring into the blank eye socks on the face mask is to gaze into the very face of history. I prefer it to the glistening replica of what it would have looked like in its heyday.

The point is that when you look at the craftsmanship of the garnet work in the Staffordshire Hoard and the Sutton Hoo no one can deny that these are talented artists, the match of anyone in the ancient or indeed the modern world. So instead let us refer to the period post 400 AD - 1066 as the Anglo-Saxon era and further split it between early (400-800) and late (Post 800 - 1066). The sectioning is a little arbitrary but this roughly 650 year period is the longest period in British history and is a time of great innovation and terrible violence.

At this point it's worth pausing to think of that other idea that's been associated with Britain for so long- Christianity. In the modern world where church attendance in Western Europe is on the steady wane, the relevance of religion in society can be over looked. To the faithful it can sometimes be overstated but it is important, particularly in understanding why many famous people acted in certain ways. Briefly going to 1066, it's interesting to note that while William Duke of Normandy in hindsight would pretend his claim to the throne of England was water tight, he successfully petitioned the Pope and got a papal blessing for his venture, complete with a holy papal banner that was there fluttering by the Norman troops at the Battle of Hastings to remind them that God was on their side. This is a little ironic because from the point of view of the English, they were faithful to Rome and had no reason to think God wasn't on their side.

However the story of Christianity in Britain is not a simple one of an ignorant people waiting to hear the word from the Gospels, and then flinging away their old beliefs to be good Christians. How integrated Britain was to the Roman way of things is debateable; we're back to that phrase again, "nobody knows for sure". It is worth thinking of Britain as the very edge of the empire, and as Christianity became the official religion of their imperial masters, it's not wild speculation to say that some locals may have been actively Anti-Christian.

While Britain did face invasion from foreign pagans, it was never likely that the Angles, Jutes, Saxons and later Vikings, actually out-numbered the indigenous population and so to say that they somehow smothered Christianity in Britain is unlikely. What is more likely is that while they were believers, there were probably more that clung to the old beliefs. What we do know for sure is that Britain lost its faith, so much so that Pope Gregory the Great in the late 6th century AD had to reintroduce it and sent Augustine of Canterbury back to his homeland to remind all the pagans that there was one true God.

Going back to Sutton Hoo, about a generation on from Augustine's mission, we have a grand pagan ship burial. What is odd is that amongst the gold for the ethereal rowers of the ship, the swords and drinking horns, there are christening spoons with Saul and Paul written on them. There's also Byzantine silverware with crosses on them. The most interesting and least mentioned thing about the Sutton Hoo burial is that it isn't a burial. While the deceased's remains would have rotted away long ago, the 1939 excavation was thorough enough to spot the different coloured soil to work out the boat shape, so it would have been thorough enough to spot the body. They didn't, nor had the locals removed it because the site showed no signs of disturbance (mainly proven by all the gold still being there). So we have a pagan burial, with Christian aspects, and no body. Could it be that the deceased was buried elsewhere in a Christian ceremony? Even if he was (and that's pure speculation), it's not exactly a clear victory for Christianity, as the locals still felt the need to drag a massive ship from the river and fill it with expensive things.

Also while the King, possibly Raedwald, may have converted (and if it was Raedwald he was a

Bretwalda- an overlord of all the Kingdoms in England) it doesn't mean that all his subjects had converted too. Christianity in early Britain was then a tough sell and one the locals didn't instantly grab with both hands. However as time went by there can be no doubt that Pope Gregory's plans worked. Not only was the whole of the British Isles Christian by 700 AD, they took their lead from Rome. To call them Catholic Christians is to put modern concepts on their theology. They were Christian; in those days in the west you were either Christian or you weren't. It was a binary choice. The Pope was God's authority on earth and at that time this was never said with a smirk, or indeed a feeling that there could be another way.

After the Romans left Britain, things were quiet for awhile. It wasn't the case that as soon as the last pair of Legionary boots left the land, the country descended into chaos, but raiding began. It is at this point I will let the Anglo-Saxon chronicle pick up the story-

"A.D. 449. This year Marcian and Valentinian assumed the empire,
and reigned seven winters. In their days Hengest and Horsa,
invited by Wortigern, king of the Britons to his assistance,
landed in Britain in a place that is called Ipwinesfleet; first
of all to support the Britons, but they afterwards fought against

them. The king directed them to fight against the Picts; and
they did so; and obtained the victory wheresoever they came.
They then sent to the Angles, and desired them to send more
assistance. They described the worthlessness of the Britons, and
the richness of the land. They then sent them greater support.
Then came the men from three powers of Germany; the Old Saxons,
the Angles, and the Jutes. From the Jutes are descended the men
of Kent, the Wightwarians (that is, the tribe that now dwelleth
in the Isle of Wight), and that kindred in Wessex that men yet
call the kindred of the Jutes. From the Old Saxons came the
people of Essex and Sussex and Wessex. From Anglia, which has
ever since remained waste between the Jutes and the Saxons, came
the East Angles, the Middle Angles, the Mercians, and all of
those north of the Humber. Their leaders were two brothers,
Hengest and Horsa; who were the sons of Wihtgils; Wihtgils was
the son of Witta, Witta of Wecta, Wecta of Woden. From this
Woden arose all our royal kindred, and that of the Southumbrians

also.

*A.D. 455. This year Hengest and Horsa fought with Wortigern the
king on the spot that is called Aylesford. His brother Horsa
being there slain, Hengest afterwards took to the kingdom with
his son Esc.*

*A.D. 457. This year Hengest and Esc fought with the Britons on
the spot that is called Crayford, and there slew four thousand
men. The Britons then forsook the land of Kent, and in great
consternation fled to London.*

*A.D. 465. This year Hengest and Esc fought with the Welsh, nigh
Wippedfleet; and there slew twelve leaders, all Welsh. On their
side a thane was there slain, whose name was Wipped."*

So the foreign mercenaries turned on their masters and took over. This is exactly what happened to the Roman Empire at roughly the same time. The whole of Europe was getting used to new overlords. It's also worth noting that the pedigree of Hengest and Horsa goes back to Woden, a pagan god. Like all new royalty, the race was on to give yourself a pedigree and what better pedigree than to be descendants of a god? Most of the Anglo-Saxon Royalty link themselves back to Hengest and Horsa and later, Anglo-Saxon Kings manage to trace their ancestry back to prophets and key figures in the Bible. Therefore if this is to be believed, the House of Windsor has in them the blood of both Moses and a pagan hunting god. Watch out! There is this modern sense that the Anglo-Saxons were somehow "proper" English people and they are a group we should hark back to. While the second part may be valid, the first part is wrong. They were Germanic and Britain fought two world wars to avoid being run by Germans again.

It also mentions in these passages Wortigern "King of the Britons". The evidence of Wortigern is slim to say the least, but if we are to take it at roughly face value, then this would imply that most of the UK was still under the control of one centralist power. However the same entry indicates this was quickly broken up into a number of Kingdoms. The Kings or Mercia or Northumbria, Wessex and East Anglia would as happily declare war on each other as they would against foreign invaders. Likewise Scotland had warring groups of Gaels and Scots, and Wales had principalities that were never able to merge into one coherent kingdom. Ultimately their one unifying factor was their overall hatred of the English, but by then it was too late and their conquest was complete. This was not to happen though for centuries to come.

So the British Isles were a patchwork of small kingdoms and principalities vying for power. However, much of Europe was like this and after the collapse of the Western Roman Empire, there were no well-structured, multi-national organisations except the Church.

What these invaders did was reshape the country. That's where we get the name England – the Angles Land (or a better translation would be Deutschland). As all invaders do, they changed the focus of the country. Sutton Hoo looks a bit "Scandinavian" to the average person, and indeed that's because the culture of Anglo-Saxon England wasn't dissimilar to Northern Europe. So prior to the Anglo-Saxons, the Brits had been largely trading with and influenced by the South of Europe. Afterwards their focus went North and remained there for six centuries. It was not until 1066 that ultimately the link was broken.

The first great piece of English literature is Beowulf. Here's the first line-"Hwæt! We Gardena in geardagum". I think you can guess the language has moved on a bit since then. It makes Chaucer look positively modern. It roughly means, "Ho! Praise of the prowess of people-kings" of course. Exactly when the poem was written is hard to say- 8th century? What's interesting is it's a classic Scandinavian saga full of drinking halls, heroic deeds and brave warriors. It's from a family of epic poetry that can be traced from Iceland to Denmark. Like all sagas, it loves a good fight and like the early sagas it portrays Christianity as something to be suspicious about. This again goes back to the question of exactly how Christian was the early Anglo-Saxon period. It should also be pointed out that the story is set in Denmark, not England. What all of this underlines is that the people of Britain were part of a society that covered all of Northern Europe, so the language, laws and literature changed accordingly.

However after the initial invasions from Europe, things did calm into a knowable *status quo*. The Welsh raided the Mercian boarders when not fighting for power amongst their own Celtic princes, and the Scottish boarders were bandit country. After that the main kingdoms of England would sometimes go to war and occasionally an overlord (Bretwalda) would rule for a few years, but no unity existed. So as the new Anglo-Saxon society emerged, things settled down and life for the average peasant was as it always was until the date that should strike fear in every reader's mind- 793.

Reading the contemporary sources for 793 and you'd be forgiven to think that you were reading Lord of the Rings, or a particularly apocalyptic section of the Bible-

"A.D. 793. This year came dreadful fore-warnings over the land of
the Northumbrians, terrifying the people most woefully: these
were immense sheets of light rushing through the air, and

whirlwinds, and fiery, dragons flying across the firmament.
These tremendous tokens were soon followed by a great famine: and
not long after, on the sixth day before the ides of January in
the same year, the harrowing inroads of heathen men made
lamentable havoc in the church of God in Holy-island, by rapine
and slaughter."

Yes, you read that right. Not just the slaughter of monks, but actual dragons were sighted. You can see why I think more people should know about this period of history.

Chapter 2 Invaders with Attitude

The Vikings are a chance to show the story behind "history". There is actually a history of how the history of the Vikings has been portrayed. In the 19th century the Vikings were all winged and horned-helmeted psychos, quick to anger and slow to grasp anything civilised. Then in the mid 20th century academics thought this was all rather one dimensional (and by then, sadly, the whole horned-helmet thing had been disproved). So you get a flurry of papers pointing out what great sailors, explorers, traders and artists they were. This is all true and this is the period when you get the revelations that they got to North America before any other Europeans. It had been sitting in the chronicles for centuries but wasn't widely known. All cities in Ireland that are pre-modern were founded by the Vikings. Dublin is a slightly mangled version of the Viking name for Blackpool. They also founded Kiev, the capital of the Ukraine, as a trading post at the end of the Silk Road and served as bodyguards to the Byzantine Emperors.

This body of newer research went so far rehabilitating the Vikings that there was a need to refocus the story because they weren't just a bunch of traders, the roots of their fame in Europe had been lost, so there was a need to say, "Yes, they were excellent boat builders but they built those boats to kill and enslave as many people as they could lay their hands on". As already noted their sagas loved to dwell on the crows pecking at the body of slain enemies left after a huge battle- not exactly Aristotle. To paraphrase Christian teaching to get to Heaven, you have to be a good, decent, upstanding individual. To get to Valhalla you have to die a good death in battle. If you died of old age in a nice comfy bed you would end up in Helheim (Viking Hell). When a Viking lord died the would be burnt in a ship with his favourite living slave added to the funeral pyre so he could serve his master in the next world. Brotherly love wasn't high on the Viking agenda.

The reference to "dragons" is often explained by the masts of the Viking ships which were usually carved into some frightening shape or other. I am not so sure. I doubt anyone survived to recount what the ships looked like, and if they did, they would have other things to worry about than ship decoration. Instead I think it's a powerful indication of how shocking the arrival of the Vikings was. The Anglo-Saxons, once raiders of the British Isles themselves, were now being raided- and it was a terrifying.

A Viking long ship is a thing of beauty. Their curves make the whole structure exquisitely streamlined. It is simply pleasing to the eye and there are some magnificent examples at the Viking Ship Museum in Oslo. They are also remarkably practical. They are one of the few ships that are sea worthy in the rough waters of the North Sea and North Atlantic, and yet their shallow draft allows them to navigate rivers, perfect for exploration, and of course, raiding. An average ship would have had 30-40 oarsmen which are a compact fighting force, so even three or four ships arriving out of the blue could deal with almost any martial response thrown at them. Pre-modern communication was slow, so that by the time a raid had happened and the news had reached a local powerbase, before any response force arrived the Vikings were long gone with all the booty (including slaves) on their way back to Scandinavia.

It was the perfect criminal enterprise, smash and grab on a continental scale. In mainland Europe Charlemagne was at his peak of power and was crowned Emperor in Rome on Christmas Day 800 (a date deliberately chosen to be easy to remember for future generations. You have to respect that level of forward planning and ego.). He was the first person to unify most of the Western Roman Empire for over 3 centuries. France, the Low

Countries, Germany and Italy were his to rule, and yet with all this power, the end of his reign would be marred by his inability to deal with Vikings. If he couldn't solve the issue with his resources and talents, what chance did the disunited Kingdoms of Britain have?

Much has been made of the reasons for this era of Viking raids. There have been in-depth discussions about population densities and even potential over-fishing of the seas around Scandinavia, but putting aside all the hard work done on herring breeding,a I think the question is being asked the wrong way round. As already pointed out Europe had already gone through generations of raiding and invasion, Visigoths, Angles, Saxons, Magyars, the list goes on and on. The Vikings were just the newest people to the age-old family business of rape and pillage, and their boat technology made them particularly hard to catch.

Probably the strangest thing is that the hit and run tactics lasted for so long. Fifty years after the attack on Lindisfarne they were still at it, attacking pretty much anywhere they chose in the British Isles (Ireland included). The Anglo-Saxons had created some preventative measures in Burghs (where the modern word Borough comes from) which were fortified positions that locals could flee to. They were by no means highly complex fortifications, but as the Vikings weren't looking for a siege, it was a safe haven. These temporary refuges saved lives and livestock but didn't solve the problem because as suddenly as they would arrive, the

Vikings would disappear across the horizon again. They didn't seem to want to stay, unlike previous raiding groups.

The Scandinavian influence on Britain therefore can be traced from the end of the 8th century to mid-late 11th century, a period of around 300 years, far longer than the Tudor period or the Georgian era and yet to many people, they are seen as peripheral to British history. They weren't. The further North you go in the country, the more reminders there are particularly in place names. Any town ending in "by" is invariably of Viking derivation: it means "farm of". Grimsby is "the farm of Grim".

The Vikings particularly loved a monastery. Monasteries were (from the point of view of a pagan bandit) the perfect place for plunder and violent fun. The communion wine tended to be of good quality as it was meant to be the blood of Christ. To the Vikings however, it was some of the best booze they ever had. Then there were the gold and silver crosses and relics covered in expensive metals. You could get richer faster raiding monasteries than scrabbling through the straw of peasant huts. Finally, monks were in many ways the ultimate raiding attraction. They didn't fight, they had a habit of chanting in a strange language or standing behind gold crosses shouting, but they were never armed. There are more than a few references in the chronicles of the Vikings (how can I put this politely) "ravaging" monks. Well they say sailors will go for anything in a skirt. Finally and helpfully, as the monks were literate, they would make highly prized slaves back in the homeland. To a Viking, a holy monastery was a shopping mall full of lovely things.

Year after year they would appear on the edge of the horizon, their square sails announcing the arrival of violence. They raided with impunity at any time of the year. When local bands of warriors would make a stand they were inevitably slaughtered, otherwise everyone would grab what they could and run away if they had enough time. It was a miserable and uncertain time that was about to get worse.

If 793 is a lost date in British history then so is 865, the arrival of the Micel Here- The Great Army. This is a shame because it was another watershed year in British history, where the rules changed and the history of these islands would alter irrevocably.

While the raiding parties had grown larger and more frequent, they were all fundamentally coming to grab loot and go away. The fleet of Viking ships arriving in 865 was fundamentally different; they were here to conquer. They had three leaders- Guthrum, Halfdan and Ivar the Boneless. After writing that I have to state the obvious fact that some Scandinavian warriors had strange names- Sweyn Forkbeard, Harald Blue Tooth- as a civilisation they pretty much win the imaginative nicknames prize (my favourite I have yet to mention, but he'll be here soon). Ivar the Boneless is definitely one of the strangest and has led to much speculation as to how he earned this name. One theory is that he was somehow deformed, possibly with a brittle bone disease, but I am doubtful. In a society based on martial prowess I am sure a person with disabilities could overcome many of their restrictions but to have something that severe would limit them from ever attaining the level of a warlord. The other option is that he may have been a berserker.

Only a few societies have created a "berserker" class of warrior. Exactly what caused them to carry out seemingly inhuman acts of endurance in terms of strength and/or immunity from pain is a mystery. Another example is the Zulus who had certain warriors imbued with drugs so they wouldn't feel pain and fight fearlessly. However the English word "berserk" specifically comes from these Scandinavian berserker warriors who, according to various sources would dress in animal skins, be immune to normal weapons, would fight with inhuman stamina and courage, who would gnaw on their shields (some of the Lewis Chessmen in the British Museum show warriors doing just this), have fits and spasms, and froth at the mouth. The exact description varies but the consensus is that while fighting normal Viking warriors was terrifying, you really didn't want to be anywhere near the berserkers.

Was Ivar a berserker? Back to that phrase "nobody knows for sure", but he was a violent warlord in partnership with two other ruthless warlords at the head of a large Viking army looking to make Britain their home. Their staging post for invasion? East Anglia. East Anglia by the later 9th Century was the weakest of the four main kingdoms of England and it was ruled by King Edmund. Edmund is not a giant of history but his reaction to the invasion was to give him a claim to fame he probably would rather not have. He raised his army and met the Vikings in a battle, which he lost. Even worse for Edmund, the victory was so complete that he was captured by the Vikings. A common mistake to make about the Vikings, after reading about all their pillaging and disregard for the sanctity of Christian sites, is that they weren't religious. They were. It's just that their religious stipulations were almost the exact opposite of Christian sensibilities. If their gods had blessed their enterprise, a victory and the capture of an enemy king no less, what better way to thank the gods than to give them something back? How about a gift? A sacrifice? A human sacrifice? So the Vikings staked Edmund on the ground, alive and conscious, and carried out the rite of the blood eagle, disembowelling him and making the bloody entrails look like an eagle. It was a slow, painful and horrific way for a man to die and it was because Edmund made the ultimate sacrifice defending his people against pagans that he was made a saint. And where did they bury Saint Edmund? In the town of Bury St Edmunds (so starting a trend of unimaginative place names that are a definite pattern in British history).

So the invasion spread. Northumbria fell and then Mercia. As each kingdom capitulated the Vikings would install one of their own as the new ruler, with a new Scandinavian ruling elite under him. All that was left was Wessex, the most southerly and richest of kingdoms. Guthrum was now the leader of the Vikings and facing him was Aethelred King of Wessex, but it was his younger brother Alfred that the main defence of the realm was to fall to and by 871 the situation was looking far from great for Alfred.

Almost on his accession to the throne of Wessex two battles were waged; both were defeats and Alfred had to bribe the Vikings to retreat from Wessex to their winter quarters of London. This shows again that the Vikings were still interested in plunder as well as conquest. The Vikings spent the next few years enjoying their ill-gotten gains in the rest of England, but then appear out of nowhere in Wareham, Dorset. Alfred led an army to meet them and again cobbled together a peace treaty but the Vikings immediately broke it killing their hostages and moving to Exeter. Alfred caught up with them and finally got a bit of luck when the Viking relief fleet was dispersed by a storm. The Vikings agreed to a truce to withdraw out of Wessex and this time they did. Alfred was engaged in a war of defence and his success rate so far was patchy at best.

It is also worth briefly stating that another Viking invasion fleet arrived in Northern France at around this time. They were led by Rollo and these "North Men" conquered a considerable area of land that was to be given the name of Normandy. William

Duke of Normandy and first Norman King of England was a direct descendent of Rollo.

Then in January 878 Guthrum carried out a winter attack while Alfred was in Chippenham. Most European armies don't fight in the winter, troop movements tend to be limited and supplies for the troops would be sparse. However if you're brought up amongst the fjords of Scandinavia, a Southern English winter is mild and it was a master stroke. The Vikings are the only group ever to invade and settle the Outer Hebrides, this further illustrates the advantages of breeding. If you're coming from South to North you get to this cluster of islands in the North Sea and think "no way", but if you're coming the other way, I guess conditions look pretty tropical. The Wessex royal court was caught completely by surprise and many were killed or captured. Alfred himself only just managed to escape.

It's at this point we get the legend of Alfred and the burnt cakes. The basic story is that after fleeing for his life, Alfred arrives at a peasant house. He was bedraggled and had no finery to alert the woman who he was. She took pity on him and offered him a seat by the oven where she was baking bread. It was a nice warm place for a traveller to rest. However Alfred was either so tired that he fell asleep or so distracted about his worries that he wasn't paying attention to the bread and let it burn. The woman returned to find her bread burnt and scolded Alfred, who promptly left.

Did this happen? Almost certainly not. However it is a good parable of how bad things were for Alfred. The richest and most powerful man in England was on the run, and his realm was on the brink of conquest by an army that had conquered all before it.

Alfred set up a new base of operations in Athelney, a marsh area and therefore safe from surprise attack. Alfred had learned from his previous defeat. He was well organised with a good communications network, and he had many loyal followers who were just waiting for his leadership. From here Alfred sent messages out across the kingdom to raise an army.

Alfred turned the tables and in the same year (878) he met Guthrum at the battle of Heddington. From the chronicles it doesn't look like a subtle battle of fine manoeuvres, but the usual Anglo-Saxon strategy of forming a shield wall and then, with a combination of archers and infantry, fighting until inevitably the battle turned into a slugging match. This time Guthrum was pushed back and then his lines were broken; he was forced to flee to Chippenham's defences. It must have been with great pleasure that after a siege where the Vikings surrendered due to hunger, Alfred was able to receive capitulation at the very site where he had been ambushed.

Here Guthrum converted to Christianity. This is unlikely to have been genuine but in the symbolism of war and politics, the one god of the Christians had clearly trumped the pagan gods, so it made sense to acknowledge that. The basic treaty that was altered after subsequent victories for Alfred essentially split the modern country of England in half in a large diagonal. Everything north of the split was now Viking ruled "Dane Law". Everything south was Anglo-Saxon and ruled by the Kings of Wessex. In the space of just ten years or so, the *status quo* of realms in England that had lasted for centuries was to be lost forever. However the deal itself is a sign itself of both forward thinking pragmatism and backward looking traditions. Alfred was never "King of England", he had been King of Wessex and this deal expanded his lands considerably, but he had no sense of unifying all the lands of the Anglo-Saxons. He also must have realised that further conquests were beyond his resources, so what we have is a deal that is wholly practical.

Alfred the Great is the only British ruler to have the title "Great" and when you consider some of the other contenders for greatness, it's odd that a man who ruled about half of England would achieve this immortality. He wasn't just a warrior but oversaw an Anglo-Saxon renaissance of art, literature, law and in essence he marks the start of the very pinnacle of Anglo-Saxon England's achievements. He had turned back the tide, he had stopped the whole of Britain being ruled by Pagans again, and he had recovered from defeats more serious than most leaders can recover from.

After his victory, unsurprisingly, he founded a navy. Now he could catch raiders as they were coming in and with their easiest sites of raiding now under Viking rule, the raiders had further to go and could be intercepted more regularly. England was no longer easy pickings and while raiding still happened, and the English defenders didn't always win, for the first time the raiding was manageable.

So a solution had been worked out and this *status quo* would continue under Alfred's son, Edward the Elder, and then into his grandson Aethalstan's reign. For an excellent overview of the entire period post Roman to 1066, for me it has to be Sir Frank Stenton's *Anglo-Saxon England*. True it was written in the 1940's, but it's still a great overview, this is the first text book rather than popular history book I have mentioned, and like all academic tomes, it's worth bracing yourself for the almost masochistic insistence to make them as dry and unemotional as possible. There are examples of academic studies also being good reads but they are the exception, not the rule.

During the period of the early 10th century the Anglo-Saxon Chronicle is full of comments of how the Wessex army rode out to fight, capture a town or rebuild. The Dane Law area of England was being rolled back, not by a master stroke, but by steady progression up the country.

However it's Aethalstan who got the title of first king of England. Indeed he went one better. After going to war with Scotland in 927 he gets a treaty from the King of Scotland, Constantine II, and become overlord of Scotland too. Indeed his armies were so effective he was the first ruler of Britain, and he was undisputed in this title. It's therefore strange that Aethelstan isn't as famous as his grandfather or indeed, most kings. He's about as obscure as it gets in history.

Scotland at this time was just as divided as England. There were the Gaels, the Scots and in the North, Scandinavian rulers all vying for power. The indigenous culture of the Picts was no longer a going concern in a mirror image of England. However before the Scots start waving the Saltire (which wasn't to be adopted until the Tudor era), it's worth remembering that the first man to rule both nations was not James VI/I, but a long-forgotten Anglo-Saxon King from Wessex. History is complicated and messy, and nationalism is one of the chief offenders of over-simplification.

This brings us to the Battle of Brunanburh. The name is not contemporary; it was such an epic conflict that for at least a generation after it was simply referred to as "The Great War". Most clashes in the Anglo-Saxon chronicle get at best a sentence. This one gets over a page.

The lords of Britain had by 937 realised that England was now the dominant power and unless something was done, they faced possible annihilation. Like any existential threat it was a powerful unifying factor. So the Kings of Scotland and Ireland, as well as Viking raiders and even mercenaries from Wales and England, gathered near the Scottish/English boarder. The exact location of the battle has been lost in the mists of time and shows one of the problems with ancient chronicles: they quite often lack fundamental details that would help future historians.

If contemporaries put special emphasis on it then it cannot be dismissed as another martial clash that had little real world impact. This battle mattered and nobody could afford to lose. At stake for all the leaders beyond personal safety there was the safety of their realms. This was too big a concentration of military might to mean there could be a round 2. So whoever lost was likely to lose their kingdom. For Aethalstan would have been all too aware of how hard Wessex had worked to create a unified and Christian England and yet this could all be lost at the hands of Scots, Irish and Pagan Vikings. For the other side if they didn't stop the nascent English nation now they would be facing a likely irreparable tilting in the balance of power.

So battle was joined, once again the Chronicles imply this wasn't a battle of finesse, where some clever manoeuvre or feint won the day but after showers of arrows it was decided with close quarter bloody infantry assault. Battle axes bit into soft flesh, war hammers crushed skulls and swords hacked at limbs. Some of the Northern army tried to flee to nearby ships but the English soldiers caught up with them and butchered them. The loss of life must have huge and indeed the chronicles agree that by the end of the day 5 kings lay dead on the field as did 7 Earls (great landowners the very pinnacle of the aristocracy). For men of such high status to die on the battlefield was rare in any period of history but to have that many as casualties could be a record in European history putting Agincourt or Blenheim into perspective. Although Constantine II fled the battlefield, it was about as complete a victory for Aethelstan as he could have hoped for. So Britain was temporarily unified and it was under Aethelstan the borders of Scotland and England were agreed and since then they largely stayed the same. For over a 1,000 years.

The union may not have lasted but Aethelstan continued the generally strong governance of Anglo-Saxon England. England was becoming one of the best governed kingdoms in Europe and its comparative unity was also a sign of strength. However with his death Edmund (Aethelstan's half brother) inherited the throne at 18 and failed to keep control of the north and Northumbria once again broke away from the union. Edmund did start regaining territory however it seems some people were keener on centralised authority than others. The problem was that while Alfred and Aethelstan were natural rulers they also had reasonably long reigns and inherited the throne at a mature age. What follows in England is decades of rulers that last for a handful of years. They weren't terrible but they were fire fighting and as "Englishness" was still quite new they were fighting an uphill battle keeping the component parts together. It also shows again the messiness of history, you would hope for a narrative of the 4 main kingdoms of England to be absorbed into one but after a brief period of genuine unification, it was broken up again waiting for a future generation to recreate the idea of England.

This can be summarised by the Viking with my favourite title- Eric Bloodaxe. Eric was from the Norwegian royal family and by now the Viking raids were more Norwegian (Norse) rather than Danish. Eric had left Norway after possibly ruling for a brief time. Eric was a classic Viking adventurer; he even had a saga written about him full of feasting, plunder and killing, lots and lots of killing. By the mid 10th century Christianity was even seeping into Scandinavia but Eric was a good old fashioned pagan and as his name suggests he wasn't one for brotherly love. What is telling about the fragility of English unity is the Kingdom of York (from Jorvik- a Viking name) would rather have a foreign pagan King with a reputation for violence than be part of the Wessex realm of England.

It is noted in the Anglo-Saxon chronicle that in search of plunder Mr Bloodaxe set fire to Rippon Minster a sign he didn't really care what the local religious customs were. The Archbishop of York (Wulfstan) was going backwards and forwards to the Wessex court and it's interesting that Eric obviously allowed this. The current King of Southern England, Eadred, gathered an army and fought Eric to the negotiation table- something of a novelty to a man of his demeanour. The people of

York were willing to look past the paganism and the burning of the occasional minster but what they had backed was a warrior who could keep them independent and in that he failed so he was exiled as he had no popular support in York. So off he went, presumably to do a bit of recreational plundering on the continent.

5 years later with a new army he was back and was again installed as King of York once more. However Eric was obviously more of a "hands on guy" and running a state was not his strong point. Only a few years later he was once again expelled and so the last independent king of English lands was out of the way, England was once again under central control. Erik had allies north of the border and it was recorded that near Stainmore he was murdered by Maccus son of Olaf. Death by violence the only way a man called Eric Bloodaxe could have gone.

Alfred the Great's father was Aethelred and he is not to be confused with Aethelred II who became king of England in 978. He came to be remembered as Aethelred the Unready which is a mangling of the Anglo-Saxon Aethelred Unraed. Aethelred means wise council and unraed means without council so the echo of the original play on words more or less remains. Aethelred is a hard man to admire, unlike the shorter lived kings after Aethelstan, Aethelred ruled for about 35 years, inherited a united realm and the land was relatively peaceful. That all changed in 991.

The Battle of Maldon is again a battle that caught the contemporary imagination so there is an epic poem written about it. Like all poems and sagas there is a huge amount of embellishment but the basic facts are a new Viking army arrived in East Anglia led by the Norwegian King Olaf Tryggvason and were met by the local Earl Brythnoth. The poem has a great line where Olaf promises to sail away if he was paid with gold and armour to which Brythnoth is reputed to have replied "we will pay you with spear tips and sword blades". This pithy reply sounds like a classic exchange that appears from time-to-time in chronicles around the world, the best one being at the battle of Thermopylae when the Persian emissary tries to intimidate the Spartans by saying "our arrows will block out the sun" only to get the response "then we shall fight in the shade." It's a little too neat to feel all that genuine but they are so good I want them to be true. Brythnoth was outnumbered but the battle focused on a causeway in a marshy area where numerical superiority was not essential to victory. The ensuing battle was again one of the Anglo-Saxon battles of attrition and his men fought bravely but Brythnoth was killed and Olaf could march further into the English interior.

Aethelred reeling from a defeat and an invasion was advised by the Archbishop of Canterbury to pay them off. You can see the logic, give them what they want they go away and then England can ramp up the defences in the meantime. Olaf got 10,000 pounds (Roman weight) of silver and he went home a happy man.

In the meantime Aethelred didn't do much so when Olaf returned 3 years later this time with Sweyn Forkbeard they sieged London. Once more Aethelred bought them off and so a pattern emerged. Aethelred was now in a vicious circle, the amounts being extorted (because that's what it was black mail on a national scale) got larger and larger which meant less money was going into the treasury for things like defence. The navy dwindled, the burh system wasn't maintained and in the meantime the Vikings came back with alarming regularity- why not? Turn up, wave your battleaxe around to get the attention of the local king and sail off with a colossal amount of treasure. It was a low risk, high reward venture.

This series of regular payment were to become known as Danegeld and while the first payment has to be seen as a practicality to buy more time and come up with a plan b, Aethelred never did come up with a plan b. That was to create a situation of a country slowly sliding into anarchy leading to one of the most shameful actions ever carried out by an English king.

By 1002 things were grim, the Vikings were arriving regularly, the annual revenues to the crown were consequently in a dramatic slump and now there were rumours of treason. Aethelred had heard that Danish settlers were waiting for and willing to help a Scandinavian takeover of his very throne. It is highly likely after 10 years of the country lurching from one ransom to another there were more than a few people hoping for a change of leadership but his response was appalling. On November 13th 1002 he ordered the St Brice's Day Massacre. This act was the deliberate targeting of men of Danish decent to be murdered on the grounds of treason.

Exactly how many died is still contentious, in the areas that were Dane Law it's likely the locals were not going to slaughter each other but in the areas near the old split agreed between Guthrum and Alfred it's likely that these were the concentrations of violence. It's worth remembering that by referring to Alfred I have just gone back about 140 years since the Micel Here arrived. Looking at Britain's modern multicultural society it's hard to think of people who have roots in the country of over a century as non-British. I myself have 2 parents not born in this country and yet I feel as British as the next man. It was a xenophobic, irrational act that was in many ways the last desperate roll of a dice of a man who was losing his grip. Many dictators in their day when they could see unrest tried to solve it with massacre but this was a fairly rare event in Britain.

It also turned rumour into fact. Now the people of Danish descent had a reason to look to the Northlands for protection and amongst the dead was none other than Sweyn Forkbeard's sister Gunhilde. So not only did this now make things personal for a Viking warlord- never a good idea, it also gave Sweyn Forkbeard a moral mandate (something of a novelty for Vikings) for another invasion. In 1003 he arrived with a large army. This time he stayed for two years until a combination of famine and a huge sum of 36,000 pounds of silver made the Norse King head home once again. Notice how the price for peace had more than trebled since the first payment of Dane geld.

For Aethelred things were desperate indeed, bribery was only attracting more trouble and his order of massacre had led to civil unrest. A primary duty of a ruler was to protect his people, not only had he failed to do that but he'd instead turned on a portion of his own subjects and attempted to wipe them out. He was broke and he had no idea what to do.

Sweyn returned in 1013 at the head of a Viking invasion fleet one of the largest so far seen. Sweyn was going to put an end to Aethelred's underwhelming reign and achieved what no one since the Romans did and conquered all of England. The English resisted with particularly effective defence of London where Aethelred was but On Christmas Day 1013 Sweyn was crowned King. He was the first Viking king of England.

He only just had time to savour the victory when in early 1014 he died and his son was proclaimed the new King by the Vikings while lingering English resistance backed Aethelred who returned from exile from Normandy. Where he stayed was important because 3 years later when the Vikings returned to settle things once and for all Aethelred and his family were to remain in Normandy binding the links of this Northern French state to the courtly life of the Anglo-Saxon monarchy. This is where Edward the Confessor was born and raised and assumed he would live out his days there.

Sweyn's son Cnut was to return and rule in England. His name can be spelt in a number of different ways Cnute and Knut as two examples but I prefer the more common Cnut because I am then living on a knife edge of being just one typo away from offense. Everybody thinks that when looking at the name, but I think I may be the first person to articulate this thought.

If people know one thing about Cnut it's that he got his feet wet showing off. This is a shame on two fronts, firstly this half remembered tale is literally only half the story and secondly he was one of the giants of early Medieval History. He was not some raider looking for booty, he was a king and his father had been a king. Indeed soon after becoming King of England he continued his conquests and by mid way through his reign in England he was also King of Denmark, Norway and the key parts of Sweden. He was the head of a North Sea empire the same size and diversity as anything Charlemagne had.

He was also a Christian King, although this can be a little over stated. He wasn't supremely pious (but then again many Christian kings weren't) however he did not represent the pagan old ways but looked to the new religion and new empire as the future of these northern realms. As pointed out earlier Anglo-Saxon England had much in common with the northern lands, culturally, economically, even in terms of DNA.

It has been said that Cnut was the best "Anglo-Saxon" king of England and certainly his reign is a period of peace and prosperity. England now was part of a vast trading network that was as broad as Iceland, France, Norway, Ireland and the Baltic regions. It is therefore a little ironic to think after more than two centuries of resisting Viking rule, when it finally came to the whole country it was an efficient system of governance. However it should be remembered that unlike earlier raiding pagans, Cnut was a royal prince looking to inherit a kingdom not an adventurer looking just for booty.

Cnut was wealthy and powerful and it was at this point we should look at the legend around him. The version remembered is he had his throne taken to a beach and there he sat on it and ordered the tide to turn away only to fail and subsequently get his feet wet.

The full tale is that some of his great landowners showered him with praise which annoyed him and declared that the greatest power on earth was the Christian one true god. To prove this he took his throne to a beach and there he sat on it and ordered the tide to turn away only to fail. At this point he turned and declared that this showed his power to be nothing compared to God. So a tale remembered as royal folly is actually a legend about the reasonableness and wisdom of a Christian King.

This powerful, wise stabiliser of a country, ruler of an empire is all but forgotten except for a legend that makes him out to be foolish with a slightly amusing name. So why isn't he better remembered? Why is he not up there with William the Conqueror or Henry V? The answer is that word that sends a shiver down any ruler's spine- legacy. Cnut ran England well for about 20 years, a decent length and as pointed out the country was peaceful and prosperous which was a complete contrast to Aethelred II's disastrous reign. He even liked England enough to be buried at Winchester rather than brought back to some Scandinavian place of internment. However on his death his lands weren't given to one overall ruler to continue this northern empire but broken up between his relatives. The empire was ultimately a short lived experiment.

Even worse his son Harald Harefoot ruled for a little over 4 years and then died very suddenly presumably from some sort of illness (there is no implication of foul play). The good news is that by him dying he did save England from a violent war because another son, Harthacnut, was set to invade from Denmark. Instead the new plan was a peaceful claiming of the throne but then managed to drink himself to death just 2 years later at a wedding feast (that must have been some party). Both these men are now forgotten kings of England and between them they lasted of only about 6 years and by now Cnut's empire was in turmoil with a host of men claiming a variety of titles.

A bit like Alexander the Great, the empire held together by one great man, essentially shattered on his death. So with Cnut and two of his sons now dead, this allowed Aethelred II's son Edward to return from exile in Normandy to become the surprise King of England. Edward had spent all his adult life as an exile and now at nearly 40 he had gone from a pretender to the throne with no actual power to the real thing. The main problem he had is real power cannot be given it had to be taken and he was given the throne from the leading landowners (the Earls) Leofric, Siward and Godwin.

Had Edward negotiated with the Earls and got on with siring a son (or indeed a daughter) English history could have been very different, but he didn't. This lack of offspring has become one of the points that is used to demonstrate his piety and indeed his title Edward "The Confessor" is a canonical title to show he's on the way to becoming a full saint although since the creation of the Protestant Anglican church it's unlikely he'll ever get the promotion. Whether he truly was celibate or not is neither here nor there what it did make him was a bad king. A king's job was peace and security and part of that was to ensure a hassle free succession. If you look at Henry VIII's reign he knew he had to get a son and this led to his almost farcical string of marriages to help ensure a male successor. As the last 30 years since Aethelred II's death had shown a country could easily lurch into war or face invasion if there was trouble at the top.

Indeed throughout history a weak succession almost invariably plunges a kingdom into civil war.

Therefore, in no way taking away from the beliefs of the man or indeed the reported miracles at his shrine and good deeds noted in his lifetime, he fundamentally failed as a temporal ruler. The story of 1066 is essentially about three major and one minor claim to the English throne. All of these would have evaporated at a stroke had Edward had children. Instead his lack of foresight on this front was to lurch the country into war and rebellion for years and to change the face of Britain forever.

Chapter 3 1066 the tale of 2 brothers

The way the events of 1066 are explained are ultimately a battle of wits between Harold and William. Two men locked in a deadly game where only one can win and the other would have to pay the ultimate sacrifice. This sounds like a great intro for a movie but I think it's the wrong way to look at the events of that famous year.

Instead I have an alternative story a story of two brothers, of respect forged on the battlefield, of rivalry in the power games of the aristocracy and with betrayal leading to personal tragedy and the death of kings. I think this would make an even better film, don't you?

As pointed out The Anglo-Saxon Monarchy was restored as the Norse empire created by Cnut faded away. So why is this period of Norse invasion not seen in the same light as the 1066 invasion? The simple answer is Anglo-Saxon England had more in common with Norway than with France. Both societies had a system of freemen who, as a form of rent, had to carry out military service. Both had strong maritime backgrounds. England had seen wave after wave of northern european invaders since the 5th century. So the languages while not identical were similar. Even war was conducted similarly. Cavalry was something that didn't exist in Anglo-Saxon England and horses were used only to get to the scene of battle. Ultimately for the average peasant in the fields, not a lot changed except the name and the head on the coins.

The invasion of 1066 in comparison brought with it the feudal system as introduced by William the Conqueror. Suddenly peasants were no longer freemen but were now tied to the land. Within a generation after 1066 castles dotted the landscape and mounted cavalry roamed the countryside to keep the peasants in check. Local landlords were no longer guaranteed to speak your own language. Whereas the Norse period of rule brought largely cosmetic changes, the Norman Conquest looked like an invasion and felt like an invasion.

By the time Edward returned in 1042 some things

had changed, and the changes at the highest levels weren't minor. The political landscape had drifted dramatically. This was the time of great power playing in the Anglo-Saxon court and nobody did it better than Earl Godwin of Wessex. Frank Barlow's "The Godwins" and Emma Mason's "The House of Godwin" are both excellent accounts of this dynasty and again the Anglo-Saxon chronicle features them heavily.

Godwin was the head of the clan including Harold and Tostig and it is to Tostig that far more attention should be paid. Since he was not the eldest son, he would have expected to find his own power base whilst protecting the family's interest as a whole. As an Anglo-Saxon aristocrat he would have been a keen hunter and warrior and would have been taught the ways of the soldier. His brother Harold is shown in several pictures with a hawk on his hand, a sign of hunting. Tostig throughout his life appeared to be a good example of the aristocracy. This probably meant that he was strong and tall, with blonde hair cut to shoulder length. Possibly he had a big bushy moustache that would have been covered in foam from the ale drunk at his father's feasts.

Before Cnut's invasion there were 4 great Earldoms. Wessex covered the whole of the South from Cornwall to Essex. In the East there was East Anglia, the centre of England was known as Mercia, and the largest Earldom was Northumbria. In the

11th century the richest of these was Wessex, run by Earl Godwin. As powerful landowners the Earls had always been hard to control, but with a King on the other side of the North Sea, they had become far more autonomous and independent.

Edward had been invited back by the Earls so that they could resist Norwegian control and try to dictate terms to the new king rather than the other way around. The plan worked. Edward was not raised as a great Anglo-Saxon warrior king. He was a religious man with a fondness for all things French. While he wasn't exactly a puppet, he lacked the authority and the unity of his people that his predecessors had enjoyed. The Earls were largely Anglo-Danish and Edward, although the rightful king of England was seen as an outsider by his own Anglo-Saxon court.

Edward made a smart move and actively allied himself to Godwin, the most powerful of all the Earls and even married Godwin's daughter Edith. For Godwin's family things were looking up. In the space of 2 generations they had gone from small time land owners to membership in the royal family. Indeed by the late 1040's Godwin's family lands were worth around £5,000. To put this in context, the royal landed wealth at the same time was valued at £6,000. In the late 1040's Godwin faced a number of setbacks but the most important one in our story is the rebellion by Sweyn, the oldest of Godwin's sons.

The task force sent to stop his raids on the South coast was led by Godwin's son Harold, but Tostig also had several ships at his command. This seems to have been his first military command. They worked well together and Sweyn was exiled as a result. The point of this is that Tostig was starting to find his own feet. He showed that he could be an effective military leader and one who knew how to work with his brother.

However Edward wanted to build up his own power base of loyal friends; so slowly and carefully he began to bring in Normans- to counter Godwin's power in court. This was the start of the chain of events that led to William's ultimate interest in England. Indeed the whole Anglo- French wrangling that was to go on for the next 500 years can be traced back to Edward's exile in Normandy. As foreigners started to get the sought after jobs at court, so Edward's unpopularity grew. In 1051 Godwin's candidate for Archbishop of Canterbury was rejected in favour of Edward's Norman friend, Robert of Jumièges. Later Godwin was able to reverse the choice, but this was to annoy both the King and the Church, further upping the stakes between these two powerful men.

Events reached a head when, in 1051 after violence in Dover, Edward ordered Godwin to sack the town. Godwin refused and raised arms against the king. It was a huge gamble, an act of open defiance and a sign of how confident Godwin was of his position and power. Edward proved to be not quite the push over Godwin had expected and ordered the Earls of Northumbria and Mercia to invade Wessex. Godwin's support melted away as a civil war, which nobody wanted, loomed on the horizon. This was particularly inconvenient for Tostig for the young aristocrat was just at this time being married to Judith, the daughter of Baldwin, Count of Flanders. Instead of Godwin bullying Edward to see things his way the country turned against him. With no other option, Godwin and his family fled abroad, Harold to Ireland and the rest across the Channel to Flanders. This was a chance for Tostig spend some time with his new in-laws.

It looked potentially as if Godwin had risked and lost everything. What made it worse was that Edward and Edith's marriage was barren, so Godwin couldn't even console himself that the heir to throne might be loyal. Indeed it was at this time that Edward put Edith in a nunnery, and took the radical step of considering as his successor, William Duke of Normandy. This was an idea so unpopular and outlandish, that this succession would never happen unless William came and took the title by force. However this move also put Edward at risk. He was a king with no heir, who had just exiled a popular and powerful English noble.

Flanders and Ireland were the perfect places for the Godwins to regroup. Flanders in particular was

a well-known mustering point for mercenaries, so it didn't take long for Godwin to create a small army to make a comeback. Within a year Earl Godwin and his family returned; and, even though Godwin died during a feast in 1053, his plans continued to work. Edith was brought back from the nunnery to be queen again. Although no chronicles record her homecoming, it's a safe bet to speculate that it was not a happy reunion.
It's at this moment that Tostig becomes far more important to the story and the history of England. In the 1040s and 50s Godwin had not only been intertwining his family with the royal line, but with other Earldoms, too. Harold, the most politically astute of the brothers, was given East Anglia. Records show that while his time as Earl wasn't that eventful, things were relatively peaceful and well run. However on the death of Godwin, Harold inherited Wessex; and by 1055, Tostig had been made Earl of Northumbria. Between the 2 brothers they now directly ruled more than half of England's land and wealth. Only Leofric, and later Edwin, and Morcar the other great aristocratic dynasty in England, could put up any effective resistance to Tostig and Harold.

Uncovering the real King Edward is hard. As mentioned his title "Confessor" sheaths him in this religious glow and a fiery man, with a real political agenda is transformed into a passive religious man withdrawn from the world of politics and filled with piety and serenity. It is hard to unpick the fantasy from the reality. However Edward wasn't getting any younger and with this new generation of Earls most people would find it hard to keep up with all the plots going on.

So in his later years he must have, to some extent, withdrawn from society to lead, at a certain level, a life of piety and hunting. But somebody needed to run England and Harold was the king's closest advisor. Indeed he's sometimes referred to by contemporary sources as the "Underking" and essentially acts as regent from this time on. For Tostig, though, this was his big chance. The family had weathered the storm of exile, political manoeuvring and Sweyn's rampage. Tostig had also been busy spreading further the family's influence in the court of Flanders. When Tostig inherited Northumbria, it was a lawless state where men were forced to travel in large groups to protect themselves from bandits. Tostig lost no time in taking control of the situation. He imposed new laws, ensuring that all captured robbers were punished with mutilation (often the nose and ears were removed), or in the most severe cases, death. This strategy, while harsh even by the standards of the day, was successful; and Northumbria came under his firm control. However this centralisation of power by an outsider was to have repercussions later.

It's at this point that 2 very famous people come into the story, Malcolm and Macbeth. As Earl of Northumbria, Tostig also had responsibility for keeping the border with Scotland safe and secure.

This was no easy task, as from the time records began until 1745; incursions from both North and South of the border were almost annual events. Sometimes it was little more than glorified cattle rustling; other times it was all-out war. Either way, the border was porous and unstable and events in the capitals of either country could create major headaches for the Earls of Northumbria. When Tostig arrived in his Earldom he was about to get embroiled in the showdown between the now legendary duo of Malcolm and Macbeth.

Because of Shakespeare's myth making, trying to get the general public to shake off misconceptions about these 2 is very hard work. This was not a simple morality tale of good versus evil. Indeed it could be said that Shakespeare is a genius playwright but a lousy historian whose plays have distorted many events in British history. As already shown by Godwin and his sons, political events in the early medieval period weren't subtle, and power was almost a mandate in its own right. While Macbeth had indeed usurped the throne on Duncan's death, Duncan perished in battle a relatively young man. Contrary to popular belief, he was not assassinated in Macbeth's castle. Indeed castles were introduced to Britain only after the Norman invasion, so fortifications in the 1050s looked very different to the stereotypical images of stone walls and portcullises that immediately spring to mind.

Macbeth had already been on the throne for over a decade by the time Tostig became Earl of Northumbria, and Macbeth was seen as a generally good ruler, rather than a mad despot with an overbearing wife. But Malcolm had been contesting the throne for some time and had been seeking and getting English help. What Tostig's initial views on events north of the border were, aren't known; but what is made quite clear is that once Malcolm and Tostig met, they hit it off immediately, eventually calling each other brother. Theatre to one side, if you back the winner in a war, you will be owed something in the future, and Tostig wanted stability. So he allowed Malcolm to use Northumbria from time-to-time as a base of operations. It's likely he gave Malcolm funds, too. As their friendship grew, all he had to do was wait for the moment of truth to arrive.

So what of Macduff, The battle of Dunsinane, and the encampment in Birnam Wood? Well Shakespeare was obviously an advocate of "don't let the facts get in the way of a good story". The showdown was, however, in many ways even more epic. Sources are sketchy, but it seems that Malcolm and Macbeth met at a stone circle near Lumphanan and fought a duel or small skirmish in which Malcolm won and killed Macbeth. Even at the time this was seen more as a dynastic change than a triumph of truth and justice. It is telling that rather than Malcolm being swept unanimously into kingship, Macbeth's stepson, Lulach was proclaimed king; and, up until his death, he continued to challenge Malcolm. But apart from a few rebellions, Malcolm was king and he kept his promise to Tostig. The only time he did attack Northumbria was while Tostig was out of the country on pilgrimage. It had shown that Tostig could not only rule his local area with an iron fist, but also influence the affairs of foreign states and build powerful alliances of his own accord.

So let's review Tostig's position. His family had been major players in British politics for more than a generation, he is married to the daughter of the Count of Flanders, his sister is Queen of England and his brother was, for all practical purposes, regent of the nation. He even had allies north of the border which led to peace and prosperity and his Earldom was firmly under his control. These are all signs of a successful man, a noble who had proven the worth of his blood line as well as underlining his own leadership abilities. Imagine one man with this much power today- books, films and TV shows would be made about him; and yet, the irony is that hardly anyone remembers him. However, at this point in our story, Tostig was one of the most powerful and well connected men in Europe.

The late 1050s and early 1060s were the pinnacle of Tostig's power and respect. He even felt secure enough to undergo the major expedition of a pilgrimage to Rome. This again shows another dimension to the man. Like all medieval nobles you may kill and take mistresses; but just like the peasants all around, you too, had to bow before God. Founding a monastery was seen as a sign of both piety and power. Paying priests to recite prayers for you and your family was a further way to ensure a connection to God and the afterlife. Making a pilgrimage was an indication, not only of wealth; but, more importantly, devotion. Travelling by horse from York to Rome would be a major undertaking even today, so it could be seen then as an act of genuine faith on Tostig's part. Heaven knows he had much for which to be thankful.

While Tostig travelled with his wife and younger brother for religious reasons, there was a political element to this trip, too. Tostig was made an ambassador by Edward charged to negotiate with the papacy over new religious appointments in England. The significance of this task again shows Tostig's position and importance in court. However his route to Rome, while taking in some political meetings to be sure, also included many pilgrimage sites. Tostig obviously took his religion seriously.

The negotiations in Rome were long and complicated and Tostig didn't get everything he wanted. However on the return journey, a Tuscan nobleman attacked the party, catching them by surprise. Tostig lost all his wealth, but escaped with his life. He returned to Rome, not only to complain, but to use this insult as further leverage in negotiations. He was a smart man. Tostig got what he asked for, plus financial recompense; and, perhaps most importantly, the papal blessing.

Tostig arrived back home not a moment too soon because in 1063 with Welsh raiders threatening the borders Harold and Tostig were tasked with defeating the Welsh King Gruffyd (like early Anglo-Saxon England occasionally a Welsh prince would become overlord however the title wasn't hereditary and the principalities inevitably broke up into their constituent parts ready for future conflict). Again Harold was the senior partner in the enterprise and he took a fleet of ships from Bristol to attack in the West of Wales. Tostig moved quickly into the North East of the country. This massive pincer movement would have required considerable planning and skill to execute it successfully and again shows the formidable military skill both brothers possessed.

The defeat of Gruffyd led to his assassination and his head was brought to Harold. Edward (through Harold) now divided the kingdom between Gruffyd's brothers and made them swear oaths of allegiance. Victory was total and was remembered for several generations in Wales.

Harold by now was Edward's indispensable right hand man (or indeed the power behind the throne) and travelled to Normandy to meet Duke William. During his crossing of the channel his ship was blown off course and instead of landing in William's lands he instead arrived at Ponthieu and was taken hostage. William acted immediately and ordered Count Guy to hand Harold over and as William was the foremost military commander in France, Guy wisely obliged.

Harold now spent a few months with William and even went on campaign with him and would have no doubt taken notes on Norman military techniques. William and Harold seemed to have got on and there had to be mutual respect as both were powerful landowners and accomplished warriors. There is even mention of Harold saving some of William's men from quick sand an act of bravery that must have impressed.

What happened next is a point of conjecture. It seems that before Harold returned to England after months of hospitality he made some sort of oath to William. However exactly under what circumstances and about what "nobody knows for sure". Of course the Norman sources all point to Harold promising William the throne after Edward's death so setting up Harold as a usurper and oath breaker when he took the throne in 1066 for himself so further legitimising William's claim to the throne.

One account even has Harold swearing the oath on a box only to have it revealed afterwards that the casket was full of holy relics so making the agreement even more binding. This is highly unlikely because verbally swearing some kind of oath in front of witnesses was taken very seriously at a time of low literacy levels. Therefore to actively trick someone about something so solemn would nullify the agreement and make the whole process pointless.

Harold may well have promised William the throne hoping that the Duke might never have the resources for a full scale invasion. Or indeed he may have promised it on the grounds that Edward wanted him to have it as compensation for all the years Edward had lived at the Norman court. What is more likely is that the oath was about some sort of mutual support which was given a new spin after subsequent events.

So Harold returned after having spent time with one of the key potential competitors for the throne of England. Shortly after his return his brother's standing wasn't to last. Tostig's taxation and harsh rule of Northumbria caused more and more resentment and in 1065 it turned into full scale revolt. Tostig's base in York was overrun and his personal guard were killed and captured. Tostig was with the king in the South when the rebellious Northumbrians began to march towards them. Edward and Harold had no choice. He had to be stripped of his title and exiled, or civil war would tear the country apart. So Tostig left the country and his Earldom was given to Morcar. It was the second time in his life that he went to Flanders as a fugitive.

Harold must have been devastated. The two brothers had already survived one exile and had worked well together building the dynasty so effectively together. It was recorded that Harold tried to compensate his brother but nothing Harold could give was to compare to the Earldom Tostig lost. If he was to return, he wanted it to be for a greater, not lesser title.

Tostig's harsh streak now comes centre stage as he was out for revenge and if that meant conflict with his brother then so be it. After trying several options in Scandinavia, his quest led him to King Harald Hardrada of Norway. Harald was everything you would expect from a Viking king. He was a huge man, strong and brave with a wild streak a mile wide. He had at one point been a body guard to the Emperor of Byzantium and was said to have bedded the Empresses. True or not this summarises the larger than life character that was Harald Hardrada. This was a man with whom Tostig felt he could do business.

At first Harald seemed to be cautious. He was new to the throne and an invasion of England was a major undertaking, however Tostig seems to have had a silver tongue, convincing Harald that Tostig could supply fighters of his own and a loyal base of supporters in England. He could demonstrate this by his family's return to power a decade or so earlier. It was just the sort of bold move that Harald Hardrada couldn't refuse and through his lineage he could claim legitimacy from Cnut's reign. The invasion was on. It may have been that regardless of Tostig's scheming that Harald would have come anyway but whether he would have chosen 1066 as the year is doubtful. As we shall see it was Tostig and Harald's actions in the north of

England that were to significantly contribute to the fate of the entire Anglo-Saxon nation.

It was to be a two pronged attack, Tostig in the South and Harald in the north. As this plan was being formulated in early January 1066, Edward the Confessor died. Almost immediately Harold was crowned king. Harold's grandparents were relatively minor land holders and Scandinavian immigrants and yet their grandson had risen to the very highest title in the land. To be fair to Harold if kings were given the title for merit he had done an excellent job of being in essence a regent for a decade or so. He was a talented general, a ruler who understood good governance and he had the connections at court to ensure a peaceful reign.

However he was not the only one with a claim to the throne. Harald Hardrada asserted his right via his ancestry with Cnut; and William Duke of Normandy staked his hopes on the slim chance that someone would believe that Edward himself had promised him the throne. As a result all these claims, England was locked into a year- long struggle to see who would rule the country.

There was however another claim to the throne from another branch of the Anglo-Saxon royal Wessex family, a boy named Edgar Aetheling. On paper he had the best claim to the throne as he was related to Edward and all the other legitimate Wessex kings. What played against him was his age, with the threat of invasion from a Viking king and a Norman Duke, the Anglo-Saxon court could ill afford an under aged king. If being a king was a man's job it was never truer than in 1066 when a strong ruler was needed to defend the realm from inevitable overseas interest. So the last legitimate heir to the house of Wessex was exiled and faded into obscurity leaving the way open for the warlords to do battle.

On April 24th Haley's Comet appeared in the sky, the first significant celestial display of this fateful year. Comets are generally seen as a sign of ill omen. Indeed the comet was seen as important enough to be included on the Bayeux Tapestry which provides another record of these early events. At this time Tostig was arriving on the Isle of Wight, an area friendly to his family. There he gathered men, money, and provisions which he then moved to Sandwich, but withdrew again when he heard that his brother was raising an army to meet him there. From Sandwich he headed up the East coast, raiding and plundering as he went. He arrived at the Humber with 60 ships, but was driven away by Edwin and Morcar, sustaining heavy losses. But he was not finished yet.

Many histories state Harold was with the army in the South to anticipate a huge invasion fleet led by William Duke of Normandy. This is in part true but it had been Tostig's staging post and he was obviously up to something so Harold was also there to ensure that his brother didn't try the same tactic twice. The two brothers were circling each other cautiously but there were other predators with their eyes on the crown in that year.

Harold had another problem, the men of the Fyrd (army) were obliged to serve for 40 days a year in payment for their lands and that time was inevitably during the summer. It was now September and coming up to harvest, which means that his men were itching to go home and desertions must have begun to be a problem. Ironically as the crowned king with all the resources at his disposal it may have been assumed that it was Harold who could play the waiting game but in reality time was not on his side and he knew it.

Tostig, while defeated was not out of the game, and he met with his ally Harald Hardrada in Scotland, a safe haven thanks to his old friend Malcolm King of Scotland. With a combined fleet they set sail and landed near York. They were so fast that it caught everyone by surprise and resistance was light. York itself quickly fell and oaths were demanded by local landowners. However Edwin and Morcar Earls of Mercia and Northumbria had beaten Tostig once, and now they were set to do it again.

On September 20th 1066 their forces met at Fulford Gate a marshy lowland area 2 miles South of York. The plan was simple. A weaker line of Vikings was put out to meet the first of the English.

As expected, the line broke and the Vikings fled, leaving the now disorganized English soldiers to march into the arms of Harald Hardrada and Tostig's elite guardsmen. They were formidable; standing there covered in chain mail, with great two-handed battle axes. They turned the English charge into a route, cutting a swathe of bloody destruction right through the centre. Many good fighting men died, not only by Viking steel but some drowned in the bog. These men were some of the North and Midland's finest warriors and would be missed by Harold Godwinson less than a month later at Hastings.

Tostig knew his brother was tied to the South waiting for William's invasion
that never seemed to be coming and it was getting late in the campaigning season. So armour, equipment and a third of the army was sent back to the Norwegian fleet. This was a chance to celebrate a daring raid that had secured a strong base in the North of England. If Tostig had waited for his brother and William to weaken each other through battle, all he would have had to do was join with Hardrada and sweep south in 1067. England would be theirs.

It therefore came as a complete shock and nasty surprise that just 4 days later, as if from nowhere, Harold Godwinson appeared 9 miles from York with the entire Anglo-Saxon army. He had just completed a forced march from the South coast, an amazing feat of endurance and skill. It must have come as a devastating blow when Harold heard that he had positioned his army at the wrong of the country and that now the North was under the rule of a Viking king and his brother.

The very next day, despite the fatigue in the English army, Harold and Tostig, brothers who had fought side- by-side were to meet face-to-face in a fight to the death. There is a legend that Harold Godwinson rode up to the Viking army and offered Tostig a third of the kingdom, Tostig asked how much land his ally Harald Hardrada would get in compensation for his efforts-

"7 feet of ground or as much more is necessary, since he is taller than other men," came the reply.

It's another great quote that sounds a little too polished to be true but the fact remains that after no agreement Tostig and Harald now faced a superior force that was better armed. Their only hope was that the forced march had depleted the fighting sprit of Harold's men. The battle was fierce but there could be only 1 winner. The Vikings had split their army and most of their armour was miles away. One chronicle reports that on this bridge a Viking warrior held off the English advance on his own perhaps the last example of a Viking berserker fighting on English soil. He wasn't brought down until an Englishman floating on a barrel stabbed him from underneath. Harald Hardrada was gripped by a Viking bloodlust and leaped into the fray showing no fear and cutting down many men. But bravery doesn't guarantee success.

Victory to Harold was total. The Viking army was shattered. Harald Hardrada got his 7 feet of land as he died in the heart of the battle as did Tostig. The battle was so savage and the carnage so great, that for over a generation the bones of the fallen could still be clearly seen on the battlefield. As this was the last Viking invasion of Britain, it also marked a major watershed in British history. A group that had been raiding and invading for over 250 years had come to an end. But the battle of Stamford Bridge had another legacy, because the wind that allowed the last few Norwegians to return home was the same wind that allowed William Duke of Normandy to land in the South. Harold, who had spent most of the year on the South coast, was once again at the wrong end of his kingdom this time with a depleted force.

Harold and his men were tired after a forced march and major battle; it would be wise to rest them and head off soon. However his tactic of arriving at the invasion point apparently from nowhere worked against one invasion force could it not work again? Harold had fought in a number of campaigns and had yet to be beaten, even better nobody, not even Alfred the Great had killed a Viking King in battle before. A third option was to wait until the next campaigning season in the north, marshal his resources, and grit his teeth as William rampaged through Southern England.

Time was now on Harold's side, one enemy was vanquished and the other had showed his hand. William would not be able to keep his own forces together indefinitely and as winter was fast approaching there was an issue with provisioning a standing army which would invariable suffer a significant rate of attrition by the following spring.

Saying all that, William was on Harold's ancestral lands- Wessex- and was closer to London where he could well organise a coronation. Then there was the cavalry factor, Harold had seen William's war machine in full swing and may well have realised that to relinquish the initiative to such a man could be a fatal mistake. There may be a personal factor to it all too, Harold had lost his brother who he was close to, maybe he just wanted to get all the threats out of the way at the same time put the dreadful events of the autumn of 1066 out of his mind and move on.

What to do? Harold was naturally a man of action so celebrations of his victory were short lived as he once again force marched his army this time heading south to deal with William, and shore up his throne once and for all.

The Bayeux tapestry shows in great detail William's preparations for the invasion. It's worth remembering he was a Duke trying to become a king, his resources were stretched to breaking point and this was a one shot deal. If he failed, even if he lived he would be close to bankrupt with his reputation severely diminished. The ships, the men, the horses, the arms, armour, mercenaries and even prefabricated castles all cost money or favours and he had cashed everything in for this one roll of the dice. The prize? A kingdom and the title of king. An impressive leap forwards for the illegitimate offspring of a family of Viking descendants.

Therefore William must have been both nervous and excited when his scouts reported that Harold and his army were assembling near Hastings on Senlac hill. He had a chance to land a killing blow to the old dynasty. He was one battle away from the crown. At the same time he knew that he was up against a formidable foe, a man who had proven his bravery to him and he was heading an alien army with no cavalry and an elite body guard of "Houscarls", men clad in long suits of mail armour, each one carrying a two handed battleaxe capable of cutting a man from the shoulder to waist in a single spine shattering blow.

On October 14th 1066 the immovable object met the unstoppable force. The Anglo-Saxons formed an almost impregnable shield wall on top of the hill flanked on either side by either wooded or marshy land that stopped any kind of cavalry flanking manoeuvre. Harold had found a way to neutralise William's chief asset. All the sources agree that the battle lasted all day- a rare event in medieval warfare. Both sides fought to exhaustion. For a large part of the day the shield wall held firm repelling frontal cavalry charges that could find no chink in the defences. The hill was starting to become slippery with the blood and entrails of the dead and dying littering the battlefield.

It was looking like the Normans had run out of ideas and then even worse the rumour went round that William had died in a cavalry charge. At that point the invaders became despondent, with no leader what hope did they have of victory and legitimacy? Some English soldiers sensing the tide had turned in their favour broke from the safety of the shield wall and rushed down the hill to attack the confused Norman ranks.

The rumour was false and William is said to have torn off his helmet to prove he was very much alive and determined to win. The effect was electrifying and the Normans rallied turning on the small group of Anglo-Saxon infantry and massacred them. It is worth noting that this sequence of events probably would have happened no matter what Harold's situation at this point. However it's what happened subsequently that may have been different had he had more, better trained men. The Viking battles in the north were acting like a delayed poison in the English ranks as the many hardened soldiers who had died at Stamford Bridge and Fulford Gate had been replaced with raw and ill disciplined peasants and they were tired. To fight for a day, even when taking turns in the front lines after two forced marches and another battle would have been a huge physical challenge and the men simply weren't as fresh as they would have been had Harold stayed in the south.

William tried his strategy of a fake route again and again in the afternoon, each time luring down a significant contingent of English infantry only to have the Norman cavalry turn and wipe them out. The shield wall at the top of the hill was thinning out. The end game was now inevitable, the Housecarls fought to the bitter end, by all accounts so closely packed around the king and his banner that as they were killed they couldn't fall to the ground. Exactly how Harold died is unclear, arrow in the eye or cut down by a Norman Knight it doesn't matter. The outcome however did.

At the site of the battle (called Battle- another imaginative name by the Brits) there is a stone marker which is where Harold is supposed to have died, but what this stones symbolizes is not just the death of the man, or even the death of a king, but the death of an entire nation. For on this battlefield, Anglo-Saxon England perished forever to be replaced by Norman feudal England, and it was Tostig, the king's own brother, who helped kill it.

Chapter 4 A man called Henry

So the man known to his contemporaries as William the Bastard (but not to his face) became William the Conqueror, King of England and Duke of Normandy. The Battle of Hastings was by no means the end of the story. On Christmas Day 1066, William was crowned King at Westminster Abbey and the mood was tense, so tense in fact that, as a roar of congratulation came from the crowd outside the Abbey, the Norman troops assumed an attack was underway and bloodshed and rioting ensued. Not a great start for a new king.

One of the things I was taught about William, which has stuck with me for over twenty five years, is that although he had big plans for his new conquest, he was smart enough to see how well Anglo-Saxon England ran itself. He put his plans on hold and saw the workings of his new government in action. What he realised and accepted was that the kingdom was well run and so changed very little of the day-to-day processes in the country, a valuable lesson for all managers.

However some changes did occur, such as the implementation of the feudal system. As a result the peasantry were tied to the land and any movement of labour depended on the local lord's consent. This local lord was likely to be a knight, a man who owned the land in return for military service to his lord (either a baron or earl) and this series of commitments led all the way up to the king, who technically owned everything.

This 'ownership' has at times been a little overstated, with the suggestion that the "Free Saxons" were chafing at the bit of their Norman overlords. True, the advent of heavy cavalry changed the nature of peasant soldier from being the core of the army, to little more than cannon fodder (although cannons had yet to be invented in Europe). This relationship was to change later.

How much Saxon peasants wanted to travel, or did travel, prior to the conquest is a matter of conjecture. Local townsfolk were probably content to stay put, as the Anglo-Saxon era had its fair share of callous dictators and bloodshed. Exactly how aggrieved the Anglo-Saxon peasantry was by its new ruling class is very hard to assess. However, having a foreigner, who could not speak your language as a local lord caused friction, and when it came to matters at the local court or festivals, it would have been all too apparent that Englishmen didn't have the top jobs anymore. William, to his credit, did try and learn English, but it just didn't stick and he had more important things to do.

This issue of language is a useful one to show integration. The first King of England after 1066 to speak English as his first language was Edward I, and he wasn't to be crowned for another two hundred years. Indeed "Good King Richard", who is remembered for his opposition to unfair taxes or even (strangely) Norman tyranny, would have spoken French first and in his ten year reign, spent less than a year in England. He also heavily taxed the nation to fund his wars, crusades and later his ransom. He may have been King of England, but he wasn't very English.

Which brings me to the most romantic feature of the medieval era- the castle. A castle is different to a fort. A fort is a defended position manned by a garrison of troops. It's a military base of operations. A castle is the fortified residence of a feudal lord. A fort has one purpose: to house troops for some sort of future military activity. A castle is a rich man's home. Yes, troops were stationed there, but it was also the focus of local governance. Sometimes coins were minted there and it was where the local lord with his family resided.

Castles are great to run around and for kids to clamber on. Many people get misty eyed at images of Camelot or Robin Hood raiding Nottingham castle (Camelot and Robin are both legendary) and want to know why people don't live like that any more? The answer is simple. If the only way you can live in your home is by being surrounded by fifty foot high, ten foot thick stone walls, peppered with murder holes, portcullises and crossbow wielding men-at-arms, then there's something profoundly wrong with society.

Two things brought to an end the era of the castle and they are complete contradictions. One was the improvement of gunpowder and therefore, siege artillery. The Ottoman capture of Constantinople in 1453 marked the beginning of the end of tall stone walls that would inevitably shatter under artillery bombardment. Different types of defences were needed. The second reason was a sustained period of peace. Castles look great and are fun to visit, but they have severe restrictions as a living place. Big, tall, thick walls make living in one invariably gloomy and cold. So it's during the Tudor era onwards that the rich stopped building these defensive works and started creating what would become known as "Stately Homes", with big open windows and far better living standards.

The castles that were converted got large windows knocked into walls. If you go to a castle, you must remember that you are not seeing something that was built once and left for posterity. They were adapted, and for centuries these adaptations were defensive. Take the Tower of London. Conveniently, the three main layers of defence are separated by about one hundred years. The central White Tower was founded by William the

Conqueror in 1086. The middle curtain wall was built in the 1180s by Henry II and Richard I. The outer curtain wall was erected by Edward I in the 1280s. However, if you look closely, you will see various different colourations of mortar and stones around windows and gateways, which suggest further modifications were added. No 12th or 13th century castle would have had large windows facing outwards as they would have been an obvious defensive weakness. William would have had a hard time recognising his original castle by the Tudor era.

So as mentioned, castles aren't a sign of everything being fine, but an indelible image of war, conquest and justified paranoia; and castles in Britain are everywhere. Some are strategic royal strongholds, like the network of northern Welsh castles such as Caernarvon. Dover castle was built as a way to assess traffic on the Channel and a key point of defence of southern England. Others were the homes of minor aristocracy, Bodiam Castle being a great example of a late castle built to show off the new found status of Sir John Dalyngrudge. The pictures make it one of the most "castley" castles in Britain, but compared to many, it's small and the moat is on top of a hill so would be easy to drain. But, with the walls reflected in the water, it's a bit like getting a 2-for-1 deal.

William's reign was not idyllic. Hastings may have won him the crown, but it took years to subjugate all the lords of England, including a particularly brutal ravaging of Northumbria, which came to be known as the "Harrying of the North". When William wisely chose to compile a directory of the value of all his lands- the so-called Domesday Book- you can see that many settlements in the north, even a decade later, had yet to recover from this brutal put down.

However, he ruled for twenty years and on his death something odd was decided that feels counter-intuitive to the modern reader. His lands were split up. Even more oddly, the eldest son got… the Duchy of Normandy. Robert as the eldest got the ancestral homelands, even though as a duke he would be lower down the aristocratic ladder than the next eldest brother, William Rufus. The youngest surviving son was Henry, who was given 5,000 pounds in silver, and no land. However according to Orderic Vitalis, William's last words to Henry were that he was going to end up with power, lands and wealth greater than his brothers. It seems the conqueror knew a winner when he saw one.

As the saying goes, when the titles and lands are hereditary, you want "an heir and a spare". William had achieved that and at one point had four sons. One died hunting but that left three, more than enough to share the family resources. Henry as the youngest was unlikely to inherit much and quite often the younger sons of nobility could expect another route to power- the church. It made sense being celibate (at least theoretically, meaning that even if they did sire children, they would be ineligible to gain hereditary control). A new bishop or abbot was always needed to be quietly prepared on the side lines, and what better pool of candidates then the men who had already been in the families of land owners.

Henry was a well educated young man and he was the first in his family to learn Anglo-Saxon English. He could also read and write, which was by no means standard in royal circles in the 11th century. However, the clerical life did not appeal and so he was going to have to come up with another plan.

However, pause for a thought at the wishes of William. This again shows the messiness of history. The links between England and France after 1066 looked solid, and even a passing knowledge of medieval history will make you aware that England and France were forever claiming each other's land. At this time the rulers still saw them as very different going concerns.

The temporary, generation long-link between England and France was severed and could have been permanently had it not been for a completely unexpected and totally unrelated event in central France.

When I was an undergraduate, studying Archaeology and Medieval History, if there was one area that was incredibly obscure, one area that had no application to the modern world, one area that only the very crumbliest of history lecturers cared about, it was the crusades- and I fell in love with them. It is a massive subject and one that was resurrected after 9/11, when people wrongly started to point to parallels and analogies to the medieval movement. I cannot possibly do it justice here, but in 1095 at Claremont, Pope Urban II preached a new type of pilgrimage.

For a medieval person, the idea of heaven and hell were far more immediate then they are now. It's impossible to compare overall religious fervour between then and now, but in a time before scientific discovery, in a time of regular violence and sudden death in society, and in a time when the Church was the only way to communicate with a higher authority, these concepts would have hung on everyone's minds far more starkly than in today's world of multimedia distractions .

Hell was a place of damnation, full of flesh-eating demons, pits of sulphur and sheets of flame and it was absolutely, undeniably real. It was a place you wouldn't want to spend five minutes in, let alone all of eternity. So if you were a man of violence, a knight whose *raison d'être* was fighting, you were going to have to do a lot of good deeds to avoid such a terrifying afterlife.

Urban preached to the European class of soldiers and knights of a guaranteed remission of all sins, a chance to wipe the slate clean with God, and a chance to do what they did best, fight. What was on offer was an organised mass expedition to the holiest city on earth, Jerusalem. Jerusalem was a city so synonymous with Jesus that to many it was simply heaven on earth, more a concept than an actual location. Medieval maps inevitably place Jerusalem in the centre of the map with all other lands spreading out from this focal point.

Urban was in essence offering a chance to ensure a guaranteed trip to heaven and a chance to get to see the land where the Gospels happened. The results were electrifying. Firstly there was a People's Crusade- a rabble of poor peasants led by Peter the Hermit which was annihilated once it reached Asia Minor. However, more importantly for our story, the First Crusade was born as thousands of nobles and soldiers followed the words of the Pope and marched to the Holy Land.

Of course such an enterprise was going to be expensive, Provisioning and paying for a military host for years that was to travel thousands of miles into the unknown against a fearsome and mysterious enemy of Turks. Indeed it was likely to be a one-way trip. Nobody had done this before and while God will provide, in the meantime financial arrangements had to be made all over Europe.

One of the nobles caught up in the call to arms was Robert Duke of Normandy. He was determined to go and fight in the name of God. So he came up with a reasonable plan, to mortgage Normandy to his brother William for the duration of his journey to and from the Holy Land. By mortgaging an entire duchy, Robert would be able to generate a massive amount of wealth quickly and only a king would have the funds available to negotiate the loan. The situation that William the Conqueror had created actually worked to the benefit of his two eldest sons. William Rufus now ruled all his father's original realms and Robert could follow the rest of the crusaders on armed pilgrimage in 1096.

Robert had his father's martial prowess and bravery, but none of his guile or strategy. By all accounts he fought bravely on the crusade and survived all the way to the capture of Jerusalem in 1099, an event not celebrated by endless praying and alms giving, but by wholesale slaughter. This frenzied act of violence against the local Muslims, Christians and Jews was such a terrible event that even the Western chronicles vividly described it, framing the slaughter in Biblically Apocalyptic terms.

Here I am however talking about events thousands of miles away from England and apparently nothing to do with Henry. It's what happened next that pulls all these stories together. One summer's morning in 1100, William Rufus went hunting in the New Forest with a retinue including Walter Tirel. Hunting was the perfect aristocratic pastime and while it was a much loved hobby, it had its elements of danger too. Horses can throw their riders and depending on the prey, the hunters can become the hunted and get gored by a stag or boar. However what happened to William Rufus was very strange. He was shot with an arrow that was fired by Walter and the king died from his wounds.

While the sequence of the following events is not in contention, the motivations are. As soon as this happened, Henry seized the royal mint at Winchester (the economic centre of England) and claimed the throne. Because Robert had yet to return from the Holy Land, Henry also claimed the title of Duke of Normandy. Very little is mentioned of Walter Tirel after the accident, but he certainly wasn't punished which is odd because he had just killed the King of England. To put that into context, a teenager who fired a freak shot at a noble walking a dog in the distance during a siege, actually hit Richard the Lionheart, who subsequently died of his wounds. Richard met the boy, congratulated him on the shot and even gave him some money. As soon as Richard died, the nobles caught the boy and flayed him until he died from his lacerations. Nothing like that happened to Walter.

Trying to prove a 900 year old conspiracy is impossible. As mentioned, hunting was dangerous and Walter may have miss-timed his shot and genuinely hit William Rufus by accident. History is full of such bizarre coincidences. In which case Henry took advantage of these serendipitous events to take control and in one fell swoop, managed to win everything.

The timing, however, is a little too good though for a conspiracy to be dismissed out of hand. Had the accident happened a few years earlier or later, things would have worked out rather differently. Robert would have been ruling Normandy and the clean sweep for Henry would have been much harder to achieve. Henry also seemed to be rather well placed to capture Winchester so quickly. He was crowned king just three days later at Westminster Abbey. Back to the statement "nobody knows for sure". Either way, Henry acted decisively and intelligently to the news, and it is this sort of response that was the cornerstone of his style.

When Robert returned, he almost immediately claimed Henry was a usurper and that he was rightful heir to both the crown of England (a little tenuous) and Duke of Normandy (he had a point there). So brotherly loved turned to fraternal war, culminating in 1106 with the Battle of Tinchebray. Ironically it was a battle that neither brother was expecting as the two armies met whilst marching to other areas of Normandy. However Robert's bravery and martial experience wasn't a match for Henry's quick wittedness, and by the end of the day Robert was not only defeated, but crucially, had been captured. Robert then spent the rest of his life (nearly thirty years) in captivity in Britain, dying in Cardiff Castle in 1134.

Henry continued to show his practical and intelligent nature by marrying the daughter of the King of Scotland. Her name was Edith and she was one of the lingering links of the house of Wessex, being a direct descendant of Edmund Ironside, an Anglo-Saxon King of England. This was a smart move as it made Henry look less of a foreigner to the English. It also further bolstered his claim to the throne and it made an ally of the Scottish nation which secured his Northern border. The only people this annoyed were the Anglo-Norman barons who wanted him to marry one of their own. To them it looked like Henry had "gone native" and to appease them, Edith changed her name to Matilda once she was queen (which was the same name as William the Conqueror's wife).

Once Robert was out of the way, Henry's reign was largely peaceful and he ruled for an impressive thirty five years. Peace and good governance led to prosperity and there was little drama during his reign, but some seeds of conflict were sown. One interesting one was that as King of England, Henry answered to no one but God. However as Duke of Normandy he had to swear an oath of loyalty to the King of France. At this time France was far less united nation than England and many counts and dukes were basically autonomous to the relatively weak central control. Even these semi-independent princes went through the motions of having a rightful claim to their title. However, for king to bow down and submit to another king creates a dangerous precedence. Did this oath giving make the French King somehow superior to the English King?

It is this point plus the intermarrying of the two royal families that was to lead to what is best described as a dynastic contest that was to start in the 12th century and end in the 15th. A temporary fix was that Henry sent his teenage son to swear the oath, so technically his son William did the duty, rather than Henry, and kept everyone happy. This lasted until the one great tragedy of Henry's reign. The English Channel may not be wide, but its waters are treacherous. They had already caused Harold to be captured in the 1060s and now this stretch of water made a more serious contribution to history. The White Ship disaster occurred in the winter of 1120 when seventeen year old William, who had only just that summer sworn allegiance to the King of France, drowned in the wreck of his royal ship.

William was Henry's only legitimate male heir. The golden rule about creating a clear succession was now shattered. Because of this Henry remarried (Edith had died years earlier) but he didn't produce another male heir. The family had plenty of nephews and cousins, but Henry wanted his own line to continue and so chose his daughter Matilda to rule as queen. Matilda was in her mid 20s but was already a widow. Henry had struck gold by marrying her to the Emperor of Germany (also called Henry) but he died, and returned to her father's side. So she was still an asset to use to secure Henry's dynasty. Henry quickly married her off to the Count of Anjou, one of the richest and most powerful French counties and on the southern border of Normandy. There was only one problem: Geoffrey of Anjou was still a teenage boy. Matilda had gone from being Empress of the Holy Roman Empire with an older and more powerful husband, to almost a mother to a count.

There was one piece of good news amongst all this: Matilda did get on with her husband and in March 1133 she gave birth to a son called Henry after her father. King Henry had a legitimate grandson and a potential successor. However, Henry was getting old and the chances of him hanging on until his grandson came of age were slim. This wasn't helped by the fact that he loved eating lamprey eels, which quite often gave him digestive problems. In the winter of 1135 after a particularly hearty helping of his favourite dish, he fell ill. Technically they didn't kill him, but his doctors gave him so many laxative treatments to try and give the king some relief, that those finished him off. There's got to be an off-colour joke about this somewhere in the story, but I'm not going there.

The White Ship accident undid many of the good things Henry had done for the nation, and it was to overshadow England for a generation. It was the biggest black mark in a long reign and it simply wasn't his fault; however he could have chosen a more acceptable successor because while he made all the barons swear an oath of loyalty to Matilda, in the 12th century the English weren't ready to be ruled by a woman. When Henry died, his nobles went back on their word and most backed Henry's nephew, Stephen of Blois, to become King Stephen. So started the period known simply as "The Anarchy".

Before we get to this period, it's worth mentioning royal names. Henry I was, of course, the first of eight kings who used the same name. The joint favourite name of English kings tied with Edward (although as we shall see later there have actually been more than eight English Kings called Edward). As time marched on, some kings changed names on accession to fit into a list of certain namesakes. This tradition was already common practice with popes. As a child, I assumed that Prince Charles, son of Elizabeth II, would invariably be called Charles III. That would make sense. Instead he is likely to take the name of George VII.

Following the history of royal names gives you a good indicator as to the success of the previous king of that name. Henry I as we have seen was a real winner, Henry II likewise grew the power of the English throne so there would inevitably be a number 3. Indeed throughout the medieval period, if in doubt Henry was the name of choice. At least England didn't give up on varying royal names. In France however you get to the point of virtual farce when the word king and the name Louis seemed to have become synonymous- there were eighteen of them.

Therefore you maybe surprised to find out that England had a king Stephen, and the fact that there was no Stephen II does imply that his was not a happy reign. Similarly, we've only had one King John, a man immortalised as the "bad guy" thanks to the tales of Robin Hood. It's hard to rehabilitate John but fortunately his son was Henry III and, as we now know because of the amount of them we know that the Henrys in general did quite well.

In England we've only had two king James (seven in Scotland), but because the last James was a pretty divisive character at a time when the monarchy was increasingly seen as the figure-head of the country rather than the political powerhouse it once was, it means there won't be another one of those. However it is strange that there haven't been more Charleses. Charles I of course lost his head in what was, in essence, a revolution but his son Charles II on his return to the throne was well liked and governed effectively. It's therefore a little strange that there hasn't been a third one.

Edward was used for 1,000 years, but the actions of Edward VIII, being the only English monarch to formally abdicate, means that the once safe name of Edward is forever besmirched and the list of Edwards will end with him. Henry VIII, on the other hand, was not a terrible ruler. True the most famous thing about him was his poor choice of wives and the second most famous fact about him was the founding of the Anglican Church, breaking the connection between England and Rome that had lasted for 900 years. But that hardly makes the Henry name toxic. Henry VI was far worse, pretty much an ultimate disappointment as a king (it didn't help that he was mad) but even after him, there was room for two more Henrys. James $6^{th}/1^{st}$ could have gone for Henry IX, and if not him, his son, but instead he was the first Charles. Will we ever see a Henry IX? Doubtful. For the time being it looks like it's Georges all the way, although we may get some more Williams.

Richards are a quick example of the law of diminishing returns. Richard I (the Lionheart) is legendary, famous in most of the world. Richard II was a disappointment and perhaps most famous for the touching play written by Shakespeare, but that wasn't real or contemporary. Then there's Richard III, not bad *per se* but because he was killed and a new dynasty came in to replace him, he would be painted as a bad guy (including, again, that man Shakespeare. In the modern world Richard III's family could have easily sued for defamation of character.). There was never to be a Richard IV.

As I have already mentioned, legacy and succession are vital to a hereditary institution like the monarchy. Being named like a previous winner somewhat eases you in. Henry V was an impressive warrior. Wouldn't you like to be synonymous with a victorious armour-plated warlord? It's an early version of "brand identity" where the abilities of one monarch temporarily rub off on the next one of the same name. My favourite example of this is Edward I and Edward II. As Edward I neared the end of his life, he just knew his son, while sharing his name, was not made of the same stuff as he was. Edward I seriously contemplated having his body broken down so his bones could be carried into battle as a sort of lucky charm for Edward II, knowing that the name alone was going to cut it (boy, was he right). As the reliquary for his bones was never created, we'll never know if this unique solution could have worked.

Perhaps the ultimate renaming comes from the current line of royalty. When hostilities with Germany broke out in World War 1, it was pointed out that their surname, Saxe-Coburg Gotha sounded just the tiniest bit German and therefore reminded the nation of their less than 100% English heritage (although as I have already pointed out, the Angles were German, too). So which name did they turn to? Well by then the Henry franchise was considered dead, so the other "go to" name was Edward, and as Edward III was a man associated with Englishness and he was sometimes called Windsor (he made Windsor Castle his base for chivalric ideals) the modern royal family chose the name of a man who had been dead for about 550 years, someone who wasn't particularly closely related to them.

Chapter 5 The Endless War (Part I the Unwinnable Civil War)

When Stephen was crowned king, he knew that it was a risky move and it was likely that it was going to lead to some kind of battle for power. What followed was nearly twenty years of civil war. This period, as previously stated, was called "The Anarchy". The civil war between two branches of the royal family in the second half of the 15th century was called "The War of the Roses". There were many other periods of war within the borders of England during the medieval period; therefore it's a little odd that the battle between Parliament and the Crown in the mid 17th century is called "The Civil War", as if none of these other wars had happened.

From around 1135 to 1485 – 350 years, almost every generation had a period of warfare that affected the nation. As the period progressed it was less to do with the aristocracy proving itself in mounted combat, and far more to do with peasant longbow men annihilating armour-plated knights. Death tolls were nothing compared to the 19th and 20th century, but then again, overall populations were much lower, too. Britain was regularly swept up in costly sieges, bloody battles, the deliberate burning and destruction of villages, crops and livestock. Between Scotland and England, if there wasn't outright war, there was regular cross-boarder raiding. In Wales this period marked the slow but steady conquest of the last Celtic lands. The Normans in Wales had the eminently sensible plan of pushing forwards a few miles each campaigning season, and then building a castle to lock down the local area. This is why Wales has so many castles.

Even if the war was in France, it led to higher taxation and again the loss of life of young men fighting on the continent. Then there was the draw of the Crusades, which not only was the realm of the aristocracy, but also all the pages and bowmen that are mentioned in the chronicles, would have been men from the peasant class who had to travel thousands of miles to see bloodshed and violence against the baking backdrop of a Middle Eastern setting.

Being in a siege was a nerve shredding experience. You would watch the enemy army building and digging, raising barriers to defend their siege engines, which in turn would rise out of the ground, seemingly from nowhere. There would usually be an attempt at negotiation. If the defenders knew no relief was likely and if they gave up at the start of the siege, they could expect to be allowed to go unmolested, ready to fight another day. However if there was a good chance of relief and they held out, then they would expect to suffer extreme privations, not only from the crash and thump of projectiles being hurled at their stout walls, but through the slow an insidious degradation of forces through disease and starvation.

Quite often agreements were made that if a relief force had not arrived by a certain date, then the castle would surrender. However on the flip side of this, if a castle defended itself after a breach was made and assault was started, then the defenders could expect no mercy. There was a cold logic to this. Better to negotiate and fight another day than be the hero and the victim of a slaughter. A lone castle would eventually fall, no matter how well designed it was; however if there was a good chance of relief, then a castle could keep a few hundred defenders safe from an entire army for weeks or months. It also meant that a castle was really only as good as the overall war effort.

If an assault came there would be the noise of screaming and the crash of weapons against shields and armour. The fighting would be up close and personal. You could look your attacker in the eye, feel his breath against your face and get sprayed by his blood and sweat in battle. There would be the sickening shudder as your weapon bit and slide into flesh, finally slowing and jolting as it struck bone. There was nothing refined or pleasant about any of this. Yet this isn't the way the period is generally remembered; there's glamour to this age. This period is remembered as the height of chivalry and castle construction. It is at this time that you get the book *Le Morte D'Arthur*. It all sounds very romantic, but the reality was brutal and scary.

Much blood had already been spilt in the history of Britain. Already we have covered numerous battles and raids, but somehow, once we get to the age of illuminated manuscripts and images of knights in shining armour, the perception is that the world was more civilised and war was somehow "nicer".

With Stephen's accession to the throne the lines were drawn for conflict. It did depend on Matilda getting people to look past the novelty of her gender and instead think of the legalities of being an oath breaker by joining Stephen but the period was marked by the fact that neither side could really land the killer blow. Of course with civil war tearing the country apart, the Scots knew they could invade Northern England and encounter little or no resistance. During this period there were regular invasions from north of the border adding to the general mayhem.

Initially it looked like Stephen was the right man for the job. He repelled invasions from Scotland; he put down a rebellion in Wales and fought successfully on the continent. On a personal level however, I don't want to overstate his successes. I once carefully constructed an essay about how Stephen was an underrated king, a bit like Richard III suffering from a bad press after the events. It was the lowest mark I ever got on an essay. It seems Stephen has no fans and it's undeniable that after a bright start, everything inexorably slid into chaos.

Matilda's side grew in strength and every ally she gained was a blow to Stephen's power and legitimacy. War dragged on, not just on the continent, but all over Britain, too. At one key point there seemed to be a respite to all this violence. After a battle at Lincoln, Matilda's forces actually captured Stephen, but despite the enmity, they could not bring it upon themselves to kill him, as he was an anointed king. To kill him (even if he was a usurper) would be to spill holy blood. However had they killed him, it probably would have saved everyone more bloodshed. He was released after Matilda's key ally, Robert of Gloucester, was captured and the warfare continued.

Here is the last quote I will use from the Anglo-Saxon Chronicle (which finishes at the end of Stephen's reign):

"...When the castles were made, they filled them with devils and evil men. Then took they those whom they supposed to have any goods, both by night and by day, labouring men and women, and threw them into prison for their gold and silver, and inflicted on them unutterable tortures; for never

were any martyrs so tortured as they were...for the land was all laid waste by such deeds; and they said openly, that Christ slept, and his saints. Such things, and more than we can say, suffered we nineteen winters for our sins."

It's a terrible condemnation of the times and the best summary of the age. The people felt as if God himself had deserted them. They had gone from God's blessed people to the damned, all in one generation.

How was it all resolved? After Stephen's captivity Matilda did rule for a time, but she was seen as overbearing and arrogant; or to put it another way, she was acting like any ruler would. The trouble was she was a woman and a woman should know her place (not my view, just the views of 12th century men). The barons couldn't stomach it and this led to a return to hostilities.

However, Matilda changed her tactics and instead of fighting for her own rule, she fought to secure the succession of her son, a male heir who everyone could agree was a rightful claimant to the throne. When Stephen's eldest son Eustace died, this paved the way for a deal. The negotiated settlement was a master stroke, and one that eventually brought peace. It was agreed that Stephen ruled until his death, at which point the crown was handed over to Matilda's son Henry, Henry II. And that's exactly what happened in 1154.

Henry II was accruing a large amount of lands in France. However he wasn't accruing them as a king, but as the Duke of Normandy or Count of Anjou, and with his marriage to Eleanor, he also acquired Aquitaine. This was great news for trade and revenues but bad news for relations between the French and English crowns. There was further salt rubbed in the wound in that Eleanor had been previously married to the French King Louis VII (see the French are already on number seven for Louis), but the marriage had been annulled.

The French King was woefully outclassed in terms of lands, wealth and even prestige. In all practical senses he was second class to the realities of the resources of the English crown. Except of course that to have the rightful claim to all these French lands, the English King had technically to become a Duke or Count and swear an oath of loyalty, in essence to carry out an act of submission, to the French crown in return for the legal entitlement to the lands. This was another flash point for war for centuries to come.

Some British historians refer to Henry II's reign as the start of the Angevine Empire, pointing out that at its peak, the English Monarch ruled England, most of Wales, most of Ireland and about half of France. This was an empire in anyone's books, except it's an anachronism. It wasn't referred to as an empire by contemporaries and the legalities, as already pointed out, showed that in the minds of the men of the age, these lands weren't some kind of unified force.

Henry gained most of these lands by marriage, inheritance and general negotiation; however he would fight when he had to, but for most of the first twenty years of his reign, things were relatively peaceful and a welcome respite from the destruction wreaked in Stephen's reign. Like his grandfather Henry I, he was a good administrator and both ruled for a lengthy time (actually both ruled for thirty five years).

It's also worth mentioning that in Henry's reign he was confirmed as the true and Christian ruler over Ireland. The Synod of Cashell in 1172 ratified this as a way to ensure that the Irish stuck to the doctrinal ideas of Roman Christianity as they were seen as semi-pagan by the Papacy, a great irony as Ireland had never lapsed from the faith, unlike England.

Three things summarise Henry's reign. Firstly, as with all European monarchs, there was always a tension with the church. The most famous argument was called "The Investiture Contest" which rumbled on for years in most Western European lands and can be summarised by the phrase "who gets to pick bishops?". The obvious response is they are churchmen, they report to the Pope, so the Pope gets to pick. Except Bishops were also major landholders, so they had a real say in the running of the country, therefore as powerful landowners surely the king gets to pick. Much was at stake and the issue was never really resolved, but it would flare up at various times, leading to the German Emperor having to stand barefoot in the snow, wearing ragged clothes at Canossa to show his repentance to the Pope. The Emperor had armies, but the Pope had the power of Excommunication. Excommunicates were beyond the law and for a ruler, being excommunicated meant that hostile powers had legitimacy in their actions against you. On a spiritual level it also guaranteed that you were going to hell, and while we sometimes see the actions of rulers as being cynical, most had a genuine religious element to their character; the thought of eternal damnation was a sobering thought for any believer. Good Christians were not even meant to speak to them: if you were excommunicated, you were tainted.

Why do I bring this up? Because the most famous thing about Henry II was his involvement in the murder and martyrdom of Thomas Beckett. It is a story that has been told in many books (Frank Barlow's Beckett is a great one to read if you want to go further) so I will give the edited highlights. Thomas and Henry started out as friends and when the Archbishop of Canterbury died, Henry leapt at the chance to make a friend and ally the most powerful churchman in the kingdom. However Thomas, once installed as Archbishop, took his role as a churchman seriously. He refused to be a puppet to royal whims, so friends became enemies as Henry's ally turned into his nemesis. It all came to a head with the Constitutions of Clarendon, a group of documents designed to weaken the link with Rome and give the king more power over the clergy. Everyone seemed compliant except Thomas who, while eventually agreeing to the terms verbally, refused to sign the document.

Enough was enough for Henry who flew into one of his well known rages. He wasn't used to being told "no". Thomas wisely fled to the continent under the protection of Louis VII who was only too happy to cause Henry a headache. Eventually the two men made peace and Thomas returned to Canterbury. The next tipping point was Henry's coronation of his eldest son (another Henry) by the bishop of London and the Archbishop of York. This was against protocol, but not law, and a snub to Thomas. Henry presumably wanted everything to go without a hitch and Thomas had shown he was his own man.

Consequently, Thomas took offense at this blatant slight to his position and authority and excommunicated pretty much everyone involved in the coronation, the Archbishop of York included. When Henry heard this, he flew into yet another rage. Exactly what he said next will always be disputed (nobody knows for sure), but the most famous version was, "Will no one rid me of this turbulent priest?". Four knights heard this, or words to this effect, and took it upon themselves to give the king what he wanted.

Did Henry want Thomas dead? Almost certainly not. We've all said things we didn't mean when angry. Did he want an unarmed churchman hacked to death in the most sacred building in Britain? Definitely not. There's an eye-witness account from

Edward Grim that tells us he was struck three times: The first cutting the crown of his head (not a killing blow but would create a severe head wound that would have bled profusely); the second, to the head, but Thomas, who had been reading vespers, still stood before his attackers and it was a third stroke that killed him. His last words were reportedly:

"For the name of Jesus and the protection of the church, I am ready to embrace death."

These poetic words from a truly holy man still have power 850 years later. His martyrdom quickly made him a saint and his shrine became a hugely potent pilgrimage site.

The fallout for Henry was disastrous. He had the right to fight wars and even debate religious privileges, but no king had the right to order the murder of clerics. Like the previously mentioned German emperor, Henry was forced to walk barefoot in a hair shirt as a sign of penitence, which I think is easy to believe was real. The knights who carried out the murder were all excommunicated and they travelled to Rome to meet the Pope himself to beg forgiveness. They were sent to the Holy Land to fight for fourteen years. For the times it was a very moderate punishment.

The second great feature of Henry's life was his wife. Eleanor of Aquitaine was one of the few women of the Middle Ages who gets as much attention as male contemporaries. She was married to two kings and was mother to two kings. She even went on the Second Crusade. The crusade itself was not a success but it speaks volumes about the attitude of Eleanor that she was willing to travel overland from France to Syria, and live amongst the male dominated world of an army (and have an affair with her uncle- but that story's for another time).

Henry II himself wanted to go on crusade and took the cross but failed to go, forever tied down to commitments and hostilities in his realm. This was to count against him in his dealings with the Pope. It is worth pointing out how the crusades and military activity happening on another continent had already shaped British history and would continue to shape British history for generations to come.

Eleanor was married to Louis for eight years and in that time gave birth to just one child. After she remarried to Henry she had eight children in about twelve years. I think it's safe to say they got on, and indeed, Eleanor ruled Aquitaine in Henry's absence for many years. Henry had a formidable mother in Matilda and formidable wife in Eleanor.

Things however soured and the third feature of his life occurred later in his reign when he fought a full-scale revolt against his sons, who were supported by his own wife. Sons rebelling against fathers is not unique, and as kings' children got to the age where they could start running things on their own, tensions would inevitably rise, so this scenario was not unusual. However with Henry owning such a large amount of land, this was a large conflict and another example of a civil war that has been largely forgotten.

Henry's children got the support of the French throne, and in the late 1180s Richard continued the war against his father, now fighting in conjunction with the King of France (Philip Augustus) and beat Henry in battle. Shortly after this Henry died of natural causes and Richard became king. Henry's final few days were spent on his death bed, knowing he had been beaten by his own son who was about to become king. Henry had grown up in a civil war and now he died in one.

Chapter 6 The Endless War (Part II England Goes on Crusade)

The year is 1189 and we come to one of the giants of history. Richard I King of England, Richard Coeur de Lion, Richard the Lionheart, Good King Richard. Richard didn't speak English. In his ten year reign he spent less than a year in total in England and his military schemes nearly bankrupted the country. So why is he remembered so fondly here in England? The simple answer is "because everyone loves a winner".

Richard was a war machine. He was one of those rare people who innately understood all things military. He was not just an immensely brave warrior in his own right, but he also understood the strategy and tactics needed to deliver victory. Wars don't come cheap and every victory leaves widows, even on the winning side. However the sacrifices made can seem worth it when your side achieves many of its goals. And that's what Richard did, time and again, against some impressive opponents. He invariably came up a winner, so much so that he's one of the few kings (like Alfred the Great or William the Conqueror) whose nickname is still remembered.

So how good was he? One way to underline his success is to look at his opponents. It has been argued (rather unfairly in my opinion) that Alexander the Great was helped by the fact that none of his opponents were particularly effective generals in their own right. It's sort of true, but it's the typical armchair general, hindsight-enabled comments that suck the life out of history. You think it's easy to fight your way from Northern Greece, through Afghanistan to the Indus River with a detour to Egypt...off you go then. However even the cynics would have to admit that Richard faced three proven military leaders in his lifetime: his own father Henry II, Salah ad-Din (Saladin) and Philip Augustus.

Some of these are better remembered than others, but the simple fact is all three men, when not fighting Richard, usually won the battle; and yet when they were up against Richard, they almost always lost. To paraphrase a much later American quote, in general he out-generalled other generals and that makes him, in military terms, quite special, and genuinely up there with the other "big" names of military history.

Again many books have been written about him and in particular the Third Crusade (try John Gillingham's excellent Richard I), but I want to give a brief run through of some of a few points that show us the real Richard. Firstly there's the issue that he was always going to be the junior partner on the third crusade. He and Philip Augustus didn't have the resources, or indeed, the same title as the German Emperor Frederick Barbarossa. Frederick raised a massive army, and although an old man, was determined to be remembered as a great Christian leader as well a powerful European ruler. This has been largely forgotten. Richard spent a fortune and carefully planned a campaign, assuming he would be a subordinate to an Emperor who had an army of 100,000 men. Richard by contrast, probably had around 15-20,000.

Richard also realised that walking from Europe to the Middle East wasted time and men and once into Anatolia, would expose any army to constant harassment from Muslim horse archers. Therefore it was Richard who changed the mode of transportation of crusades to ships- faster, easier and more efficient but also more expensive. It did however revolutionise the whole crusader movement. As a result of his crusade he landed in Sicily. His capture of Cyprus was not a great military feat, but moving the island's leadership to Western Christian authority allowed it to be a base of operations against the Turks well after the fall of the Kingdom of Jerusalem and into the height of the Ottoman Empire three and a half centuries later. On a more personal note this is where he married Berengaria of Navarre (she has the distinction of being the only Queen of England who never visited England).

After arriving in Palestine he found out that Frederick Barbarossa had drowned in a river in Anatolia and his huge army had disintegrated (so proving Richard's use of boats more efficient than a long march). Some Germans still made it to Acre, but the entire makeup of the crusade had altered beyond recognition. From being a key lieutenant, Richard was now the man in charge. Had an old man not lost his footing on a riverbank, things would have turned out very different and Richard might have been one of these warlike kings who gets admiration in the circles of military historians but nobody else had heard of.

Richard led the crusade in a successful siege (Acre), a pitched battle (Arsuf) and a daring raid (Jaffa), showing he had mastered the main types of military engagement. He was also smart enough to realise that to capture Jerusalem would be pointless as it couldn't be held once he left. Despite his rival (Philip Augustus) returning home before him, leading to an inevitable snatching of Richard's lands in France, he stayed on to set up the new crusader states as effectively as possible. He was a patient and strategically minded ruler, as well as being a brave man in battle.

Before we get too misty eyed about him (and it is easy to be distracted by his almost story book tales of daring), we must mention the terrible moments on the crusade. There was a massacre that even the chroniclers are uneasy about. As pointed out in my introduction, if the contemporaries had issues, then we have to take it more seriously than later revisionism.

After the siege of Acre, Richard had over 2,000 Muslim prisoners of war. Saladin by now, knowing that Philip Augustus, Richard's great rival, had sailed back home knew he could play for time. Richard knew the same, so after negotiations for the men's lives started to drag, Richard basically smelt a rat. Richard could have returned the troops with some kind of lesser deal but instead, he marched them out into the plane beyond the city and had his troop execute all of them. Thousands of unarmed men, under his protection, were mercilessly and brutally slaughtered. While it is true that Richard couldn't afford to waste any more time, and it's true he didn't have the manpower to keep such a large force locked up, this was a very coldblooded solution to the problem.

Indeed as soon as you start equating people's lives with being a problem, you are on the very slippery slope to dehumanising them, and then euphemisms like "final solutions" or "collateral damage" or "acceptable losses" start being used for terrible acts of violence. This was cold-blooded murder and it made Richard's contemporaries as squeamish then as it does the modern reader. It was strategically the right thing to do; it was morally the wrong thing to do.

At the siege of Acre Leopold V (from Austria, so part of the German contingent that made it to the Holy Land) planted his flag on the battlements first. Richard didn't like this, seeing it as his victory, and had it torn down and replaced it with his banner. A fairly bold challenge. Also in the wranglings that went on in the Holy Land during his time there, Richard was implicated (rightly or wrongly) in the death of Conrad of Montferrat, Leopold's cousin. Richard had made a dangerous enemy.

This gives us an insight into another flaw in the man because on his return journey, while he hadn't planned it, Richard decided to travel incognito through Leopold's lands. This is the part of the Robin Hood legend which is true and as usual, the bit that sounds the most fantastical is actually based on bizarre historical fact. Richard was detected and Leopold got his revenge, imprisoning Richard and literally demanding a king's ransom for his release.

England at the time was being run in his absence by Eleanor, Richard's mother. So another part of the Robin Hood legend turns out to be true because punitive taxes were raised to pay for Richard's release, after additional taxes that were needed to pay for the crusade (the Saladin Tithe). However none of this was because Prince John (Richard's younger brother) was a pantomime villain wanting lots of gold (for no clearly explained reason), but because the country was paying for "good" King Richard's decisions.

What was Richard thinking? Why did he take such a risk? The answer is by now the familiar "nobody knows for sure". However it's worth remembering that Richard was a bold man who took risks, and more often than not, they paid off. Had his subterfuge worked, it would have been another victory on his list as he fooled Leopold and got home using craft and guile. While this is one way of looking at things, the other is that Richard was a reckless adventurer. He'd made a number of risky moves in the Holy Land and now he was ready to gamble again, and while that would be fine if he was a knight, he wasn't. He was a ruler and if he had been a little more sensitive to that, he could have found a similar but politically safer route home.

John doesn't exactly come out of this exonerated because while the money was being raised for his release, he and Philip August did actually offer substantial sums to keep Richard in prison. Richard as a crusader could count on Papal support. Putting a crusader in captivity on his journey to or from the Holy Land was against the rules of pilgrimage, so the Pope excommunicated Leopold and anyone who held him. However by 1194 Richard was finally released after a cripplingly large ransom had been paid.

But before we come to Richard's epic return to France, it's worth having the debate about his sexual orientation. It's a topic that has led to numerous historians arguing and contradicting each other; and of course, like many great debates, there can never be a definitive answer. One argument is that while he did a lot of campaigning and was kept in prison, he still had time to sire an heir, and without doubt Richard had no legitimate children. However if Edward II a king who had to be gay (more on that later), was able to summon up enough courage to do his duty and have children, why couldn't Richard?

Then there's the deliberate misreading of Richard lying in bed with Philip Augustus- so were the two of them lovers? The answer to this one was "absolutely not", and while it might be fun to think of the ensuing war between them as the ultimate lovers spat, the fact is, the phrase is to do with a PR stunt to show solidarity, which has subsequently been either accidentally or deliberately misinterpreted.

Of course the problem is with all these old chronicles is that they were designed to say what happened and put who they were writing about in the best possible light. The idea of the "man behind the name" is something that comes much later, which is why we only get hints of the real personalities or personal motivations that we have come to expect from a modern biography.

There seems to be some evidence of Richard chasing girls, but on the other hand, he seems to have to make confessions for other types of possibly gay indiscretions. We are all humans with our own complex feelings and emotions running through our heads. These people were no different, but because of the extant sources, we just didn't get their thoughts written down. Who knows what was going on in their minds, but he's unlikely to have been a standard bearer for Gay Pride.

So Richard returned home where John immediately asked for forgiveness and Richard accepted John's desire for reconciliation. With Philip Augustus however, things weren't as simple. Richard had lost control of most of his French lands so he now had to reassert his authority. With his usual efficiency at war he began to do so and the symbol of his desire to dominate France can be seen by Chateau Gaillard.

Chateau Gaillard was not a chateau in the more modern sense, but a castle, and at the time the most impressive one in Europe. In the three years it took to construct, it took two years of England's entire revenues to build, a colossal expenditure on just one military project. It is however an example of a new breed of castle, greatly evolved from the simple Motte and Bailey designs of the previous generation. It was a declaration of intent and a projection of Richard's power in France, written in stone. To Philip Augustus it was a red rag to a bull. Philip boasted he would take the castle "even if the walls were made of steel." Richard retorted that he would defend it "even if the walls were made of butter."

Ever since I first heard of this monument to Richard's power I have been fascinated by it. When my parents took the family on a holiday to Normandy, I wanted to see the site of this fortress that dominated the Seine valley. Sadly, today there's not much to see, but even that adds mystery. After the build up I remember the palpable disappointment of my parents when we turned up to a crumbling ruin, so I can't say it's a "must-view" location. But just standing there, you can see that Richard chose the perfect location for a defensive site. It was a key site of conflict and siege for hundreds of years, and eventually it was torn down. It had been the site of so much interest by either French or English armies for so long that in the late 16th century, the French king ordered it to be demolished once and for all. Once again Richard's legacy echoed through the centuries, long after his death.

Richard wasn't just building, he was fighting and pushing back Philip Augustus. By 1199 almost all Richard's lands were back under his control again; at this rate it wouldn't be long until he took the Ile de France, the area of French Royal control based around the Paris region. However, in a minor siege at the minor castle of Chalus-Chabrol, Richard went out at dusk to walk his hunting dogs and a young boy took an optimistic shot at the distant figure and mortally wounded the King of England. It was another one of those freak events that had huge implications for history.

As already mentioned, Richard asked to see the defender who had hit him. He gave him a purse of coins and ordered that nobody should harm him, quite frankly, one of the coolest death scenes in history. Even as he lay dying he was the stuff of legends. Richard died, saving Philip Augustus an end game he was likely to have lost and Richard's retinue went back on their word and tortured and killed the boy who had shot him.

So we come to John, a man so different from his elder brother it's hard to see them coming from the same family. John and Richard were chalk and cheese, but the biggest difference is that John was a loser. John lost Chateau Gaillard because even though it had withstood assault (a French soldier had got in via a new and unbarred latrine that John had ordered to be installed- John doesn't help his own reputation.), the garrison realised that there was no relief force coming. Surrender was the only way to avoid a death sentence, showing once again that a castle can be as brilliantly designed as possible but in the greater scheme of things, they can't win wars in their own right. The fall of the castle and the city of Rouen meant that Normandy was now under Philip Augustus's control. In a few short years since Richard's demise, all his gains in France had been lost by his brother.

Then John faced a revolt from his barons. Yet another civil war broke out, only this time the King did emphatically lose. He even managed to lose the backing of the church by getting into a political storm over the election of the new Archbishop of Canterbury, which lead to him being excommunicated. John had lost militarily, politically and even spiritually; he was a defeated man. What to do with a defeated king? The idea of deposing a king hadn't evolved yet and the thought of a republic would have been anathema. So the great landowners created a document, a great charter (which is what Magna Carta means), and in 1215 got him to ratify it (he never signed it but added his royal seal) at Runnymede.

Magna Carta's importance has been a little overstated. In essence it says that nobody, not even the king is above the laws of the land, the first time this idea was articulated in Western European history. While this is true, the document is not some great emancipation proclamation, nor is it an early declaration of fundamental human rights. There's a lot in there about farming, inheritance rights, fisheries in the Thames, the sort of things rich landowners care about. It's also worth noting that as soon as John agreed to it, he quickly raised a new army and started fighting again, so nullifying the charter through his actions (that were supported by the Pope). It was a dead document almost as soon as the wax on the seals had cooled.

The turmoil in England and the comparative tranquillity in France allowed Philip Augustus to offer a helping hand to the rebels of England, and in 1216 Philip's son Louis (yes, another one) landed in England with an army to "help". With John in the north and a French army in the south, it was starting to look like 1066 all over again, exactly 150 years later. The chances were good that the two crowns would be united, with dominance going to the French monarch.

John finally had the upper hand with his own nobles, but with the French army arriving, the balance tipped back against him. Further bloodshed was imminent, and indeed foreign rule also looked imminent. Then John did the best thing he ever did for his country. He died. At a stroke, the reason for the baron's rebellion ended. It also gave no legitimacy for the French army to be in England. So Louis and his troops went home, presumably very frustrated that fate had dealt them a bad hand, knowing that they had been so close to something so historic. The English nobles in turn rallied round John's son Henry, who was quickly crowned Henry III.

Henry was a boy on his father's death, so he had to have advisors. These advisors ensured that Magna Carta was ratified again, and it's this action that makes the document so important. It was now the essential document that a king had to agree in advance of a smooth coronation. It was already becoming a symbol to say "I will rule lawfully and not arbitrarily" and for generations to come, it or a modified version of it, was agreed at the start of a king's reign. It was these subsequent actions, referring back to the document, that made the charter momentous, not the actual events of 1215.

Henry's reign lasted for over fifty years and can be seen, by-and-large, as a break from all the warfare. There were some exceptions, but Henry's reign saw some important changes that weren't to do with bloodshed. Henry was the first king to come to the throne with a written promise to show he was going to rule by the laws of the land. Although Henry, and indeed, all the kings for the next few centuries would rule like the absolute monarchs in Europe, it turned out that this was an inadvertent safety valve for change. Although the first parliament was while John was still king, it was under Henry that it becomes an established institution that would very slowly start to eat away at the powers of the monarchy. All this ultimately came to a head in the mid 17th century in what is called "The Civil War" (ignoring the dozens of other ones), but that was the tipping point. Before the Civil War the monarch had the upper hand, afterwards, it was parliament with the power.

Parliament and the continuing traditions of charters like Magna Carta are why we still have a monarchy today (instead of beheading them in a town square or shooting them in a basement). It allowed the transition of power (again, very slowly) from a central unelected official, to a wider group. Let's not get too dizzy with the concept of democracy. In the 13th and 14th centuries, what the king said was what happened, and parliament wasn't full of wise, common men but rich land owners, who used the institution for selfish ends, just as a king might. But the idea of governing through consensus was here to stay, and that's important.

That's not to say that Henry was all for the erosion of his power. Throughout his reign (once he was old enough), he regularly tried to fight against the restrictions of Magna Carta. He also tried to undo the damage of his father's failures in France and tried to win back the northern territories of Normand and Anjou (it's worth remembering that he still held Gascony in southern France). Therefore Henry kept up the royal hobby of going to war with France, once again making a mockery of the idea that "The Hundred Years War" was somehow a special period of enmity between the two crowns.

While I seem to be a little misleading in my initial statement that Henry's reign was relatively quiet, we have to remember this was over a fifty + year period and the perception of contemporaries was that the country was not blighted by war and destruction. Part of a king's job was to be a warrior and defend the country's (and therefore his) interests. A state of low level constant warfare was almost assured. It's worth pointing out that post-World War II, we are experiencing the longest period of peace in Western European history...ever.

Henry's biggest problem was the hugely powerful noble Simon de Montfort, who was Earl of Leicester and Chester. Simon de Montfort was son of the famous Simon de Montfort (a little limited on the imagination of naming the heirs of the family though). The first one had fought in a particularly nasty crusade called the Albigensian Crusade in southern France. By now the crusades embraced any group that threatened the power of the Roman Christian faith. I mention this because Simon died in the siege of Toulouse, showing he was not just a military leader, but a man who was willing to take risks and fight in the most dangerous theatres of war. He took a direct hit from a rock hurled by a siege engine, a very quick and very messy way to die.

His son followed in his father's footsteps and was a brave man of action. Simon was so powerful he had married Henry's sister. The two men were of similar age and as an ultimate sign of trust between the two, Simon was sent to be governor of Gascony. However here he was an outsider, and the status quo was disrupted by this noble from England. Simon tended to want to do "the right thing". Twice he took the cross, the act of declaring he would go on crusade, which was becoming a right of passage for young nobles to prove their piety and bravery all in one go. Twice he was thwarted by the king who declared that he was too important to the running of his lands to go. Therefore when he started to clean up some of the nepotism, excesses and inefficiencies in Gascony, the locals pushed back, declaring that Simon was abusing his power.

Simon was acquitted, but Henry, who had at times fallen out with Simon, ensured he stayed in France to keep him out of the way. However there was a general disgruntlement that Henry was showing too much favour to his cronies and in-laws, that the king was abusing his power rather than ruling wisely. This was probably the most common complaint by landowners in any country against a hereditary monarchy. Some favouritism was par for the course, but it seems that Henry's was either too overt or too consistent in picking the favourite for the job, rather than the right man.

Eventually the nobles gravitated to Simon de Montfort as the rallying point of this disgruntlement. In 1263 he returned to England to initially plead his case, but tensions rose to the point that, only through force of arms was anyone going to get anywhere with the argument. So civil war broke out. This seemed pretty rash because, at this stage, although Simon may have had popular consent on his side, he didn't have a large army, nor had he really had time to solidify his support. Henry acted quickly and brought Simon to battle. Henry decided to "blood" his son Edward who also fought in the Battle of Lewes in 1264.

Edward showed the potential that would make him one of England's greatest warlords. He defeated Simon's left flank, but in the rashness of his youth, he pursued the retreating contingent, taking him away from the battle. Simon managed to keep the rest of his force together and defeat the main body of Henry's army and when Edward returned, he was also defeated and captured on the field of battle. For Simon the outcome couldn't have been more emphatic despite facing a larger and better equipped army, he had not only won, but now had the king and heir to the throne in his custody.

But what to do with a defeated king? This was a dilemma that had faced the nobles after Stephen's capture and again, after John's defeat. Yet again the barons were faced with the problems of what to do with the figurehead of government under their control. The laws all flowed through the monarch, and of course, the coronation is a public declaration that the king is crowned and blessed by God himself. Surely no man can cast aside such a person? To summarise this, the best quote has to go to Louis XIV who simply declared "I am the state." That was some 400 years later, and by then the monarchs of England were different in their interactions with the mechanics of governance; but in the middle of the thirteenth century, Louis's summary fits the situation perfectly. Nobody quite knew what to do next.

Except for de Montfort, who invoked a parliament of elected officials, the first time in Western European history that elected officials gathered to rule the country. The birth of the modern concept of parliament started here, and for about a year, Simon de Montfort was in essence, the first republican ruler of England. The phrase itself is incredibly anachronistic, but for a year, the country got on with running itself -without the direct influence of the king.

This status quo was simply too novel and to keep it going, Simon had to make too many concession to potential enemies, both foreign and domestic. Inevitably, the tide turned against this alien way of ruling and, on the most practical level, Prince Edward escaped and started to do what he would inevitably be best known for: he went to war.

It all culminated in the Battle of Evesham. Simon was awaiting reinforcement from one of his sons (another Simon; it seems the de Montforts were more novel at creating new systems of government than they were at coming up with children's names). When he saw the banners of the approaching army, he recognised them as his own, but joy soon turned into shock when he realised it was Prince Edward displaying the banners he had won in the run up to this battle. For Edward, this was payback. He had been defeated, imprisoned and watched as the country slid into anarchy and the man responsible for it all was in front of him. Edward positioned his troops at the top of a hill, forcing Simon's smaller army to fight and charge uphill. This was not a great historical battle, because it was over before it started. The outcome was the unsurprising annihilation of Simon's army and his death at the battle. Normal service was to be resumed and Edward had shown everyone what to expect once he had the crown.

Henry ruled for seven more years, and then it was Edward's chance to show everyone what he had in mind for the throne. Henry III was a little obsessed with a distant ancestor- Edward the Confessor. To honour this king, Henry ordered the rebuilding of Westminster Cathedral to enlarge his shrine, the building that still stands today. Henry was so in awe of this Anglo-Saxon ruler he even named his first son after him, so resurrecting an Anglo-Saxon name in a very French family line. This makes it a little ironic that Henry's son is now seen as Edward the first, when he was named after another English king called Edward. There was actually two other King Edwards in the Anglo-Saxon era before that, so by my reckoning, we've had elevn of them, not eight (a good pub quiz question). Edward I became known as that to differentiate him from his son and grandson because, for the first time in English history, we had three kings in a row, all with the same name. He was the first of the three Edwards and not actually Edward I.

Chapter 7 The Endless War Part III – the Brief Unification of Britain

Two things are now worth noting. Firstly, Simon de Montfort is the first person to get any serious consideration in this book who wasn't "royal". One of the advantages of looking at the time period of a king's rule is a pleasing, but false, sense of the beginning, middle and end of a story. However as time went on, the monarchs themselves had less say in the running of the country than they did in the past; and while the tipping was yet to come it had started. Simon's moment in history is a good time to pause and point this out.

Secondly, with Edward I, we get to the first truly contentious period of British history. Even though these are events from 700 years ago, the echoes of his actions still reverberate on these islands today. I want to take the four main ones and work through them.

Empires
It's strange to think of the British Isles as an empire, but it was. At the height of his power, Edward ruled Ireland, Wales, Scotland, England and parts of France. The last part was not technically as king, but the rest of it, he absolutely was the man in charge. You can use whatever title you want, but he was de facto ruler of all those territories (if this gets Welsh or Scottish readers fuming, wait; I've yet to get to you).

The point is that one of the key things the war between 1939 and 1945 did was to start setting some ground rules about expansionist and acquisitive wars. Nowadays it's almost impossible to build an empire. True there are other factors like cheap explosives, the ubiquitous AK-47 and the mobile telephone/social media that give the insurgent advantages that local populations could only dream of even a hundred years ago; but putting technology to one side, the word "empire" is now synonymous with "evil", and it's very hard to get any support in taking over another country.

However (and I will go into more depth on this later) in the Middle Ages, you did it to the other guy before he did it to you. It's not a pretty way of looking at things and it's also quite blunt, but it was the truth of the matter. Might was right and if you didn't expand into that undefended territory on your borders, than your enemy probably would and make your life hell. We've already seen it with Cnut, who had no real claim to the throne of England, but gave it a try, which paid off handsomely. The same goes for William the Conqueror. More recently in our story, Philip Augustus had no real legal right to take all the French lands away from Richard and John, but he could, so he did.

Those were the accepted rules of the day, and therefore, those are the rules we should judge these people by and not some modern interpretation of morality.

Scotland
The Scots came to Edward for his help in attempting to quell their own bloody civil war. Scotland hasn't had that much attention so far, but the history of Scotland is just as complex as that of England, with many groups vying for power. Scotland was not an idyllic land of misty highlands and outstanding whisky, defiled by the English. It had its own group of selfish and violent nobles who would happily go to war with each other, and frequently used England's wars in France to raid the north of England for no other justification than they could. Therefore, when the English came in force to fight, they tended to win (don't worry I'll get to the great big exception a little later); and they did this because Scotland was hostile and that's what hostile, forces do to each other.

Had Scotland allied with England rather than France, 500 years of messing about could have been saved and both countries would have prospered. Scotland never really gained much from the "Auld Alliance" with France, except for legitimising raiding in England. But France didn't pay Scotland the sort respect it gave to the Holy Roman Empire, Spain or even England in terms of marriages or alliances. France saw Scotland as a weapon to be used against an enemy, and not as an equal partner.

Scotland had famous people before the Act of Union in 1707, but they only became world famous because of the British Empire. Once Scots and Englishmen worked together, Scotland really started becoming more than a local power. Compare the fast economic improvements in Scotland in the first 100 years after union and as part of a global empire, with the previous 500 years of fighting the English.

Which brings me to William Wallace. He may have been turned into a beautiful and emotive (if completely historically mangled) movie, but so was Lawrence of Arabia. Both are, at best footnotes in history. It's also worth remembering that no matter how poetic his defeat or how noble his cause, he lost; and losing isn't what Scotland needed in a ruler against Edward I. William and Lawrence are both examples of Interesting stories, but on the world stage of historical players, nothing special- Sorry.

Wales

Wales had no list of kings prior to Edward I. It wasn't actually a country, more an area that was culturally connected by the Welsh language and Celtic traditions. Wales was made up of a group of principalities which would happily and regularly fight against each other. They not only fought the English, but made deals with them too, sometimes colluding to gain their own chunk of an enemy's territory. Llewellyn ap Gruffyd, a famous Welsh "freedom fighter", made a peace deal with Simon de Montfort, showing he was open to political realities and not just noble concepts of freedom and fighting the English. Indeed, exactly how "English" the invaders of Wales were is also up for debate. As the nobles of England, they were all Anglo-Norman from the same blood lines of William the conqueror's Norman army. You could say that while England was conquered in just 20 years by the Normans, Wales did very well resisting the Norman invasion of their country all the way into the late thirteenth century.

The Welsh princes' biggest issue was that they never made overseas allies. Scotland had France (although how likely France would come to Scotland's aid is debateable). Wales didn't have a major power to back it, and who would want to? With no fixed ruler, the principalities were small in size, resource and usefulness. Florence was smaller than Powys, but had banking; Bruges was smaller than Anglesey, but they had a trade network; Wales didn't have many bargaining chips, so without external support, it was inevitable that it would be absorbed by a much larger and richer neighbour.

Similar to Scotland, once areas were incorporated under the English crown, then there was access to a larger world, greater availability of trade routes and markets for produce. Cardiff was the largest city in Wales, and yet it was one of the first places to be conquered. Indeed the geography of Wales with its mountainous regions, particularly centrally, meant that the north of the country found it easier to communicate with the north of England than with the south of Wales, and vice-versa.

Edward didn't start the conquest of Wales, but he ended it; and while it can be lamented that Wales wasn't treated as an equal partner, there was no reason to do so. There were no kings to negotiate with; the population, arable land and overall resources were all significantly smaller than those of England. If the tables had been reversed, the Welsh kings would have done no differently to the principalities of England.

Anti-Semitism
This is where a very careful path must be tread. First, let's put Edward's actions in context. Almost every time a crusade was declared, the poor would stand no chance of joining in. But how to show some solidarity? How to strike back against the haters of Christianity? The answer was, inevitably, an attack on the local Jewish population- and this happened across Europe. Generation, after

generation, from region to region, the Jewish communities suffered again and again.

The modern observer finds this to be blatant anti-Semitism. To the medieval man, it was acceptable. The Jews were "other"; they defied the Church and were money lenders (a trade forbidden to Christians). They also kept away from the rest of society (who could blame them when massacres were so common place?), which led to various myths such as Jews sacrificing Christian children (there are saints still recognised by the Catholic church, like St. Simon of Trent, who was a child allegedly killed by Jews. Probably the poor boy was assaulted and murdered by a medieval paedophile, but the blame invariably went to the Jewish community).

None of this is acceptable now, but I am writing about a time when the Jews of Britain were technically the king's property and he could tax them as he chose. This small group generate great revenues, in return he was meant to protect them, but in practice, he tolerated them.

Edward had more than a few similarities to his great uncle Richard the Lionheart. Like Richard, he was a complex man who did some bad things as well as good. So it was with the Jews that Edward blots his mark on history, as Richard did with the massacre of the prisoners. However, I think Edward was no more anti-Semitic than the next man (which is to say he was anti-Semitic, but not especially so for the time).

Edward's wars and castle construction were very expensive and the Jews were a source of revenue for him. First he squeezed them with taxes; then, under trumped up charges, had 300 killed for coin clipping. Devaluing the currency was a serious offence, and to be fair to Edward, that was the usual punishment for the crime, although it was rather convenient that the deaths of these key Jewish figures led to more wealth coming to him. This move would have been a tactic the mafia dons would recognise.

Then in 1290, with the Edict of Expulsion, he exiled all the Jews from England, an order that was to last nearly 350 years. This was not a new idea. The Kings of France had already done this twice, many years earlier, and it was not motivated by some irrational hatred. What it did do was wipe the slate clean of his debts to them. Edward needed the cash; it wasn't motivated by simple anti-Semitism. Just like Richard, it can be judged as the strategically right thing to do, but morally wrong.

Battles and sieges were par for the course, and death was just an everyday occurrence in these times, but the expulsion of an entire ethnic community definitely tarnishes his image in modern eyes. It is, however worth pointing out how incredibly happy it made the rest of the country when he did it; and Parliament signed off on more taxes because of the "pious" actions he had taken, showing there were greater bigots than Edward around at the time. The Jews were not to return to England until the time of Oliver Cromwell in the mid 17th century.

For more on Edward, try "A Great and Terrible King" by Marc Morris, a superb (if a little obsessed with exchequer rolls) history of Edward. As already mentioned, Edward had definite similarities to Richard; both went on crusade, both were high effective warriors, both knew how to build a state-of-the-art castle. Edward's legacy was more permanent, but on the other hand, he never did battle with a "great" opponent. William Wallace was no Saladin or Philip Augusts, so it could be said that Edward was never tested to the extremes that Richard was.

The 8th crusade is one you've probably never heard of, and there's a reason for that. It was all a bit of an anti-climax and Edward's role in it was as a Prince, subservient to the King of France, Louis IX. There was no equivalent to the siege of Acre or battle of Arsurf for Edward, so legends and popular folk lore did not spring up. There was however, one moment where Edward could have ended up a footnote to history. He was very nearly assassinated.

In English we get the word "assassin" from a secret society called the Hashishin. It is ironically a derogatory term meaning "the users of hashish" in Arabic. It was alleged that these poison blade wielding hit men, who would fight to the death, were inspired by drug addled dreams. This wasn't true. As the modern world shows us, all you need to have is enough faith, backed by the wrong teachers, and you can get a man to sacrifice himself for your cause- no drugs needed. They did however, inspire fear in both Muslims and Christians. In the Holy Land both faced attacks from this Muslim extremist sect. An attack by one meant almost certain death.

One of these assassins, posing as a respectable envoy, managed to convince Edward's men that he should have a one-on-one meeting with Edward in his own private quarters, where Edward would be unarmed. The assassin lunged at him with his poisoned blade, and while he did cut Edward on the arm and even managed a glancing blow to the head, Edward was able to fight him off with a nearby stool. So the heir to throne had to fight to the death, hand-to-hand, with a member of the most feared assassination team in the world- and he won. This is the stuff that legends are made of. In one version Edward's wife Eleanor sucked the poison from his wounds. Had the assassin succeeded, English history would have been very different. Edward had yet to sire an heir, so the next 100 years of English history would have had completely different rulers.

But Edward recovered from his wounds and while his actions on crusade showed his bravery they didn't make the same impact as Richard's. Once crowned in 1272 Edward was to embark on one of the most energetic and successful series of conquests yet seen by an English king. He is known as "Long Shanks" for his height, "Hammer of the

Scots" for obvious reasons, but also "The flower of chivalry", to many contemporaries both at home and abroad, he embodied the medieval ideal of what a warrior king should be.

By the end of the first decade of his rule, Edward could claim domination over Wales. There were later serious rebellions but in 1284, the Statute of Rhuddlan incorporated the remaining Welsh lands into the English administration. Edward was thorough. He wanted to ensure that Wales couldn't slide back into rebellion, so he went on the most extensive and revolutionary castle building scheme yet seen in the British Isles. They incorporated the latest technology, the newest designs, and these castles were monsters.

Beaumaris was never completed, but even in its half-finished state, you know it's a formidable fortification. Nowadays it's land locked, but originally, it had one side on the sea front to allow resupply by ship. It's also perfectly concentric, a new system of defence in depth, where siege engines would find it much harder to make any impact on the walls. Corners, which were always a structurally weak point of attack, have been completely avoided by adding semi-circular towers making the structure stronger and giving a wider arc of fire on any attackers.

Conway was built specifically for English settlers in Wales, and indeed, anybody Welsh found there after dark was presumed to be a saboteur and faced the death penalty. This is why I call it

Conway. It was built by the English and named Conway; to make the name more Welsh by renaming it "Conwy" misses the point of its origins and history.

Caernarfon, the jewel in the crown of the Edwardian network of castles (Edward II was born here, which led to the later designation of the Prince of Wales for the next in line to the throne, a title that exists to this day). The locals wisely tried to attack while it was under construction because they had to know that once it was finished, nothing short of an army would be able to take it. The walls had distinct bands of colour around them, reminiscent of the walls of Constantinople, which had kept that city safe for nearly a thousand years and were a symbol of Roman power. Edward had built his own miniature Constantinople in North Wales to show his imperial power to the Welsh. They are English authority written in stone.

These are but a few examples. Castle construction was hugely expensive (generating the debts I have already mentioned) but the strategy worked. Wales may have had the occasional rebellion, some serious, but they all fizzled out and the English were never far from a safe base of operations.

Edward had achieved what everyone since King Offa of Mercia in the days of the multiple kingdoms of Anglo-Saxon England had failed to do; he had brought Wales under the rule of the English crown. From here on, when the French Chronicles refer to "English" armies, they actually mean a mix of

English, Welsh and quite often, Gascon soldiers. Welsh longbowmen in particular, helped England to some of its greatest victories on the continent.

Edward could have stopped there, but he didn't because of a freak accident, of the kind that crop up more often that you'd expect in history. Alexander III King of Scotland is best known for being in a hurry. He had been married to one of Edward's sisters and the two men were on good terms with each other. But with great sadness to both men, Alexander had witnessed, not only the death of his wife, but a number of his children, too.

This put the middle-aged king in a precarious position; he had run out of male heirs and also a queen with which to produce more. So he quickly remarried and in the meantime, made his granddaughter (Margaret only a toddler at this point) his heir. These were all sensible precautions followed by a spate of bad luck that was to change everything.

In 1286 Alexander made his hasty decisions to acquire an heir. He had finished his business and a celebration of his new marriage in Edinburgh when he decided that he just had to see his young wife that night. The weather was terrible and he was advised that he should wait until conditions got better, but he had one of the more pleasant duties of a king to attend to, so with a small retinue, he went off into the storm in the dead of night. What exactly happened that stormy night we'll never know, but Alexander got separated from his party and he never made it to his destination in Fife. It seems that along the way, his horse stumbled and the king was found the next morning lying dead on the shore with a broken neck.

Dynastic disaster struck Scotland. The king was dead, the queen had been in the country for only a few months so had no real support, and the throne now potentially was in the hands of a child, Margaret, Alexander's granddaughter. Already the wolves were circling their prey. John Balliol made a claim for the throne and the Bruces, a powerful family, backed Margaret's claim. It was civil war and none of this was down to Edward. The group of guardians appointed to rule for Margaret until she arrived from Norway (she was the daughter of the King) and was old enough to rule did their best to keep the peace but tensions were high.

However Scotland had a potential saviour. Edward was seen as a great diplomat as well as warrior. He had been involved in a number of continental disputes, both as antagonist and as conciliator, and he was viewed as a wise ruler, one who could work through the different grievances and come up with an independent solution. Why not ask him for some help?

Edward's solution, readily agreed by the Scottish nobles, was that his first born son (who was about the same age as Margaret) would marry her, and together they would be the rightful rulers of both nations, uniting the two crowns of Britain. It was a simple and elegant solution that gave Scotland the footing as a partner, not subject to the English throne. Edward had pulled off another diplomatic triumph.

So Margaret, aged just seven was sent from Norway in 1290. True, there would be a long period of stewardship under the guardians, but in the long term, both nations would benefit from this union. However the North Sea, even in summer, is a rough place to be and this little 7 year old girl fell ill on the journey. At the Orkney Islands things got worse, and she died. The fate of two nations had rested on Margaret and her sad demise was to lead to centuries of further warfare between the two nations. It was one of the great missed opportunities of British history.

For Edward this political tragedy was met by personal tragedy when Eleanor, his wife of 46 years, died. He was, by all accounts, grief stricken and as her body was carried south for the funeral, he ordered a cross to be built at everyplace where her body had been overnight. That's why the London station Charing Cross is so called, because it was one of the twelve places marked with a cross. The original stone cross was destroyed in the civil war; what stands today is a Victorian interpretation of the original. Although he remarried, it is a unique sign of royal mourning.

With Edward's diplomatic plans thwarted in Scotland and with no wife to perhaps temper his bellicosity, Edward pushed harder and harder to gain recognition as ruler of Scotland. John Balliol objected, of course, but by no means all the Scottish lords rallied to his cause. After all John had openly defied the wishes of Alexander III, the last undisputed king of Scotland and Edward had tried to arbitrate a solution and was a formidable king from a major royal household, trumping John in pretty much every possible comparison.

Eventually the situation led to violence, and in 1296, Edward invaded and swept through southern Scotland. There was a brief battle at Dunbar, but apart from routing the Scottish army, it was not a clash of particular note. After a brief siege of Edinburgh and the capture of Stirling castle, Edward had won. John Balliol capitulated, and while Edward was never crowned King of Scotland, something Scottish Nationals love to point out, he was in every other sense, King of Scotland. Robert The Bruce didn't feel secure enough in his claim to crown himself king until 1306- ten years later (and after the murder of one other potential claimant to the throne). Edward took with him on his return journey to England, the Stone of Destiny, the great slab of rock all the medieval kings of Scotland had been crowned on. Edward made a niche under his own throne to store it. It was not returned to Scotland until 1996.

In those ten years between Edward's campaign and Robert's coronation, we have the man, the legend, William Wallace. Most of what has been written about him over the centuries has either been for entertainment (mainly by a bard called "Blind Harry"- doesn't sound that reliable does he) or for

Scottish national propaganda. The actual facts are pretty thin. It's likely he was a military man before 1298, and there are hints he may have been an archer- possibly even having served on Edward's Welsh campaigns. But notice my language: "likely", "hints", "possible"- it's back to the phrase again- "nobody knows for sure".

What we do know for sure is that from seemingly out of nowhere there came a Scottish minor noble who fought a successful battle at Stirling Bridge, where Wallace cleverly used the river and bridge as a way to break up the larger English army and destroy them. It also showed that heavy cavalry would not always win the day against infantry. It sent shock waves through England.

Wallace followed this up with a punitive raid into England where he sacked a number of towns in a display of Scottish confidence and violence not seen for generations in England. Edward responded in the way he knew best: he went to war again. Despite now being nearly sixty (an old man by medieval standards), he led a campaign into Scotland to fight this new and unknown foe. In the summer of 1298, they met at Falkirk where Wallace pulled his men into Schiltrons, layered walls of spears and poleaxes held by the infantry, designed to repel cavalry who would come up against these forests of steel at their peril.

However, despite the fact that Wallace had picked another good area to fight against superior numbers, the old master used his Welsh longbow men to break up the Schiltrons and let his cavalry reek havoc on the remaining Scots. Wallace, wisely, disappeared and for the next few years, the Scots would not be lured into another pitched battle against the English. Instead hit and run raids would occur, but strategically, the Scots had nowhere to go and once again, Edward was in control.

William Wallace was captured in 1305 and was tried for "treason and atrocities against civilians in war". Wallace himself made the valid point that he couldn't be a traitor as he'd never sworn an oath of loyalty to Edward in the first place, but on the second count, he was undeniably guilty (even though Edward was just as guilty of that himself in both Wales and Scotland). William Wallace, after being declared guilty on all counts (it was an English court after all), had the dubious distinction of being the first man to be hanged, drawn and quartered. That is he was hanged until almost dead, then castrated and disembowelled, then beheaded and then finally, chopped into quarters, where the remains were put on spikes in certain public places. It would be hard to think of a more brutal way to die.

However, once Robert the Bruce declared himself king, Edward again went north to do battle. It was actually his heir Edward II, who won the Battle of Methven, but in what was to become the usual pattern for Edward II, he had no grasp of the politics of the situation and military victory turned into political defeat as his heavy handed actions led to growing support for Robert's claim to the throne.

Then in 1307, just south of the border, Edward died. He was a shrewd man and he knew his son had weaknesses, but he did his best to set up some protection for his son and heir. But it would prove fruitless.

Already, with Richard I, we have looked at a king's sexuality and in that section I made the bold statement that Edward II was gay. Therefore may surprise you to find out that Edward II had five children. Yes, you read that right; that's five kids. If he didn't like the ladies, he might be able to grin and bear it to get an heir, and maybe even a spare, but five? Contemporaries cast no doubt that they were his either. Surely there had to be a part of him that liked heterosexual love making. However the two great loves of his life appeared to be men, not his queen.

So we are back to the frustrating part of history where the truth was never written down. Indeed, had Edward carried out his rule with the occasional secret dalliance on the side with some guys, we would all be none the wiser. The reason why many historians side with homosexuality was because of Piers Gaveston. It's one thing to have a lover (of either sex); it's quite another to elevate that person above what was acceptable at the time. Edward I spotted this before his death and had Piers exiled, but shortly after his death, Edward II brought Piers back, disobeying his father's wishes to the general disgust of the nobles.

When Edward II went to marry the king of France's daughter, he made Gaveston regent in his absence. Indeed, on his return to England when Edward held a feast in honour of the wedding, the new Queen Isabella was placed in a less important position than Piers. Even though she was only thirteen it was her celebration; she was of royal lineage and being outshone by some minor noble. Gaveston knew that he was becoming a very wealthy and powerful man because of the king's favours, and while all kings had their favourites, the privileges being bestowed on this very minor noble outstripped any demonstrable reason. Putting it simply, it had to be love; there was no other explanation.

Edward II is a serious contender for the worst English king in history. He managed to fail in war, lose the respect of the barons, and lead the country into civil war. He also showed another side that was generally a symptom of poor governance; he was fixated on the respect he needed to be shown to him. That's not to say that kings didn't demand respect, they did; but they got it because it was earned. However with kings like Edward II, John and Richard II, the more they failed, the more they demanded this respect and the more it annoyed the nobles. Edward had already managed to exacerbate feelings of contempt from the Scottish nobility; and now, with Piers, he was playing a dangerous game with the English lords.

This all came to a head in 1311 when the lords, led by the Earl of Lancaster, demanded Gaveston's exile. Edward reluctantly agreed. This was to be the second time Piers had been forced into exile. It wasn't long however until he was back again by the king's side, to the fury of Lancaster and the other nobles. In 1312 Lancaster and other barons hunted him down and beheaded him. That was one way to ensure Gaveston couldn't return to the king's side.

But in one sense they were wrong, Edward was so grief stricken that he kept Piers's remains with him for weeks. Lancaster and the other lords begged forgiveness for the execution (it's quicker to beg forgiveness than ask permission) and Edward reluctantly agreed. Besides he realised he needed their help.

Robert The Bruce had been busy after his earlier defeat, and over the next seven or eight campaigning seasons, he had won back most of Scotland. Almost all of Edward I's hard won gains had been lost. So Edward, for a change, decided to wage war in Scotland and carefully brought together one of the largest armies yet seen in England.

The plan basically had three goals:

Firstly, tactically, the force would ensure Stirling Castle's security. Stirling Castle was often a focal point for war because it was seen as the gateway to the Highlands, controlling much of the traffic between the Highlands and Lowland Scotland.

Secondly, the size of his army would impress on the local population that resistance was futile.

Thirdly, it was hoped that after years of insurgent warfare, Robert The Bruce couldn't resist a pitched battle that could win back, in one battle, all that been lost.

So Edward rode north with an army of approximately 25,000, knowing that Robert would be lucky to get a third of that number onto a field of battle. Lancaster didn't go, but he sent the required number of troops The ranks were full of Welsh archers that had already proven their worth in the Scottish wars, and there were even Scottish nobles and their retinues who were hostile to Bruce.

As they headed into Scotland in the high summer, their progress towards Stirling was good. By June 23rd they could see Stirling Castle. The army had arrived in time to force a relief compromise (remember all those rules about sieges? Edward had arrived in the allotted time, so the Scots were, by their own terms obliged to retreat). However Edward was not a wise military ruler and wanted to do battle, assuming that a bigger army meant inevitable victory.

In reality, he couldn't have avoided conflict even if he wanted to because the army was already starting to break up into its component parts, and the vanguard engaged with Scots. Edward I would never have allowed such a breakdown in the chain of command, but throughout the battle of Bannockburn, Edward II was only nominally in charge of his own army.

The Bannockburn itself was a minor tributary to the River Forth, and it seems the English almost have mythical bad luck fighting battles in Scotland near rivers. Edward's army, although huge, lacked agility as well as cohesion. This can be summarised by a "legend" that actually happened.

Henry de Bohun was an English nobleman who, shortly after crossing the river, saw Robert The Bruce without armour on horseback, carrying a battle axe. Henry used his initiative and charged at the relatively defenceless king. Henry, on the other hand was riding a war-horse clad in the latest armour and was about to win the battle before it had even properly begun. Much to Henry's surprise, Robert did not flee to his troops, but stood his ground, turned his horse at the last moment, and smashed his axe down so hard on Henry's helmet that he split both the helmet and Henry's skull in two.

This moment of sheer bravery and skill gave the advantage of morale to the Scots; their leader was a man of action and bravery. Like Wallace, they used Schiltrons to keep the superior English cavalry at bay. The general location of the battle, a mixture of marsh and wood broke up the larger English formations so that Robert could concentrate his forces on the piecemeal English army. This focussing of arms in front of an enemy army is a feat carried out by only a few truly great generals, so Robert was a talented military leader. However he was helped by Edward's unimaginative tactics and the lack of overall control of his forces.

The second and final day of the battle saw Robert pushing his massed ranks into the heart of the English host, which had run out of ideas and the will to fight. As Robert threw everything he had at the English centre, Edward's army broke and ran, some men drowning in the route.

The Battle of Bannockburn was one of Scotland's greatest victories over the English, and it was vital. Although the level of losses as a proportion of troops were quite similar, Robert had the field and Edward II, never a born warrior king, had had his big gamble badly backfire, ensuring some breathing space for Scotland. Had Robert lost or indeed, been killed by Henry de Bohun, then Scotland would have run out of options, resulting in a more humiliating capitulation than the one Edward I imposed.

Edward returned, defeated and cowed. He was down but not out. A wiser ruler would have learnt from his previous mistakes and come up with a plan B. Instead Edward became besotted with a new favourite, Hugh Despenser (who was also Piers Gaveston's brother-in-law). It was the same Edward making the same mistakes. Like Henry III

Edward was deemed tyrannical, and arbitrary in his laws and favours. Hugh, like Piers, was only too happy to receive all the gifts and titles; but again, unlike a normal royal favourite, he wasn't particularly gifted at anything. Favouritism was acceptable if the person was a great fighter, or administrator or a reciprocally generous lord; but Piers and Hugh just didn't know how to play the game.

It is worth mentioning that there is less circumstantial evidence about Hugh being Edward's lover; it could just be that Edward was besotted and Hugh knew how to play the king. Either way, the relationship mirrored the situation with Piers, and everyone had to know that this game was unlikely to end well for at least one of the players.

In 1321 the Earl of Lancaster (the same one who had helped execute Piers) rose up with a group of powerful nobles in rebellion against Edward and the Despenser family. Edward knew he had to do what he already had done with Gaveston, and in order to keep the peace disown both Hugh and his family, much to the joy of the nobles. The lords weren't stupid, and there was a bit of a clamour to become the king's new favourite, to be lavished with gifts. This backfired spectacularly on Lancaster who was defeated in battle, brought to a tribunal and sentenced to death. He was beheaded in front of Edward who must have been overjoyed knowing that he had got his revenge for Piers Gaveston.

However England was now slipping into anarchy. Powerful nobles were secure one day and beheaded or disowned the next. The rule of law was becoming sporadic, and with the Despensers returning to power, no one was quite sure who would prevail.

Things got worse with France demanding Edward pay homage for Gascony, which he was legally obliged to do; but as stated before, English kings were loathed to do so on the grounds that it implied a master/servant relationship between the French and English crowns. Then Edward came up with a plan. He could send his wife, as she was from the French royal family and would therefore be the perfect envoy. While she was in Paris, Edward II could come up with a compromise (like Henry I had done) and send his son Edward to do homage for Gascony.

It was a sensible solution and the events that would spiral from this choice were unknown to Edward at the time, but while all this looked great on paper, it was one of the biggest political blunders in English history.

By now Queen Isabella had grown weary of her husband's infatuations with men (to be fair what wife wouldn't?) and she knew that she had married a failure of a ruler. By getting her son, who was also the heir to the throne out of the country, she had all the bargaining chips, while Edward was left with the reviled Despensers and a hostile aristocracy. Had Isabella returned with Prince Edward alone, she would have gone down in history as one of the "good guys", saving England from anarchy; but she fell in love with Roger Mortimer, a rich, handsome and brave noble. Now we have an unfaithful Queen using her son as a bargaining chip and keeping him prisoner. So she goes into the "bad guy" category.

In 1326 Isabella and Mortimer invaded England with the young Edward in tow. It was a huge gamble. The invasion force was tiny but counting on popular support. The gamble paid off, and Edward found he couldn't raise a reliable force to counter his own wife's march on London. Anarchy and reprisals started. Hugh Despenser's father was captured by a group loyal to the deceased Earl of Lancaster and killed him in revenge.

Edward was captured by Lancaster's son and taken to Kenilworth Castle. Now we have the replay of King Stephen after his defeat, or King John after his or indeed, King Henry III with Simon de Montfort. The nobles in all these cases had the very real problem of what to do with a defeated king, because while there was no doubt that Edward was a weak ruler, he was still the anointed King of England. If you want a job done right, get a woman to do it. Isabella did what many great lords had feared to do for centuries: she forced Edward to abdicate. A completely new and legally indefinable idea. Could a king abdicate, even if he wanted to? Nobody knew, which meant that even though Edward was out of the way, he was always going to be a rallying point against Isabella and Mortimer.

Exactly what happened next "nobody knows for sure". What is traditionally stated is that Edward, after being forced to abdicate, was moved to Berkeley Castle where he was murdered in 1327. The legend is that Edward was killed by having a red hot poker shoved up his rectum, a reference to his homosexuality. However no contemporary chronicles state this and it is a later fabrication. The fact that he was killed is generally accepted. But I always remember a rather strange fact that I was taught and is picked up in Ian Mortimer's excellent book on Edward III "The Perfect King" (do try it, it is an excellent read). In it he points out that twice in Edward's early career, a lone traveller (possibly a religious man) claiming to be the king's father, arrived in court. Edward III greeted him with great warmth and gave him a place of honour at the meal.

The great thing about conspiracies is that the perpetrators never write anything down, so the lack of evidence proves the validity of their ideas to some. The expected absence of proof is not, however, the same as proof. So was it likely that one of the most unpopular king's in English history was killed in prison to do away with an inconvenient problem? The idea is not unlikely. But for someone to go up to the new king of England and declare he is his father, when he knew he wasn't, would be virtual suicide. And for the king to react in any way other than throwing the man in prison or beheading him on the spot has to raise questions.

Edward had dinner with him twice and treated him as an honoured guest, twice, maybe there was a happy ending for Edward II afterall? Either way, Edward II was no longer a going concern to English history.

Chapter 8 The Endless War part IV (Armageddon)

Once upon a time there lived a brave prince. The prince was sad because he was a prisoner in a castle. He was in prison because his mother, the queen, and his evil stepfather ruled the land after killing his father, the king. The people wanted the prince to be king because the wicked queen and stepfather ruled the country so harshly and so unjustly.

Ok, I am exaggerating slightly (but only slightly- Roger Mortimer was never married to Isabella) about the early period of Edward III's reign. It sounds like a fairy tale, but then again, a lot of his reign does. However in 1330 things were looking grim for Edward. Mortimer and Isabella were poor rulers basically running England, Ireland and Wales for as much personal gain as possible while Edward, aged 17, was essentially under house arrest in Nottingham castle. Technically his rule had already begun in 1327 with the "death" of his father, but in reality he was a helpless prisoner. It's worth pointing out that he was already married and even had a son (Edward known forever to history as the Black Prince), showing that teen pregnancies aren't a modern phenomenon.

However Edward lived under the shadow of Mortimer who knew that sooner or later he would either have to make way for Edward or remove him from the equation as he'd done with Edward's father. Then in October 1330 at the castle, Edward gathered together his most loyal and trusted companions who staged a hugely daring raid and captured Mortimer. Edward showed decisiveness beyond his teen years and had Roger Mortimer executed and forced his mother into permanent retirement from politics.

Despite the decadent nature of their rule, one of the biggest grievances against Roger and Isabella was a very generous peace deal with Scotland which Edward used as an opportunity to rally the nobles to his side and declared war.

The Scots vividly remember that Battle of Stirling Bridge and Bannockburn, but they forget the 1332 clash called the Battle of Dupplin Moor. Edward wasn't present, but throughout his career he was able either to lead armies into overwhelming victory or pick men who could do it for him. So what we have is a very small (2-3,000) Anglo-Welsh force, led by Anglo-Scottish nobles against Robert Bruce's illegitimate son (also called Robert) who had 10,000 men. Indeed the Scots were so confident of victory, being in the unusual position of numerical superiority, that they paid the small force little heed. Even better for the Scots, the battle site was by a river and by now we know what happens to English armies near Scottish rivers. The British force (a technically correct term) crossed the river in the dead of night and found a flanking position to the Scots. The next morning the Scots, panicked by the unexpected movement of the enemy, formed up their Schiltrons and charged at the enemy. Schiltrons are an excellent formation against cavalry, but are woefully vulnerable to archers, as Wallace's defeat a generation earlier had proven. The small force had very few cavalry, but its main host were longbow men, and the Scottish army was butchered. Robert Bruce junior was one of the casualties. The small force was alleged to have lost only thirty three men; the Scottish casualties could be measured in the thousands.

This forgotten battle is mentioned, not to show up earlier Scottish success, but to show that Edward's army had perfected a new way of fighting. Throughout Edward's (and other English King's) battles in France the story is almost always the same, a smaller English army beats a significantly larger French force with far more heavy cavalry because of careful positioning and lots of archers. Dupplin Moor was the dress rehearsal for far more famous battles.

As a result of his victory, Edward got a far more reasonable treaty with Scotland. Then he then turned his mind to a larger prize because in 1337, he declared himself the rightful heir to the French throne. He had a claim via his mother, albeit through the female line (and because the new King of France Philip VI had just as dubious a claim to the throne, the situation could be debated with no clear-cut answer). This point is conveniently referred to as the start of the Hundred Year's War, but war with France, as I have already shown, was virtually a generational act by now. It also saw war with Scotland as France's ally but again this was hardly a new development. All Edward did was raise the stakes, but the game itself had been played since 1066. I avoid using the term "Hundred Years War" (a valid option) because nobody at the time called it that and this period lasted longer than a hundred years anyway.

The most critical battle of this entire period is the Battle of Sluys in 1340. I doubt it's one you've heard of, but it was both a technically highly difficult battle to execute successfully and it was a decisive victory for England, which would shape the nature of the war between England and France for generations to come. Bold statements I know, but allow me to explain: you see Sluys was a naval battle.

What all leaders fear is invasion and with England, a fleet was needed to do the job. Edward knew this. He also knew the French were working with the Genoese to build a large fleet of about 200 vessels to be loaded with men and landed somewhere in the south of England. Edward pre-empted this and raised his own fleet, with Flemish allies, of around the same size.

This was not a battle on the high seas but at the port of Sluys. When the French saw the enemy navy in the distance, they lashed their ships together in lines with chains and then watched as the English fleet manoeuvred around them. The French and Genoese had crossbowmen; their bolts were lethal, but Longbows were even more deadly and could be fired far more quickly than a slow loading crossbow. Most of the battle was vicious hand-to-hand fighting but through sheer bloody-mindedness, Edward's army captured most of the enemy fleet and killed nearly 20,000 enemy soldiers and sailors with only a few thousand losses on his side. The sea turned red from all the blood and the waters were thick with the corpses of the slain. Edward was in the thick of the battle and suffered a wound from a crossbow bolt, but it was nothing serious and only added to his growing reputation as a brave and dangerous military opponent.

Sluys created two kinds of damage to France's war machine:

Firstly, they lost men. Sailors and marines were harder to replace than peasant troops. The training involved in creating an effective navy took time and skill that couldn't be solved by just adding more men.

Secondly, they lost ships, which were very expensive to replace and again took considerable time and effort to rebuild.

Sluys stopped any thought of invading England for decades and gave the initiative to England for about the next eighty years. Few victories give that much breathing space to a nation.

The next few years involved Edward regularly marching around northern France, laying siege here, stirring up trouble there, but infuriatingly, Philip VI would not commit to a battle. This is the period we start hearing of Chevauchées. It's obviously a French term and what it basically means is murder and plunder. This period is seen as the height of medieval chivalry where knights are bold and ladies wait in castles for their knights in shining armour to return to be read romantic poetry. I guess that might have happened somewhere but largely it was a time of brutal, bloody and muddy violence.

The idea of a Chevauchée was to show the locals that their king was not protecting them; it was a scorched earth policy. It also solved the problem of re-provisioning armies as they marched across hostile territory. It also incentivised people to join Edward's army: go to France, risk your life but potentially get rich. To many it was appealing. Some English people wonder why the French aren't friendlier to us. While we may have helped them with the Germans twice, that's nothing compared to the centuries of English armies wandering around the French countryside, stealing anything that wasn't nailed down, and not just killing their men in battle, but sometimes women and children, too. This period was not glorious; it was brutal.

However by 1346, the English had made a nuisance of themselves long enough to finally lure the French King into battle at Crecy. Edward had an army of about 15,000 against a host of about 40,000. The French were disorganised and over-confident due to their superiority in numbers.

The French tried to beat the English at their own game by sending in their Genoese Crossbowmen first. That didn't work because of the superiority in both range and rate of fire of the longbow men. Also Edward had a new weapon: a handful of very early cannons that fired large spear-like projectiles that could easily rip through armour. The situation was further confounded by the fact that, traditionally, Crossbow men wear a shield on their back (a pavise) to protect them as they reloaded, but these shields were still on the baggage train in the rear. So they had to turn their unprotected backs to Edward's archers. It was a massacre. The Genoese fled under a hail of armour-piercing arrows and the mounted French knights were so disgusted by this display that they added to the casualties by hacking the crossbowmen down as they fled, to get them out of the way so they could charge the English lines and show them how it was done.

As the French nobles charged forwards, they did so into a shower of arrows. The arrows used were not the traditional flat-headed spade shaped arrows that spring to mind, but instead were tipped with a steel spike, inches long, designed to puncture the plate armour the knights wore. If it didn't hit the man, it would certainly lame the horse, and soon the field was covered with writhing horses and men. Lightly armed Welsh and Irish irregulars would sortie out and jam small knives in the visor slits of the knight's helmets, cold steel violating living flesh, the face and eye sockets turned into a bloody mess, so killing another French noble. The bodies were starting to pile up. Each French assault added more to the pile and the ground started to churn with the dead, the dying, blood and entrails, making the next wave of attack against the English even harder to carry out.

Finally, one group of French knights managed to engage with the English knights and started to push the English back. The Black Prince was in this wing of the English force and there was concern that he might need assistance, but Edward calmly said "let the boy earn his spurs" and refused to send help to see how he would perform. The danger soon passed. By the end of the day, English casualties were very light a few hundred men killed and only two knights (two members of the nobility) dead. By comparison, total casualties on the French side was closer to 6,000 (mainly the crossbowmen) and 1,500 of those were French knights and dozens more of the most powerful nobles in the land. It had been a very heavy death toll for the French aristocracy.

Crecy is sometimes called the moment that chivalry died. Before Crecy most major battles were won or lost by the nobility, either dismounted and armour clad, or on horseback charging at the enemy ranks. They had high status in society partly because they were the big scary guys no one dared to mess with. However at Crecy, most of the killing had been done by peasant archers and most of the deaths had been at range, and not in hand-to-hand combat. The armoured knight was proving to be less an invincible medieval tank, and more a lumbering target.

There are many stories springing up from the battle. One is about the blind King of Bohemia, who was on the French side, and demanded he and his knights charge at the English all tied together so he could find his way. His helmet, with three ostrich feathers, was found after the battle near his corpse and given to Edward, who made this the symbol of the Prince of Wales, is still used to this day and the image is on many two pence coins.

It was also after this battle that Edward created the Order of the Garter, the oldest, most elite and most prestigious chivalric order in Europe. Knights of the Garter were the king's closest friends and the original twenty six members were all fighters at Crecy, and not all of them were English either. It was an international society of the most elite knights alive, the most prestigious club ever. No one but a close personal friend of the monarch or a prime minister is going to be allowed in. Linked to this is also the founding of St George as the patron Saint of England. George was always seen as a warrior saint and so evolved into being the protector of knights; however after Edward's stunning successes, he felt he could claim that St George was showing his favour to English knights in particular. And that's how a Palestinian-born Roman soldier became the patron saint of a country he never visited.

As we've so often seen, no matter how overwhelming the victory, it rarely puts an end to the issue. The Scots did soundly trounce the English at Bannockburn, but veterans of both sides of that battle were present at Dupplin Moor. The same can be said for Crecy, because it was not the last time, even in Edward's life that English and French armies would do battle again.

At roughly the same time as Crecy, a far more important conflict was being waged. The siege of Caffa has never had the same attention paid to it as Crecy. Caffa was a Genoese trading outpost on the Black Sea cost in modern day Ukraine. These trading posts were vital to the Italian city states as they were the frontier zone between East and West and were the most westerly points on the Silk Road. They were cosmopolitan walled towns which were the medieval equivalent of the Wild West. Caffa, however, had caught the attention of the local Mongol warlord, Janibeg. He proceeded to siege it with thousands of men. The inevitable unsanitary conditions led to an outbreak of disease- so far, so routine. However, this illness was different. Soldiers were collapsing with fierce fevers, they were convulsing, their vomit was black and they started to break out in black sores and lesions. The victims usually died within a few short days of first showing the symptoms.

As the siege of Caffa progressed, Janibeg's army was being devoured by this pestilence. So the Mongols decided to get their revenge on the miserable trading outpost and used the dead (rather than rocks) as missiles to be launched by their siege engines. These rotting and highly infectious cadavers would have exploded on impact, spreading rancid offal and stinking decomposing limbs all over the town.

Janibeg lifted the siege, but the Genoese had had enough (what with this and what happened to their crossbow men at Crecy, Genoa wasn't having a good time of it) and set sail back to Europe, bringing with them the incubating disease. The Great Pestilence, the Great Mortality, the Black Death had arrived in Europe.

The Museum of London has a section on the Black Death and on one wall it projects the names of the cities affected by this terrible plague. The roll call starts with exotic sounding places like Astrakhan and Caffa, and then the more familiar like Constantinople and Rome, before we get to names like Marseille, Paris, Dover and London. It is a simple and elegant way to show the remorseless creeping of this great illness as its infectious tentacles crept through the countries of Europe.

The Black Death is a good example of how bitchy any area of learning can get. For one hundred years the Black Death was associated with Bubonic Plague (Yersinia Pestis). Then in the 1980s a zoologist called Dr Graham Twigg started to point out some inconsistencies in the patterns of disease between Bubonic Plague and those described in the chronicles of the day regarding the Black Death. Initially he was condemned, the historical community had made up its mind on the grounds that the historian Francis Gasquet had linked Bubonic Plague with the Black Death in 1893 (with little or no research), and that was good enough for historians for the best part of a century.

Dr Twigg was an outsider, a zoologist and not a historian, which didn't help his case initially. Most academic communities don't like outsiders; it's an intellectual version of "you're not in my gang". On many occasions there is good reason for this, as already pointed out, some areas of history get hijacked by insane ideas that historians have to calmly correct. Atlantis theorists, New Age ideas or just plain bad history, like *1421* by Gavin Menzies (and his follow up books), which claims the Chinese did just about everything except invent the computer in the 15th century.

However this default defensive position gets in the way of new ideas and Dr Twigg had a point, which led to a fairly vicious battle of claim and counter-claim over the biology behind the Black Death. *Return of the Black Death* by Susan Scott and Christopher Duncan is an example of research pointing out the uncomfortable discrepancies between the realities of Bubonic Plague transmission and patterns of outbreak, and the extant descriptions of the plague itself. They make the fair point that if it was spread mainly by rats and fleas, how come the forty day quarantine (when it was properly enforced) worked? Fleas don't know what a quarantine zone is, but humans do. Surely this shows most of the transference was human to human. However Scott and Duncan themselves try to dismiss the hard evidence of finding evidence of Yersinia Pestis found in a plague pit.

The evidence now strongly suggests that Bubonic Plague was the main culprit, but it certainly doesn't answer all the questions. The most likely explanation is that the overall culprit is a mix of bubonic and pneumonic plagues (an airborne version of the same disease), possibly with a few other nasty bacteria/viruses following in their wake, preying on a weakened population.

This particular controversy illustrates a fundamental issue with academia. You don't get noticed if you agree with everything that has gone on before. So everyone is looking for a new view. It's a little easier in science when you can in theory discover something completely new- The Higgs Boson, for example. It's much harder to do that in history (news just in: it turns out the French won at

Crecy and Edward III was actually a Turk in disguise). Instead there are very heated arguments about interpretations and nuances of certain actions. It gets very technical, very quickly. That, or there are secondary issues going on.

All History is seen through the lens of your country. Trying to learn everything that happened in all cultures in 1066 is impossible, and a little pointless. So by definition, in England, 1066 is a big deal, but not so much in Russia. With China's rise in its world standing, it is keen to prove to the rest of the world its historical worth. There is a certain anxiety to this. China was hugely powerful, but when it met the expansionist forces of Western Europe in the 19th century, it was humiliated. This humiliation lasted for generations until with Mao it not only got a nationalist leader, but also got a man who had no qualms in stunting growth, one who so mismanaged the economy that millions ended up starving to death or languishing in prison. Any price was worth paying as long as he stayed in power.

No wonder China now wants to remind everyone of its very impressive imperial past. For millennia is it was at the global pinnacle of learning, art, law and order. However it is selective in what it wants to recall. Mao, for example, is still revered, his massive blunders costing tens of millions of lives are side stepped, ignored or denied outright. China has suffered external threats by everyone from the Mongols to the English, so the modern interpretation is that foreigners tend to be untrustworthy or evil; the (Han) Chinese are best.

There isn't a lot of nuance in it, and yet, if I have one overall point to make it is that history is complicated with few outright "good guys" and "bad guys". No country is "best". Compare Chinese history to modern British history, with all the hand wringing in the UK about the empire. I am very proud of the fact that Brits are uneasy about the imperial past. Some imperial victories will always be a bit glamorous (e.g. Waterloo), but we are aware of the slave trade and our mistreatment of Ireland etc. I think this is the right way to look at things.

Historians have heated debates on the very old stuff, but politicians can whip up all kinds of unhelpful sentiment on more recent events. History can be a weapon that justifies actions or attacks opponents, and I am aware that the further I travel along in time, more readers will have opinions about some of the people and events I mention, some of which have no easy answers and may clash with the mild views in this book. Of course the ultimate compliment is if I niggle both sides of an argument; then I know I'm being fair.

Whether people are arguing because their research is being challenged or because someone is re-editing history so that their country comes out better, things can get very nasty indeed. I have tried to steer an "interesting" course through history, but I know I will have annoyed people. One thing I do know is that, as I do not have a doctorate in history, there will be some academics who will scoff at an amateur; but I am trying to be populist, so being able to recite the Gesta Francorum in its original Latin isn't necessary. Likewise I am sure it will be said, "how on earth can he write about x without mentioning y? He's missed the point/over simplified/is misreading the situation." I have had to summarise to get 2,000 years of history into a relatively short book, but I don't think I've said anything wildly controversial. To those I have offended, I apologise; it was never my intention to do so, (and I'm saying this as I write the actual text), but if you've read this far, I must be doing something right.

Meanwhile, by 1347, the plague had reached France. By 1348 it had spread across the Channel and was cutting a swathe through England. Europe had experienced many outbreaks of disease before, by the sheer virulence and extreme mortality rate was bringing society near to collapse. Looking at things from a French aristocratic point of view, it had lost many key nobles at Crecy and now, a year later, their peasants. Knights and family members were dying in their thousands. The microscopic pathogens took no notice of titles; low born or highborn, millions died vomiting up their own putrefying blood. It would take years to return to some kind of normality.

What the exact death toll of the plague across Europe was we'll never know, but the general consensus was between 30-50%. A population may be able to recover from this level of mortality eventually, but society will change. There are thousands of abandoned villages all over Europe from this time. There simply weren't enough people to keep them going, so the remaining population migrated elsewhere. This was, according to Feudal law, technically illegal; a farmer had to work on the lord's land in payment for their own plot. The peasantry was in essence tied to the land, but with so much death, the survivors could move from region to region with no problems. Of course the lords themselves were quite often dying, too. The clergy, with its commitment to looking after the sick, was particularly badly affected, in some cases wiping out entire religious populations.

Let's put the deaths into perspective. Some have estimated that as many as one hundred million died in this outbreak of plague. By comparison, in the first thirty years since the discovery of HIV 30 million have died from AIDS or other HIV related illnesses (according to Avert 2012 figures). HIV is more insidious because symptoms may not manifest until years after contact with the virus therefore massively increasing the chance of the virus spreading. With Bubonic Plague the victim becomes sick within a month and dies within days. It's like a biological wildfire that incapacitates its victims so quickly it will burn itself out- unlike HIV. The horrifying thing about the plague was that it came back again and again, never at the pandemic scale of 1347/8, but when it hit a town or city the death rate was familiarly high. And it kept coming back until well into the 17th century. London was suffering from plague when, in 1666, it had the great fire. It never came back to London again; and while it's tempting to say the pathogen was killed off in the fire, the plague continued elsewhere in Europe for a couple of more generations. It was blind luck that stopped any further outbreaks in London.

We now take a short break from all the death for a necessary bit on social history – I told you I'd avoid it when I could. Under the feudal system, the king owned all the land (yes, the Church had separate rights, but ecclesiastical history is complex and for the sake of simplification, the church also technically owed their lands to the king. This conflict of interest has already been briefly mentioned with Thomas Beckett). The king through this basic conceit, could raise taxes and also demand men. The more land you had, the more knights or soldiers you were required to produce when the king summoned them. This all worked fine until two things occurred. Firstly, a large proportion of the population dies and secondly, when there is fighting abroad. To fight wars in France it took a lot of time to ship armies from England to France and the armies weren't obliged to serve indefinitely.

This led to a system that modern historians refer to as "bastard feudalism" because the same principals existed, but this time, the landowner could pay the king the value of the men he owed for service. This would allow the king either to pay for a standing army or to hire mercenaries. The king therefore had flexibility, which would lead to a core of an army that was even better versed in martial abilities than before.

The second part of this was how to raise cash from the land when a significant proportion of the farmers have died? The answer in England was to switch to wool. Arable farming is labour intensive and still happened in many parts of Britain, but there was now a steady rise in the number of shepherds, where only a handful of individuals are needed to look after a large flock. Sheep, likewise need less maintenance than cows- and sheep produce, milk, meat and wool. All of this could generate the revenues that would pay for castles and raise armies. Sheep would pay for future English wars in France.

Society adapted to the Great Mortality. Populations migrated, economies changed gears, and humans got on with their lives. The 14th century is sometimes referred to as the worst century to have ever lived in Britain: war, apocalyptic plagues, even the weather was worse than usual. It didn't have a lot going for it, and yet (and this is my final nod to social history for the time being), Chaucer would show us another way of looking at things.

Nowadays "writer" or "poet" or even "philosopher" is a full time job. Not so in the past. I love the idea of Socrates being a hoplite soldier in an Athenian Phalanx, brandishing his spear and shield, all those great thoughts pouring through his head as he killed and maimed as part of an army.

Today it seems these literary people need to be left alone with their thoughts in order to produce their work, whereas in the past, the writing may have been their first love but they also needed a proper day job, which makes them far more interesting in my opinion. Even in his day Chaucer was lauded as a great writer, and he is the considered to be the father of English language literature; but that didn't stop him being a royal official, carrying out various diplomatic and regulatory duties, as well as fighting in sieges and battles too.

Here's the opening line of his greatest work The Canterbury Tales:

"Whan that Aprille with his shoures soote the droghte of Marche hath perced to the roote and bathed every veyne in swich licour."

Let's be honest, the English language still had a way to go from this point. Despite what some scholars say, like Beowulf, you need a modern translation for the average person (like me) to work out what he's going on about. However, unlike Beowulf, you can at least now see what individual words mean; and overall you can comprehend that it was showery in April in the 14th century, just as it is now.

Chaucer was In Edward III's royal circle and spent time as a soldier, a courtier and a diplomat. He saw the workings of feudal society from the very highest vantage point and yet wrote about a cross-section of society, bringing to life what would have been a very drab and depressing time, demonstrating that even in the face of such adversity, humans were the same then as now. You can read about vulgarity, humour, bravery and pride and his rogue's gallery of characters give us a glimpse of real people in the 14th century.

By 1356 life had returned to a routine and just to prove this, Edward sent his eldest son, Edward "The Black Prince", to the south of France to carry out a Chevauchée in to the French heartlands and relieve English forces while he stayed at home to run the kingdom. Edward dutifully obliged and started to build a reputation as a formidable military leader in his own right. France now had two wolves to deal with and it was time to teach the pup a lesson.

The Black Prince ran into some bad luck at Tours where, because of bad weather, he could neither carry out a successful siege nor burn it to the ground (bad luck for him. I am sure the occupants considered it pretty lucky). King John II of France heard of this and moved as many of his mounted forces as he could south. Even though he had disbanded much of his infantry, he knew he would still outnumber the English raiding force.

King John had his eldest son with him (the Dauphin), and so it was a chance to see how the future kings of France and England would compare. Edward was cornered on a Sunday and he knew that he stood little chance, outnumbered as he was by approximately four to one. Therefore he spent the day trying to negotiate his way out of the situation using the Papal Legate as a diplomatic go-between the two armies. He tried a promise of a return of lands and castles, of money, of a guaranteed truce, but John was having none of it. He could smell victory and saw this as a chance to undo the damage of Crecy. He had The Black Prince cornered and begging for a deal.

On the next day the French King split his army into four divisions, each one about the same size as the entire English force. The Black Prince chose an uneven area of ground, covered in vines, and split his forces into three tiny contingents behind a thick hedge of thorns and shrubs. If the French wanted him, they were going to have a hard slog to get to him.

The first wave of the French army assaulted the English position. While archers did their worst, this was not the same as Crecy. The knights were able to engage with the English lines of men-at-arms so this battle was down to lethal hand-to-hand fighting. However the first line of French broke from the assault and got in the way of the second attack. This second force was led by the Dauphin and they had to trudge over the same vines, now littered with dead and dying French knights. He engaged with his nemesis the Black Prince, and the two opposing forces hammered away at each other. The English were starting to tire, but they were desperate men, with no way out, and a cornered animal fights with a savagery that often makes the attacker think twice.

Using modern parlance, Edward's men "wanted it more" than the French who broke and ran. At this point, from the French perspective, it seemed they were up against a savage enemy in an impregnable defensive position. The truth was otherwise. The English by now, after hours of hard fighting, were on the brink of collapse. It was said that all of the English army was either exhausted from their efforts and/or wounded; and while they had done a mighty job resisting half the French army, the other half was still there.

Or it was until The Duke of Orleans, leading the third division of the French army, thought the routing of the Dauphin signalled the end of the battle and headed off with him.

It was a reprieve, but a short-lived one, for now the French king approached with his battleaxe in hand (which, by all accounts, he used very effectively). His own host was still fresh and while the English didn't have to fight the Duke of Orleans, they still had to fight the battle all over again against an equal number of fresh troops.

At this point one of the battle hardened veterans standing next to Edward muttered something about the situation being hopeless. The Black Prince roared at him:

"You lie! You miserable coward, while I am alive it is blasphemy to say we are beaten!"

With that he screamed at the oncoming French host, jumped over the hedge and led his men in one last desperate push. There was no safety of a hedge anymore and the fighting was brutal, as both sides sought to end this on their terms. However once the two sides were engaged, a tiny English force of cavalry and a couple of hundred archers appeared at the French rear. Such a small contingent could make little practical dent in the French forces, but it created an illusion of reinforcements. The cohesion of the French force broke down as they panicked about potential attack from the rear.

The Black Prince had not only won a victory every much the equal of his father at Crecy, but now he had the King of France as hostage, too. Edward broke open John's provisions and had a feast to celebrate his victory with the French King present. It got worse. When John came back with Edward to England, he was kept in (luxurious) captivity with David II King of Scotland, who had been held captive for ten years.

To pay for his ransom David II was to try and negotiate with Edward III the Kingdom of Scotland over the next few years. Although this never came to anything, it did pacify the northern borders. The French, however, did their best to raise their ransom in gold and these huge taxes, compounded with a weak Dauphin as ruler and a nation still only just recovering from the Black Death, tipped the balance in England's favour for a decade. The Black Prince had proven the phrase "like father like son".

Chapter 9 The Endless War Part V – The Problem with Consistency

The issue with dictatorships is that they focus, naturally, on the ruler. Some are remembered as utter tyrants, Hitler being an undisputable one. The whole of government is moulded to mirror the leader. Consequently, if a leader wants to rule a country efficiently, picking wise councillors without an onerous taxation system, then things should run OK. Get a poor ruler- be they insane, blood thirsty, arrogant or indecisive- and the whole edifice crumbles. This is the problem with dictatorships: they are only as strong as the boss and few are up to the job.

By and large England was lucky. Every time it got a bad king, it was followed by a good one, not morally good, but someone who could bring the whole system back from the brink. The other coincidence is that while England, like most countries, would occasionally implode into civil war under poor kings, the solution was quite often rather novel release valves via new legal systems: Magna Carta, Parliaments etc. This was quite unique. Other countries regained regal power when a new winner came on the scene, quite often with an even more ruthless commitment to absolute power. In this period the differences between the power of the English Monarch and the Russian one were less obvious, but later on, without the pressure releases of an effective parliament and a rule of law that applied to all, the result was bloody messes like the French and Russian Revolutions. The closest England came to revolution was the parliamentary Civil War in the 17th century, which is why we still have a monarchy to this day.

However, after all of Edward III's great successes, his biggest issue was that he lived a long time and even outlived Edward the Black Prince (probably the greatest prince never to rule as king). So the throne went to the Prince's young son who was crowned as Richard II. At the same time, the Dauphin Charles went from being a rather weak regent to being a canny king, so the balance of power tipped in favour of France.

Having a young king is not a disaster if there are effective replacements, and Charles V of France, while an effective ruler, was not a heavy-weight leader of the same standing as Philip Augustus or Louis IX. The signs were not inevitably poor for England, but as Richard grew up, it became apparent that he was never going to be a great ruler.

Now enter from stage left, William Shakespeare. Richard II is remembered for two reasons: the Peasants Revolt (leading to the one joke about medieval history- "sire the peasants are revolting") and Shakespeare's play.

Let's deal with Bill first. William Shakespeare is probably the world's greatest playwright. The standard of quality goes from exceptional to legendary in his dozens of plays and sonnets. He is the cornerstone of the English language, and he is an industry in and of himself. Somewhere in the world someone is always putting on one of his plays, writing a book about him or adapting one of his stories to film.

Understanding the English written word without Shakespeare is like learning about the history of food without mentioning meat. However, cards on the table, I think there's a difference between important contributions to language and literature and a great night out. A Shakespeare play can be a hard slog for a modern audience. As for the argument that you have to read it and understand it before you go and see it, I don't know of any other entertainment where in order to understand it, you have to read a book about it first. It's too much like hard work, in my opinion. Even worse for historians, he has become more famous than many of his subjects.

Nowadays there are many grumbles about Hollywood playing fast and loose with history all for the sake of a good story. This may be true, but it can be argued they are just following in the noble tradition of the great bard, who never let facts get in the way of a gripping tale.

Julius Caesar's last words were not, "Et tu Brutae", but more likely, "Ahhhh, stop stabbing me!" -but they aren't as poetic. As we have already seen, the real Macbeth bore little resemblance to the haunted ruler in the great play. Then there's Richard II. Most people who have read or seen the play have fallen in love with the forlorn king who has been unfairly manipulated by his courtiers, and who is then imprisoned. There are some cracking speeches, too.

"Now is the golden crown like a deep well, that owns two buckets, filling one another, the emptier ever dancing in the air."

And the great-

"This royal throne of kings, this sceptred isle,
This earth of majesty, this seat of Mars,
This other Eden, demi-paradise,
This fortress built by Nature for herself
Against infection and the hand of war,
This happy breed of men, this little world,
This precious stone set in the silver sea,
Which serves it in the office of a wall

Or as a moat defensive to a house,
Against the envy of less happier lands,--
This blessed plot, this earth, this realm, this England."
(Shakespeare put this into the mouth of John of Gaunt rather than Richard)

These are beautifully crafted phrases that, quite frankly, make my attempt to write look like an arthritic spider has lurched across the page. However their beauty belies the fundamental truth that it's largely made up. For those who feel sorry for Richard, it's worth remembering that Henry I, Henry II, Henry III and Edward III had just as ignoble starts to their careers; but they overcame their difficulties and were effective rulers. Richard should not be mourned as some king who was never allowed to shine, but more the poor, vain ruler that was not up to the job. Like John or Edward II, he was a man (thirty two) by the time he was deposed, more than enough time to have grasped how to rule and become an effective king. He was a loser and in the game of crowns. While the rewards can be beyond the wildest dreams, failure is the very grimmest of options.

Then in 1381 there was the Peasant's Revolt. Whereas previous uprisings had been nobles against king, this was the agricultural class against the system. Wat Tyler, John Ball and others raised a peasant army and marched on London, demanding fairer treatment of the common man.

With palaces burning and the streets filled with rioters, Richard II, aged just fourteen at the time, met them and promised them pretty much anything they wanted if they would just go away. Once the host disbanded, there was a draconian crackdown and the leaders and large quantities of normal folk were executed in retribution.

The revolt failed, but this uprising combined with the growing importance of archers on the field and the depleted population following the Black Death (with the subsequent returns of the plague) meant that the common man had to be taken more seriously. They were needed to keep the economy and the war machine going. So while initially everything remained the same, it can (just like Magna Carta) be seen as the opening of a door to new ideas of governance and responsibility to the people.

Elegant monologues and soliloquies to one side, Richard II was a loser, the sort of preening, arrogant lightweight that was not needed by England while it continued it zero sum war with France.

Charles V had learnt the hard way not to engage the English in open battle, so while Richard was largely ineffectual in England, Charles got on with his own Chevauchées against the lands owned by Richard in France and sieged any available castles he could, knowing that the English neither had enough troops to hold onto all their lands, nor had any decisive central direction from Richard II.

What happened over the next few decades was a gradual but constant decline of English power in France, with no embarrassing pitched battles that massacred a significant proportion of the French aristocracy. Charles refused to play his enemy's game and campaigned on his own terms for limited goals. And year after year it worked. No wonder the French would remember this king as Charles the Wise.

Eventually though, Richard's weak leadership was to cost him dear. Although there was not the spectacular clashes of Matilda and Stephen, nor the dramatic turning of a wife against husband like Isabella and Edward II, there was instead another member of the royal household, Henry Bolingbroke, who would make a grab for the throne in 1399. Richard was imprisoned and then died under mysterious circumstances.

Henry IV had arrived with a swift coup and assassination that would have made even a mafia don blush. One of the issues of Edwards I- III was their issue. They all had a large amount of male children, and they in turn had sons. By 1399 a significant part of the aristocracy could trace their ancestry to a King Edward. In Henry Bolingbroke's case, his father was John of Gaunt who had been one of the regents for Richard II and a son of Edward III. It was a good claim, but not the only one, and both he and his son would have been painfully aware that their line lacked the simple succession of almost every other king since William the Conqueror.

Playing in Henry's favour was the perception of him as a glamorous king, a return to the past. He was every inch the dashing warrior, having gone on crusade; but as the Eastern Crusades by this time had faded away, he fought with the Teutonic Knights in their Northern Crusades into Pagan, Lithuania. He also went on pilgrimage to Jerusalem, so showing the right balance of royal pedigree, action man and devout pilgrim that would appeal to everyone.

However, a little like Stephen who also had all the right attributes initially, Henry IV's reign was blighted by rebellions. These ultimately would use up resources and hamper attempts to regain the lost lands in France. Probably the most famous opponent to Henry was Owain Glyndwr, a Welsh noble who raised the spectre of a rebellious Wales. It started with Owain's neighbour, an English lord Baron Grey de Ruthyn, illegally seizing some of his land. Owain appealed to Parliament, which was the correct procedure and shows that he was more than happy to comply with the English legal system. However, it seems de Ruthyn was a bit of a pantomime bad guy and would keep pushing Owain for no other reason than avarice. He was a supporter of Henry IV, so could ensure that the rulings went his way. Owain was subsequently branded a traitor, to which he retorted by proclaiming himself Prince of Wales (it's worth noting he never claimed to be king, which would have put him on equal footing to Henry) and he quickly built support in the areas of Wales furthest from English power bases.

War broke out, Conway was sieged, skirmishes were fought and in 1402 Owain got a taste of justice by capturing and then ransoming de Ruthyn. A year later it seems France wanted to help him to further divert English men and resources away from the English ruled areas of France. As the English laws became more draconian over their long- held territories in Wales, so it turned the ethnically and linguistically different Welsh population against English power.

By 1404 Owain felt secure enough to have himself formally crowned as Prince of Wales. It's this act that the modern Welsh Independence supporters point to as proof of an independent Wales, but it was not ratified (the free Irish and Scotland didn't back Owain) nor did the situation last very long. Bluntly, anyone can crown themselves, but without recognition, it's all a bit fanciful. So while it's a great tale and a rebellion with a noble impetus, Owain was being as much the canny politician as Henry IV. Like William Wallace, it's the modern interpretations heaped on these brief moments of history which have distorted them.

In 1405 the French landed forces and while their deployment never came to anything, it was a sign of how serious things were getting for Henry. However the earlier victories of the Welsh forces (many of which would have been veterans from

French engagements, with plenty of the dreaded longbow men in their ranks) were drying up and now the victories were going to the English.

Then Henry's son, another Henry or Hal, as he liked to be called, began to get involved in the fighting and strategy at the impressive age of just twenty (once again showing what Richard II could have achieved had he been able to get his act together). Hal had obviously been learning from the French and deployed a similar tactic of blockade and siege, avoiding pitched battles which had a nasty habit of unknowable outcomes. Just as it worked for Charles V in France, so too, it worked for Hal in Wales.

Despite Owain being able to raid as far as Birmingham, it was ultimately game over for the rebellion by 1409. Hal didn't finish the campaign unscathed, having been hit in the face by an arrow, leaving a livid scar on his right cheek, which is why his contemporary portraits are in profile from the left. Owain faced two insurmountable problems. The first was the simple fact that his resources were tiny compared to England's, and no amount of clever marshalling of men and money could save him in the long run if he was up against a competent opponent. The second problem was Owain wasn't up against just a competent enemy, but Prince Hal known to history once he was crowned as Henry V. It's worth remembering that because some of the men firing arrows on Henry V's side in France had once fired them at him in Wales. It's not insane to suggest that the man who shot Hal in the face may well have been one of Henry's archers at Agincourt, singing his praises.

Owain may have lost the war, but he was still a free man. He was never captured or killed by the English (and they really tried to hunt him down). His rebellion was killed off with many of the key nobles executed, but Owain himself slips from history and into legend, the perfect poster boy for any nationalist movement. But let's stick to the known facts. Apart from 1412 when he led a small but successful raid, he vanishes from written history. However in 1413, Henry IV died and Henry V needed peace in Britain so he could finally get the resources of the realms focussed on France. He subsequently repealed a number of the more onerous and racist laws against the Welsh, which took much of the logic of the rebellion away. After fighting the revolt with steel, Hal ultimately killed it with kindness.

But Owain was just one thorn in Henry IV's side during his reign. He faced revolts in a number of areas of England throughout his reign; and of course, the usual disruptions from Scottish nobles, be they supported by the Scottish King or otherwise. In short, Henry IV's reign echoes the disastrous reigns of John or Stephen. He had usurped the throne and paid the price because anyone who wanted to ignore a new law or ruling could question his legitimacy. Henry did try making things as legal and "right" as possible. He held a large number of parliaments and even had the Byzantine Emperor visit, which added kudos to his own stature, but did nothing to address the issue of legitimacy.

Henry V, on the other hand, was the rightful son of a king and had already proven himself a capable ruler as his father, in the later years of his reign, frequently fell sick with a mysterious illness. What the country needed badly was stability, and Henry had already proven he was the man for the job. It was also fortunate for Henry that while he was a capable ruler, the French crown went from Charles V (the wise), to his son Charles VI known to history as "the mad".

Just as England and Wales were regaining the stability they so needed, France was sliding into civil war at the very point when it could have finished off the English lands in France once and for all. For this period leading up to the end of Henry V's reign, Juliet Barker has written two exceptional books "Agincourt" and "Conquest". They are breath taking summaries of this period and come thoroughly recommended.

We now come to another giant in English history- Henry V- the steel clad victor with the famous coat of arms and a terrible haircut. For once Shakespeare's portrayal of this king seems to fit the reality fairly closely. Henry was cut from the same cloth as Richard the Lionheart and Edward I. He was tough, brave and fundamentally knew the brutal art of warfare. He ruled as king for just nine years (Richard only ruled for ten), but he had already been an effective ruler due to his father's illnesses for a handful of years before that.

Henry may have been an exceptional warrior, but he wasn't bad at diplomacy, either. He ensured the British Isles were at peace before casting his full attention on a weakened France. But before he could go to war, he needed a case for it. He used Owain Glyndwr's French support as one cause, but he had the usual fall back of a claim to the French throne. To bolster his claim he negotiated with the King of Hungary who later became the Holy Roman Emperor to recognise his claim to the French crown. Sigismund was only too happy to oblige as he knew that France would be preoccupied with English incursions, so wouldn't be threatening his empire.

Henry now had a cause to go to war, had peace in his lands and knew the French were unlikely to get any continental allies. His thorough planning put him in a strong position. Even better for Henry, the French aristocracy was in the middle of a bitter civil war between two groups- the Burgundians and the Armagnacs. Both sides claimed the power of regent over Charles when he fell into one of his frequent bouts of madness (and Charles really went to town with his delusions. At one point he feared rising from his bed because he thought he was made of glass and would shatter). This was the background to Henry's arrival at Harfleur in 1415.

The siege of Harfleur has gone down in history as very average. Henry executed it well, the city was a good choice as it commanded the shipping on the Seine River, and with it under English control, Henry could threaten Paris. The defences held out for a month, but without any relief from either the king or the Dauphin, they had no option but to capitulate. So Henry returned to English-held Calais with a solid if unexceptional victory. The effort hadn't really matched the reward, and at this rate, it would take forever to make a real impact against France.

On the way back, Henry's depleted and disease-ravaged army met the one thing Henry wasn't really expecting. Ironically Henry's actions were seen as dangerous enough to end the civil war and unite the bitter foes. In late October, at the very end of the campaigning season, Henry faced a massive French army. The exact numbers are in dispute, but a rough estimate is that Henry's 7,000 men faced a host of around 35,000. They were outnumbered around five to one.

Poitiers had seen a similar situation, but in this occasion, the imbalance between the sides was even greater, and Henry knew that his men were in poor shape after the siege. Also Charles d'Albret of the Armagnac house, standing in for the mad king, was a formidable general.

Henry's one hope was the longbow men. Most of his army was made up of archers who needed to work in perfect unison to stop the formidable French cavalry in their full plate mail armour. The ground didn't favour cavalry; it was thick, muddy and recently ploughed. The river Somme flowed nearby and 500 years later, the English would be back in the same area complaining about the mud. The field of battle was shaped like a giant funnel, with the small English army at the narrow end and the large French army at the wide point, the sides flanked by thick woods. This was to prove to be a key advantage to the English the next day.

That night Henry mingled with the troops to make them feel like a cohesive army, fighting for a man they knew. This is the battle that created the phrase "band of brothers". To avoid getting too noble about this build up, it's worth pointing out one other, more cynical motivation. Most of the English forces were bowmen, or in other words, commoners. They were worthless as prisoners and would be killed rather than held to ransom if they surrendered. By contrast a large contingent of the French army consisted of the very cream of nobility, and so worth a fortune if captured. The bowman had everything to lose including their lives (with no safety net of an honourable surrender) so they had every reason to make sure it didn't come to that.

On the morning of the 25th of October, Henry addressed his men, reminding them that he was the rightful king of France and pointed to the earlier victories of English armies in similar situations. It was all very noble, but the truth was that things looked very grim for Henry's small and sickly force. The French, on the other hand, had avoided pitched battles for a generation, and many nobles had fathers or uncles who had been slain in the earlier English victories. Some French accounts emphasise this by describing the jostling of a number of lords to get into the vanguard, just itching for revenge. They knew the power of the English archers, but if they could close quickly, their superior numbers and the fact that longbow men were lightly armed and armoured, would mean the French would win the day and perhaps even have an English king for ransom.

So the French advanced as quickly and eagerly as they could. The difference in the two armies was almost immediately apparent. The English knew the drill (literally) and fought as a co-ordinated unit. The French, by comparison, were keen to engage but were a mass of individual units whose loyalties and commands were contradictory and disorganised. It was a bit like Bannockburn, with the sheer size of one army actually being its weakness.

Problem number two for the French was that the land had been recently ploughed, and so while they advanced on foot, they were in full plate mail armour (approximately sixty pounds of steel), slipping and sliding through the thick mud. Looking out of the full-face helms of the period, huffing and puffing away through the muddy troughs in the field, it would have been a claustrophobic experience made deadly by English and Welsh archers firing volleys, not just from the front, but also from the sides in the forest, too. Many knights were mounted, but while they may not have been as drained by the charge across the battlefield, they were badly organised; and their horses were easy targets for the archers.

The third problem was that as the mass of French knights got closer to the English lines- the wedge shape of the field meant the knights started to bump into each other and a crush developed in the French front lines. Some accounts talk about French front ranks so tightly packed, they had difficulty actually defending themselves; and indeed, some of the dead had no room to fall to the ground. Unbeknown to the French, they were being funnelled into a kill zone, with arrows coming at them from three directions, bodies of the dead and dying as well as the living, reducing their already compromised mobility, and a line of English men-at-arms glistening in their own steel plate mail in front of them. One final unpleasant surprise for the French was that the English front line bristled with sharpened stakes hammered into the ground. This further broke up the French advance and impaled some of the horses as they charged in.

The French were being butchered and their corpses started to pile up in front of the English front line. Henry was seen on several occasions at the fore of the battle his armour adapted to hold a crown on the helm, with his coat of arms emblazoned on his chest. He made a tempting target for the French, but was also a rallying point for the English. Here was a great warrior king who was willing to risk his own life with his men. The English defensive line held firm.

The French broke off, and this allowed Henry to gather the thousands of captives together. Around this time a small French force managed to attack the English baggage train in the rear, but it was a hollow victory in the greater scheme of things. By now Henry had clearly won the day and it was time for the French army to leave and fight another day. However, the French organised into another assault and the previous butchery now turned into a massacre. Henry's army was tiny and to defend all the prisoners and continue the battle was impossible, so Henry declared "no quarter", a phrase still in use today, meaning total commitment, but in Henry's case it meant no prisoners.

This is the act which Henry is most criticised for. At first glance it sounds a bit like Richard and the slaughtering of his prisoners at Acre. This though was different. The battle was still happening and had Henry done "the noble thing", we would have read that Henry snatched defeat from the jaws of victory and lost the battle of Agincourt. To win, Henry had only one choice: get rid of the prisoners. Some of the blame belongs to the French; their battle plan was in tatters and another assault was extremely unlikely to win the day. They had to know that with such a small army and with another attack on the way, Henry would be in no position to release a retinue of soldiers to play prison guard. The French were sacrificing their own countrymen's lives in a pointless assault.

The day ended in more bloodshed than was needed, but war is war. Does it really matter if the casualties in the battle died behind the English lines or drowned in the mud (as some French knights did)? It was always going to be a terrible waste of life, no matter what happened on that St Crispin's Day. By evening, 450 of Henry's army were dead and 4,000 French were corpses on the field. It had been another epic victory for the English.

England went wild when it heard of their king's miraculous victory at Agincourt. The French slumped into despair, their best troops dead, a key town lost left with only a mad king to sort everything out. Things did not look good for them. Fate it seemed was with Henry, and while he never managed to pull off another Agincourt, the initiative and momentum were with him. Every year more castles and towns fell to the English, while the French remained divided. Only Mont Saint Michele, the monastery come fortress island in Normandy refused to surrender; and indeed, over the decades, it was besieged many times. It was never captured but this was a minor victory against the juggernaut that was Henry V.

The French really had no option. A house divided cannot stand and with a compromised ruler, the French had to come up with something. What was agreed was the Treaty of Troyes in 1420. It was the simple solution that we have seen before. Charles VI remained king until his death, at which point Henry V became king of both France and England. As Henry was in his mid-thirties, the deal was one he had to take. For good measure, he married Charles's daughter. For France it meant stability and effective governance by a proven ruler; for England a well deserved rest from war. In fact everyone won, except the Dauphin (another Charles), who had just been disinherited from one of the most powerful thrones in Europe.

It could have been a case of "and everyone lived happily ever after" except the unexpected happened- Henry died young. In fact, he died just weeks before Charles VI. At least Henry had a son; unfortunately, he was just nine months old, and so began the longest regency in English history as Henry VI slowly went from baby to king.

It was quickly agreed at a parliament that Henry V's two brothers would act as the main regents. John, Duke of Bedford would continue to fight in France for English interests, and the domestic government would be supervised by Humphrey, Duke of Gloucester. Both men had excellent pedigrees and both were effective rulers in the absence of a king. It's a little startling that these two immensely powerful men, who could have been tempted to carry out their own coup or usurpation of the throne, didn't and honoured their elder brother by backing the interests of his young son for the next decade or more.

The Duke of Bedford even managed to fight another key battle in 1424. The Battle of Verneuil was an important moment in the political balance in the wars in France, and yet, it's been all but forgotten by all sides. This time the French side had a significant contingent of Scots, led by the Earls of Buchan and Douglas. The Scots had played a part as French allies earlier, and they were often to be found in the garrisons of besieged towns or castles. At Verneuil however, they made up a significant proportion of the army faced by Bedford, a fresh contingent to this endless war. Also the French forces had a significant amount of Lombard heavy cavalry in the very latest plate mail armour, which even covered the horses.

This time the English were again outnumbered but by a less epic 2-1 rather than the 5-1 of Agincourt. Still the advantage lay with the French and their allies. The battle took place in August after a hot dry summer, and the English archer's stakes could not be pounded into the ground, so they were lacking their now standard defence against heavy cavalry. They would have to try and break the Lombards before they could reach the vulnerable archers.

The French saw this and a mass cavalry charge ensued. To the horror of the archers, their armour-piercing longbows were not doing the usual damage to the Lombard heavy cavalry; and the right flank of Bedford's army crumbled as the freight train of armour-clad cavalry smashed into the lightly armoured longbow men. Like a hot knife through butter, the knights carved their way through the infantry and onto the baggage train in the rear.

What saved the English was the usual lack of cohesion to this polyglot army. Bedford himself routed the French men-at-arms and chased them back to Verneuil's moat where many armour-clad French knights drowned. The Scots remained steadfast but when they saw the French and Lombard Cavalry concentrating on the English baggage for booty, they remained to finish the job of winning the battle despite being deserted by their allies. With Bedford returning to the main battle, the Scots were now outnumbered and by the end of the day, the Earls of Buchan and Douglas, as well as a significant proportion of their troops, lay dead. As the sun set on another bloody battle, the English had suffered a little over a thousand casualties against nearly ten thousand of the Franco-Scottish army.

Verneuil was a close run thing but the outcome showed once again that small English forces could manage to defeat larger French ones. For the English, it solidified their hold on Normandy; for the Scots, it was decisive in another way. While Scottish mercenaries and the occasional small contingent would fight with honour on the French side, Scotland would never muster as large an army to fight along French kings for generations. It had removed the potential for large Scottish reinforcements to refresh French armies from the equation.

So the Bedford, Gloucester regency was working; England had the stability it needed while gaining success in war with France. Bedford even managed to keep the split going between the Burgundians and the Armagnacs, with the Burgundians backing the English and recognising Henry VI's claim to the throne. While things would have been better with a functioning king, the country was in safe hands in the meantime.

However in the same year that success was being sealed at Verneuil, a twelve year old girl was having powerful visions of saints in eastern France. Four years later this teenage girl asked for permission to visit the French royal court. She had just correctly predicted another English victory, a battle which has gone down in history as the Battle of the Herrings. A small French army of four thousand attacked an even smaller English convoy of equipment and food, including barrels of herrings (hence the name of the battle). The English, led by John Fastolf (that's not a typo he was a highly respected military figure in the 15th century and not to be confused with Shakespeare's fat bumbling drunk), corralled the supply wagons together and turned them into a mini-fort, complete with the anti-cavalry stakes; and despite the French (and a Scottish contingent) having canons, they were beaten off. In their retreat, they were counterattacked and routed.

Quite frankly, predicting another English victory wasn't exactly hard but it was enough to gain safe passage to meet the Dauphin where the Maid impressed Charles in a private meeting. Her name was Jehanne (Joan) d'Arc. I have already mentioned some national icons and am aware that by stripping away the myths and legends, and only looking at the historical evidence, I may annoy a few people. However, while Owain Glyndwr or William Wallace may get the blood pumping for some, they aren't officially canonised saints. Joan d'Arc is also used as a feminist icon, or at least, as an example of a woman struggling to gain recognition in the face of the elitist patriarchy's misogyny. She is integral to the French National psyche. She also blurs the lines between history and belief. To her supporters, she is a holy woman who selflessly led French armies to incredible victories. To her detractors, the Dauphin looked to a delusional young girl and used her for his own cynical political gains. As always in life, the truth tends to lie somewhere in between.

Personally I have an issue with people declaring that "God's on our side". Apart from the obvious question, "how do you know?" it does somewhat imply that the other side has done something to offend God and are now paying the price. The person who declares divine backing will also invariably proclaim an imminent victory. If it transpires that a loss then occurs, it's not that God's on the other guy's side, but that God is invariably punishing the losers for some unspecified sin. To put it another way, no matter what the outcome, God gets the credit/blame.

If God had chosen this moment to reveal himself to France in the form of a teenage girl, it does lead to a few uncomfortable questions. Prior to this, almost every major battle had been a humiliating

French defeat for the last eighty years (3 generations or so). That plus the Black Death makes one wonder exactly how sinful were the French to need this much punishment? The other main question is if she was a divinely inspired leader, why did the divine spirit leave her just as she was gaining some momentum, which then led her to her own spectacular demise. Her military career lasted just three years and her success rate against the English, both strategically and tactically, was nowhere near a divine 100%. Putting it another way, if piety is associated with military victories, then Edward III or Henry V should be saints too, because they had better military records than the Maid of Orléans.

Initially Joan exploded onto the scene, but the idea of divinely inspired young women didn't start with her. There were a number of them in the medieval period. Perhaps the most famous other one was Saint Catherine of Siena, who in the late 1300's, led the Papacy back from France to Rome and created truces amongst the warring Italian city states. Women had got involved in wars before, as we've seen with the likes of Matilda and Isabella. However for a sixteen year old girl to strap on full armour and ride into battle leading troops and declaring that she was receiving holy visitations was a wholly unique package, and by all accounts, electrifying to the beleaguered Dauphin's supporters.

Joan was a zealot. To her the conflict was a holy war and that made the English, not just an enemy, but their very presence in France, sacrilege. Consequently in her first notable action in a siege at Jargeau, she broke with chivalric tradition and did not allow the English garrison to negotiate terms, which as we have seen, is the standard procedure in such a situation. The English defences were successfully stormed and largely slaughtered, unnecessarily. Joan had raised the stakes and shown the French army how to win again.

Then it was to Orléans, the pinnacle of her success, where a three month siege by the English was dragging on. Within days of her arrival, the English left their defences, but didn't do so in a panic. At about the same time came the Battle of Patay.

Here is an example where myth overtakes reality. Joan was at the battle but it was all but over by the time she was to play any part. It was not her efforts that gave the French victory, but the decisive actions of French noble La Hire.

What happened in this situation was that the French vanguard of the army (just 1,500 men) met a sizeable English force of about 4,000 led by two of the most formidable English generals of the day, John Fastolf and John Talbot (known as the English Achilles for his prowess in battle). However the English archers gave away their position too soon, so the French heavy cavalry was able to flank them and annihilate them. Fastolf, realising the battle was over almost as soon as it began, retreated, leading to John Talbot's capture by the French. Losing a battle and a key general were major set backs, and in retrospect, more important than the lifting of the siege at Orléans. This French victory had very little to do with The Maid. A victory is a victory and the French didn't really care who was responsible, but it's worth noting, to demystify Joan d'Arc, that she was sometimes given too much credit.

The Maid of Orléans made another prophecy: the Dauphin would be crowned in Reims as the rightful king of France. However Reims was still deep in English held territory and this was a bold prophecy to make. Bedford ,was all too aware that this own claimant to the throne was a young boy who had yet to have a coronation in England or France so if Joan's vision was correct, it would be a blow to their claim to the throne of France.

Joan d'Arc didn't need to fight now. The news of her victories went before her and her fiery letters reframed this battle between two royal households into apocalyptic language of angels and damnation. She was on a crusade to rid France of the English curse. Towns welcomed the Dauphin and this teenage girl, dressed in male clothing, with rapturous cheers into their cities. Bedford seemed powerless to resist.

On the 16th of July 1429, Charles with Joan did the seemingly impossible; they marched into Reims without a siege or battle. The crowd was ecstatic and the next day Charles was crowned and anointed at the Cathedral (although the traditional coronation regalia was in English hands, waiting to be used for Henry). France now had two kings and war resumed, with the Maid at the forefront fighting for her newly anointed monarch. Meanwhile the noble La Hire, victor of Patay, was busy besieging towns like Louviers and generally not getting the same credit or interest as Joan.

Paris became concerned, as Joan's next move was to slowly tighten the noose around the capital held by the enemy. Bedford tried to set a trap in August, but the French refused to be lured into another Agincourt, so both sides cautiously manoeuvred around each other.

Then Joan arrived at Paris itself, and with no thought to her own personal safety, stood in front of its walls with a standard bearer and roared at the defenders-

"Surrender to us quickly, in Jesus' name. If you don't surrender before nightfall we shall come in by force whether you like it or not and you will all be killed!"

A crossbowman responded by shouting-

"Shall we? You bloody tart."

And promptly shot her through the leg. Another crossbowman shot and killed the standard bearer. This has to be one of the best retorts in the history of sieges.

It was not a great start for Joan and a few days later the siege was broken off under Charles's orders. Some have said that if Charles had persevered, he probably would have captured Paris. I think it's unlikely. While the events around Joan have already confounded a lot of well-established precedents, Paris was well defended and motivated to keep The Maid at bay.

The next spring things went badly wrong for Joan. She went to the town of Compiègne to relieve it from an Anglo-Burgundian siege. She attacked the Burgundian camp and was surrounded. It is worth noting that her final battle was against a French army and it was her countrymen who handed her over to Bedford.

How you feel about the next and final phase in Joan's life is about as divisive as it gets in history. Bedford had a mortal enemy in his hands, a unique being who had turned the tables on decades of English superiority, partly through unbridled bravery, partly through demonstrable piety. She had added a religious dimension to the war, casting the English as unholy (which was news to them) and going against the chivalric codes with various unnecessary massacres. She was the enemy's secret weapon, which gave them an advantage both militarily and psychologically, as a symbol. This was only going to end one way.

The other way of looking at this was that the English had a vulnerable teenage peasant girl in their midst. She was imprisoned and had to fight off attempts to rape her; she was bullied and subjected to ridicule, with no support from her benefactor Charles.

Books, films and documentaries have been made about her; she is another figure who has become an industry in their own right. Almost all of this is from the modern French perspective, which turns Bedford into a pantomime villain and Joan into a clear-cut heroine. As has been seen however, she raised the stakes, she showed no compromise in her views and wouldn't have expected any in return.

Her trial was not a military one, but a religious one and it was fixed from the start, breaking even the rules laid down by the inquisition, which was hardly fair to begin with. Joan did an excellent job of defending herself, showing that she was intelligent and eloquent, and this after the notes of trial were later altered to further condemn her.

Her best exchange was a theological ambush. She was asked if she was in God's grace. It's a trap because according to church doctrine nobody could know this, so if she answered "yes", she would indeed be a heretic; if she answered "no", then she would be admitting to a fraud. Instead she replied with the elegant-

"If I am not, may God put me there; and if I am, may God so keep me."

This didn't do her any good, and to Charles's shame, he made no attempt to negotiate for her, pay a ransom or try to free her, even though she tried to escape on several occasions. Bedford was dealing with a threat; Charles however, was needlessly sacrificing a loyal ally. On May 30th 1431 she was burned at the stake for heresy. She was nineteen.

Like Magna Carta, like Parliaments, Joan d'Arc was the start of something; but at the time, the powerful legacy was not immediately apparent. In Joan's case almost all her victories were reversed by Talbot, Fastolf and Bedford in the next few years after her death. Bedford also ensured a lavish coronation for Henry VI in the winter of 1431, when he was aged just nine to counter Charles's claim to the throne. Henry's coronation systematically trumped Charles's. Henry had the correct coronation attire and was crowned in Notre Dame in Paris. While this was not the traditional cathedral of a French King's coronation, it was bigger than Rheims.

In every way Henry had the better claim, but ultimately, it didn't matter anymore. The reality was that Bedford and the others were fighting more than French armies; Joan was a symbol of France. In the 15th century people associated themselves with a region, but slowly, the idea of a national identity was forming. The reality was that the Norman French simply had more in common with the French from the Isle de France than with London, and no amount of archers can stop that.

As all the wars in France have demonstrated so far, the French invariably had more men, more resources and more land; and because the English had failed to plant the killing blow in the previous two centuries, they had missed their opportunity to ever do so.

Just twenty five years after her death, there was an enquiry into Joan's life and trial, and she was exonerated. There was good reason to do so, but the politics behind making her a saint were more partisan. The war between England and France, while dragging on for another twenty years, was starting to have a certain inevitability about it. The English resources grew thinner, and then disaster struck as the Burgundian and Armagnac factions were reconciled. By the end of 1450 only Calais remained English in the whole of northern France. Cherbourg was sold to the French in the same year, a sign the English just couldn't match the resources of the French crown anymore.

Chapter 10 The Endless War part VI(It ends! Sort of

Don't worry about the write up, ...it'll be fine.

While things had been going badly in France, events over the channel were sowing the seeds for another convulsion of violence in England.

Three things were bubbling under the surface to create a toxic brew:

Firstly, as already pointed out, there had been so much successful breeding by kings that most of the aristocracy had links to the crown. These potential claimants were nullified if the king was strong. Everyone seemed to want to give Henry VI, the son of the great warlord Henry V, the benefit of the doubt. But the wars in France had begun to split the nobility of England into two distinct factions: one centred on the so-called York branch of the family tree, and the other around the Lancastrian branch. The names are misleading because the lands these families had were all over England, Wales and Ireland, but it's by this shorthand that the two power bases were known.

Secondly, with war in France all but at an end, England was awash with veterans of these wars who knew no other living. While becoming a mercenary on the continent was an option the reality was that if anyone wanted to, they could very easily hire battle hardened veterans for an instant and deadly fighting force in England.

Thirdly, lighting the fuse to disaster was Henry VI's insanity. Modern geneticists could have warned them of the dangers because as Henry's mother was the daughter of mad French king, she was likely to be carrying some of those damaged genes in her own DNA. After all that waiting, after all that hard work by Gloucester and Bedford, their efforts protected a failure of a ruler. Henry is another serious contender for the worst king in English history. It may not have been his conscious fault, but after humiliation in France, what was needed was a strong hand from the central point of power. Instead this was a man who would lapse into catatonic states at key points in his reign.

This era of dynastic warfare came to be known as the War of the Roses (due to the symbols of the two houses); its name conjures up images of romance, and once again, it is a battleground for historians. Some claim that seeing it as a civil war is over-emphasising the battles, and in reality, it was more of a dynastic spring clean with some violence as a consequence. Others point to the scale of casualties and see it as a bloody home-grown continuation of the levels of violence that had become commonplace in France.

It's also a confusing period of history. Henry VI was deposed and then made a comeback; so he was king twice. His usurper, Edward IV, similarly reigned twice. Then you get Edward V, considered a king in retrospect; but as he was a boy who disappeared under mysterious circumstances, he plays no real part in history but makes for a great conspiracy theory, immortalised by that man who is always playing fast and loose with English history- William Shakespeare. Of course this period also brings us to Richard III who gets a similar treatment from the great bard, turning an adequate ruler and brave warrior into one of the most loathsome villains in theatrical history. He never deserved to be remembered that way, and there's even a society dedicated to rehabilitating his image (particularly after his body was found underneath a Leicester car park in 2012). I'm not a member, but I agree with them.

This jostling and positioning of partisan rulers was to last a generation. However the good news was that this was to mark an end to civil war in England and dynastic based clashes in France as the default setting for England and Wales. Further spasms of violence would happen, but they were to be the exception rather than the norm.

Henry's weak grip on the throne was challenged by Richard Duke of York who had increasingly begun to defy the king's court, and most importantly, the queen's. Scuffles had broken out before 1455 but in that year you get the first open conflict with the 1st battle of St Albans (obviously nobody called it that at the time) took place. In the greater scheme of things it was a minor skirmish, with only a couple of thousand soldiers in total involved. The Yorkists, however, managed to kill a number of key Lancastrians, but the fighting seeped into other members of the House of Lancaster and dripped down into the next generation, too.

Henry VI did come up with a novel solution to the problem in 1458 by creating "Love-Day", where the main nobles involved in the battle at St Albans walked arm-in-arm to St Paul's Cathedral in London to show no hard feelings. Mortal enemies were forced into reconciliation to the cheers of the London crowds. It didn't help, as the issues were too great to be solved by this rather naive PR stunt.

Richard Neville, The Earl of Warwick, was pivotal in the early period of this fighting. In 1459 Richard of York was forced into exile after losing a few too many battles. However, his supporter Warwick fought on his behalf, and at the Battle of Northampton, captured Henry VI. This battle is an example of how the War of the Roses wasn't a case of minor skirmishes. The total amount of troops on the field were roughly 30,000, huge for an English civil war, and would have been considered a decent size in the French campaigns. Warwick was able to capture kings and back other kings and so came to be known to history as "The Kingmaker".

However in 1460, Richard and his son were both killed at the Battle of Wakefield, so things looked like they could finally settle down. Unfortunately shortly after that, at the Second Battle of St Albans (it was bound to happen and was this time much larger with tens of thousands of soldiers), Henry VI was captured again. The fundamental issue with this period is the same as Stephen and Matilda's in that neither side could land the killing blow. Just as some momentum was reached by one side, the leader was captured or key personnel were killed, or a must-win battle was lost and so the advantage moved to the other side.

A good example of this was that just a year later in 1461, there was an epic battle at the Yorkshire town of Towton. This was one of the largest battles ever fought on English soil and part of it was fought in a blizzard. The Yorkists were outnumbered but were led by Edward IV and Warwick, and received reinforcements later on. Not unsurprisingly given the previous descriptions of battles of this time, the pivotal role went to the longbow men. The Lancastrian archers fired blind and into the wind, meaning many of their arrows either missed their targets or fell short. Gusts of snow also obscured their view and they fired so furiously that they ran out of arrows. The Yorkist archers were more cautious and had the wind with them. They fired into the Lancastrian ranks and even pulled out spent missiles on the ground and returned them to their owners. It was like a hail storm of steel landing on the lightly armoured longbow men.

This, plus a well-timed cavalry charge, led to the bloodiest battle on English soil. The total casualties are estimated at nearly 30,000, and when you consider the casualties on the first day of the Somme were 60,000 with a much larger population overall, you realise these were exceedingly high losses for a medieval battle. This struggle for dynastic dominance was not a lacklustre affair, as some have suggested.

For most of the 1460s, Warwick backed Edward and he was handsomely rewarded, not only with lands in England, but with titles and responsibilities for the navy and the few remaining outposts in France too. However it wasn't to last, and when two men fall out spectacularly, there is usually a woman involved. On this occasion it was because Warwick had been painstakingly trying to negotiate a marriage between Edward and the French King's daughter, only to discover that Edward had married in secret, so wrecking his plans and showing a lack of trust in Warwick.

The results weren't immediate, but the two men drifted apart. Warwick started to court Edward's brother Clarence, potentially to be a new king. This dance of power went on for months as the three men circled each other, cautiously, to see who would gain the upper hand. In the end, Clarence felt that blood was thicker than water and threw his lot in with Edward, leaving Warwick outmanoeuvred.

Henry VI did manage to sire a male heir, Edward, but he died aged just eighteen at the Battle of Tewkesbury in 1471; and Henry VI was murdered in captivity in the same year. In the spring of 1471, Warwick "The Kingmaker" also died in battle (at Barnet), so three key figures all perished within a few months of each other and gave Edward IV some breathing space. This was a very dangerous period for the nobility; it was possible to be king or lord one day, and a corpse the next.

During the latter stages of Edward IV's reign, things did settle down; but he died unexpectedly (of natural causes in 1483), with no adult male heir, so plunging the country again into uncertainty. Edward's brother Richard of Gloucester took the throne and became Richard III.

As you may have gathered from my summary, there is far more to be told about this period of intrigue, rivalries and war. Overall though, the point is that none of this was pre-ordained. It was never going inevitably to end with a young pretender called Henry going for broke at Bosworth Field and beating the respected king and general Richard III. Any one of these players could have won; even "Love-Day" conceivably could have worked (ok maybe not). Edward IV could have lived long enough to install an adult male heir; Edward, son of Henry VI, could have lived and conquered all; and even Clarence, with the backing of

Warwick, could have been the founder of a dynasty. Only hindsight makes it "obvious" who was going to win. The reality was that this was a maelstrom of vanity and hubris wrapped in a lust for power. Had fate smiled on a different person, we would have had a very different 16th century and may never have had the need to break from the Roman Catholic Church.

Of course all this fighting in England meant there was no real attempt to keep the French from the remaining lands in France. The south western lands were also absorbed by the French crown, which now left Calais as the lone outpost on the mainland. This port was a whisper of the former dominance of English power in France, never to be regained.

Henry Tudor was of Welsh origins (he was also born and raised there, with Welsh ancestry- so you could claim that he's the first Welsh King of England) and had a very tenuous claim to the throne, with two barriers. The first problem was his claim was derived from the female line, never seen as legitimate as the male one. This is further complicated by that line involving an illegitimate connection, which all but wipes it out as a claim in the eyes of the laws and what was social acceptances at the time. After all, if every bastard a king sired could legitimately claim the throne, there would be have been even more wars across Europe.

As we have seen however, Henry was not only was a winner in his day, but the founder of a dynasty; and this was to ensure that history would remember him kindly. After all if Henry's claim to the throne were to be examined too closely by the next generation, then Henry VIII would have had a tough time keeping his own throne- the same for Edward VI, Mary and Elizabeth, too.

In 1485 Henry took the highly risky but decisive strategy of landing in England (his earlier scheming had got him exiled) and met Richard in battle at Bosworth Field. Had Richard survived to fight another day or indeed won (he had the larger army), Henry Tudor would be a footnote in history. What Henry did in the battle was to rather rashly attack one of Richard's allies near a marsh. Richard, seeing this, led his household guard in a charge to kill the enemy leader and end the rebellion once and for all. He got close, really close. Henry's own standard bearer was killed in the initial clash. However Henry's men outnumbered Richard's personal ground and the marshy ground gave him little chance to manoeuvre. Seeing the danger, Richard's men offered him a horse to get back to the Yorkist lines (he therefore would never have had to call out "A horse, a horse, my kingdom for a horse!"). He refused the new mount and fought on foot, perishing there in the heart of the battle. Almost any other outcome would have meant victory for Richard, but as it was, Henry won the battle and the crown.

To Henry's eternal credit, he finally ended this generation long war and brought stability to the English crown for the next century. He married Edward IV's daughter, so uniting the houses of York and Lancaster again and combined their respective symbols of a white rose and a red rose into the white and red Tudor Rose, a literal illustration of the union he had brought to the country.

Henry now ruled over England, Wales, Ireland and Calais. The English would continue to claim a right to the French throne, in the same way that the Papacy would still occasionally call for an eastern crusade. While the language was strong, everyone knew the reality of the situation, and the chances of Henry VII being crowned king of France, like Henry VI, was remote. Instead, after so many years of civil war, plague and wars in France, Henry brought peace. His reign wasn't violence free, but in comparison to the blood-soaked previous three centuries, it was a virtual oasis of calm.

Here I am going to fast-forward again, just as I did with Roman Britain, and go past all the Tudors. Why? You may well wonder, but my answer goes back to the start of this book. Some periods have more written about them than others. To be honest, if I really wanted to sell a truckload of books, I should have done one on the Nazis; they almost always sell well, hence the glut of books on World War 2. The 1540s are not twenty times more interesting than the 1440s and yet, by my rough estimate, there are about twenty times the amount of books written on the Tudor period than the times immediately before or after. There is so much written about them that even the Tudor loving novelists and historians are running out of topics. In recent years there has been a trend to write more about the period of the War of the Roses, and to be honest, it has just as much sex, violence and intrigue as the Tudor period. It's a good area to move into this earlier era.

Henry VIII did a number of important things in his lifetime and yet even five year olds know him for his six wives and being fat. Show a picture of a painting of Elizabeth I and there are many times more correct guesses regarding identity as opposed to showing a painting of Henry V. I have nothing new to add, and unlike some of the events I have described, you probably know the rough outline of their reigns. Chances are good that you know about Henry VIII needing a divorce and splitting from Rome, Mary and lots of burning of Protestants/heretics, and Elizabeth and the Spanish Armada. So I will gloss over these one hundred and twenty years and keep Hilary Mantel's publishing career going (my apologies to Hilary Mantel).

Chapter 11 People Power

Possibly the most important thing that happened in the Tudor period was not the ephemeral politics or beheadings, but that in 1497, Humphrey Gilbert became the first European to set foot in North America since the time of the Vikings. This was important for two reasons-

1) It would eventually lead to the formation of the hugely powerful and globally influential country of America.
2) It can be seen as the start of the British Empire, which would take another 200 years to reach a critical mass in terms of size, but would eventually become the largest empire the world has ever seen.

It was an inauspicious start. Having found this new land, they decided to call it "Newfoundland", so winning the award for the most literal naming of an area- ever.

Meanwhile back in the old world, in 1603 Elizabeth I was dying. After forty five years on the throne, having shown England and the rest of Europe, how effective a female monarch could be, she was fading away. Elizabeth was famously referred to as the Virgin Queen, and in later years claimed, to be married to England. This is great for noble speeches, but continued the perennial problem of continuity. An heir was desperately needed to stop civil war or invasion. England did not need another war, so a delegation of nobles, led by Sir Robert Cecil, approached the King of Scotland, James VI, to become King of England. He had a bloodline that could be traced back to the English throne, and as a Protestant was an acceptable choice.

Elizabeth died in the spring of 1603. James travelled south and was crowned to great adulation and general relief. This is a little stranger than it first appears because a few years earlier, James wrote a book called "The True Laws of Free Monarchies". In it he writes about the divine right of monarchs and how they are higher than ordinary people, having been ordained by God to rule. He was a believer in absolute power and looked to the Biblical kings to prove his point. This is worth remembering when reading the King James Bible (the standard english language Bible) because in it, kings are generally seen as both powerful and divinely anointed. Many are heroes, so echoing

James's vision of how things should be. An English King, however, was no longer all-powerful.

The situation was odd because James, the "divine" and all-powerful king, did not conquer England. He didn't demand the throne either; he was politely offered it by a committee. It was a sign of how effective the English system of government was working, without the need of a king. English monarchs weren't quite figureheads yet, but the systems of how to rule the country were no longer automatically flowing through the king, and parliaments could keep things going without royal direction or interference both in theory and practice.

James's accession to the throne of England also unified the crowns of England and Scotland. The dream that goes back as far as Athelstan was realised again and this time, the union was to be permanent. The two countries had yet to be unified, and in that sense, you could see James as a mini-emperor as he ruled two separate lands with conflicting viewpoints. James's ruling of both nations, however, brought an end to the "auld" alliance between France and Scotland. In the future, France would have to find other partners to cause mischief against the English. It also started the inevitable process of union. The two countries that had been separated for so long by almost continual war, were similar in too many ways for them not to coalesce once the crowns were combined in one monarch. It wasn't a smooth transition, but it had begun.

James is a king who tends to be quickly summarised, and then the story moves on. This is probably because all his achievements lacked instant glamour. Theories on government discourse on the rights of Catholics in England, and peace treaties with Spain are in many ways more important than a Battle of Poitiers or a crusade, but they aren't as instantly interesting to read about.

However the one event in his reign that is remembered, is the gunpowder plot. In 1605 Robert Casement and his dozen other co-conspirators (including the far more famous Guy Fawkes) planned one of the worst devised terrorists plots in history. Parliament was partly to blame. In the past, leaders in Europe had been assassinated; there had been poisonings, stabbings and even the occasional shooting, but nobody had been deliberately blown up.

At this point in history, the Houses of Parliament (which were on the Thames River) had storage rooms beneath them that traders would rent to store cargoes. These goods were constantly coming off or being loaded onto the ships that plied their trade on the Thames. The cabal rented one of these rooms, directly under where the opening of parliament would be taking place, and filled it with thirty six barrels of gunpowder. They had plenty of time to plan this because the parliament was delayed from the spring to the autumn due to another outbreak of plague in London.

The big question is, of course, what was Guy Fawkes's motivation? The simple answer is that as a Catholic, he felt victimised by a protestant government and hoped that by removing a king with a weak claim to the English throne, he could bring about either a Catholic king or a ruler that was far more pro-Catholic. This is worth remembering as in recent years, Guy Fawkes (and the mask popularised in the comic and film V for Vendetta) has taken on the new image of a freedom fighter against oppression. He has become the common man struggling against the machinery of dictatorship. This is modern revisionism at its worse. He was not a libertine or a member of a pro-democracy movement; most of these phrases would have meant nothing to him. He wanted a Catholic monarch to be running his country and was happy to kill hundreds of innocents to achieve this.

He deserves no sympathy because he showed none himself. There is no need to feel sorry for idiots with bad plans, and the last addition to the conspiracy was Francis Tresham who sent an anonymous letter to his benefactor warning him not to attend this parliament, hoping he might not alert the authorities. For the plan to work, the barrels of gunpowder would have had to remain undetected for weeks before James arrived. While this part of the plan almost unbelievably nearly worked, it was overall, one of the most optimistic schemes in history. It's amazing the scheme got as close as it did to a successful conclusion. Far more rigorous plans have failed.

As it was, the benefactor alerted the security forces and Guy Fawkes was caught red-handed under the Houses of Parliament on the night of the 5th of November. Some went on the run, and there was a shoot-out in a house three days later where the rest of the group were either killed or captured. The survivors were then tortured into confessions and executed. A plan that should never have worked, didn't, which is unsurprising. However to this day, on November 5th, we have Bonfire Night where we burn a "Guy", in theory, an effigy of Guy Fawkes. Most people know the rhyme-

"Remember, remember the 5th of November, gunpowder, treason and plot."
"I see no reason why gunpowder, treason should ever be forgot"
(The second line is less well known)

Of all the enemies of the state there have ever been, in the gallery of rogues that have caused bloodshed in the British Isles, it is bizarre that Guy Fawkes is the only "bad guy" that's remembered and annually cursed. What is equally odd is the actual ring leader, Robert Casement, has become all but forgotten.

James responded to this attempt on his life and wanted to create a fairer rule for his Catholic subjects. In 1606 Parliament came up with a compromise and created an Oath of Allegiance for Catholics. It said that the king was the highest authority in the land so whatever he decreed trumped the Pope, an attempt to keep the politics out of Papal interventions in England. This was still within living memory of Pope Pius V creating the Papal Bull (decree) Regnans in Excelsis, which made the assassination of Elizabeth a holy act on a par with going on crusade. Now Catholics who swore the Oath could hold offices and go about their lives as normal; the ones who didn't were considered troublemakers (with some justification).

The Irish, however, were not to convert to Protestantism, so bringing a religious angle to the age-old rebellions that would frequently erupt. As Scotland and England now had a common king, it was going to be harder to make the two go to war. For Spain and France, Ireland was the new weak spot.

In 1607, on the other side of the world, a group of settlers landed in North America. They founded a small settlement with a defensive fort which they named in honour of the king, Fort James. They called the town Jamestown and the nearest river- go on guess; the James River. Other settlers did little better getting bored of naming everything after the king they named the local area which reminded them of England but was new- "New England" continuing the underwhelming naming conventions of British explorers.

Unimaginative naming wasn't England's only problem in the new world: Britain was seriously behind in the rush for riches derived from this new continent. Prior to the Tudor era, France had always been England's public enemy number one; however after 1492 and Christopher Columbus discovering the Caribbean Islands (and spectacularly misnaming them the West Indies), the Spanish had arrived (not literally) in Europe like never before.

Spain and Portugal had slowly been carved out of the Muslim kingdoms of the Iberian peninsular, so now with total control of the land south of the Pyrenees and a new continent to explore, the Spanish and Portuguese were in the unique position of having far larger resources than they'd ever had before. Cortez and Pizarro were adventurers who took on entire civilisations. Both bands of men had a huge technological advantage over their Aztec or Incan opponents. They had also created an inadvertent biological weapon by opening up these populations to virulent European diseases to which the conquistadors had natural immunity.

These points may help to explain how hundreds of men took on armies of tens of thousands and won, but they were still tiny bands of adventurers taking on vast empires. They were the right mix of brave and ruthless to carve huge fortunes for themselves and followers, while shipping similarly colossal amounts of booty back to the motherland.

The South American colonies were built on violence and plunder. There was no real attempt to turn these territories into self-sufficient regions in their own right. They were to be exploited as much as possible. It was a miserable, cynical business that was ratified by the Pope on the grounds that the locals were godless heathens who carried out human sacrifice. They were. But this is, of course, an imperial view of local customs, and while nobody can defend human sacrifice that didn't mitigate the wholesale slaughter and mismanagement going on.

The British were fundamentally different in their approach. Their goal was less about plunder (let's be honest- mainly because they never encountered any easy pickings) and more about settlement and later, trade. The Protestant work ethic was in full swing, building towns from scratch and starting to learn how to grow crops in the local environment. That said, farmers generally aren't rich and the ones in America certainly weren't, so these modest starts to empire were dwarfed by the treasure ships regularly heading across the Atlantic to Iberian ports. Spain could afford anything it wanted and was now the premiere force on land and sea in Europe.

England had been fighting against Spain, partly through small forces sent to the Netherlands where there was almost constant war (the Dutch fought "The Eighty Years War" against Spain), but mainly through privateers. Privateers were, in essence, government backed pirates. Britain couldn't possibly win a full naval engagement or a large set-piece battle against the Spanish behemoth. So instead it would send small groups of fighting vessels to get some of that Spanish gold.

The later 18th century pirates that have for some bizarre reason become child friendly, didn't tend to board treasure ships; they grabbed whatever the merchant vessels had and sold it. In the 17th century however it really was a case of grabbing ships full of treasure in the Caribbean. Sailors could grow very wealthy if they joined in these raids and knew that they would be protected if they could get back to England.

The Spanish were furious about this officially sanctioned robbery (they had a point), so James created a peace treaty which meant that Britain could spend its money on development, not war. James's reign was one of improving government and a continuation of the golden age of literature and theatre. He may not have had his own Agincourt, but the country was better off for it. Indeed towards the end of his reign, Europe exploded into one of the bloodiest and widespread wars that ever happened on the continent. Later it was called the Thirty Years War (1618-1648) but gets little attention in the UK because we were peripheral to the events. But that's a good thing that's worth mentioning.

In my introduction I said that this war is still considered by many to have damaged areas of Germany more than World War II. (For an excellent book on this period do read Peter H. Wilson's *"Europe's Tragedy").* This conflict drew in Sweden, the German states, Switzerland, France, Italian city states, Spain, and the Low Countries. Britain, by contrast was an oasis of calm, occasionally sending over protestant armies but it was on English terms and never caused any damage to the English economy or country. Wilson has estimated that over this period 170,000 British soldiers fought in the wars (about 42,000 of those were Irish fighting for the Spanish). Overall though, this kept British armies up-to-date with current military trends; and in general, Britain grew stronger as Europe devoured itself.

James died peacefully in 1625 and his son Charles became king. Charles had obviously been reading up on his father's view of monarchy because he tried even harder to push back parliamentary power and increase the royal prerogative. This was not unusual. Spain and France had absolute rulers and any Christian king only had to look at the Old Testament to find dozens of just rulers ordained by God. Charles didn't appreciate that his situation was different. Since the times of Henry III, Parliaments had been instrumental in governing the country. Added to that the precedents of Magna Carta, Parliaments raising taxes for the endless wars with France, and the fact that it was the nobles who invited Charles's father to be king, meant his situation was irreversibly different to those other examples.

There was simply too big a gap between the way Britain was governed and the way he thought it should be. As already stated, Magna Carta may have started a trend, but it had been a trickle of legal and governmental adjustments. But that had been four hundred years earlier, and by now that constant trickle had led to a vast lake of legislation and social acceptances that was ultimately to make Charles's attempts to be an absolute monarch flounder.

Charles started provocatively by marrying a Catholic princess, so offending pretty much every Protestant and Puritan noble in Britain. He then went back on his father's policy of peace and actively went to war with Spain. The good news is this did increase his Protestant credentials; the bad news is the English minnow was now fighting the Spanish shark. While this was part of the larger Thirty Years War, so ensuring that Britain didn't fight on alone, it was going to be a hugely risky and expensive venture.

To pay for all of this he tried to raise taxes without a parliament, something that the members of parliament were not going to tolerate. At almost every turn Charles was going against the grain, perhaps to prove that he was supreme ruler or maybe because he was a poor decision maker. As the saying goes, "pick your battles" and it seemed like Charles was picking every available fight; he couldn't win them all.

In 1628 Parliament brought Charles the Petition of Right, which laid down everything the king could and couldn't do without consent from Parliament. This document is as important in the formation of the modern legal framework as Magna Carta, but it doesn't get the same attention. It says many things but some of the key ones are that taxes have to be raised via Parliament and not the king, nor can you be imprisoned without cause (an issue that's still a hot topic today). This last point stopped Charles throwing into prison anyone who didn't want to vote for his unpopular taxes.

The Petition of Right, just like Magna Carta, could have solved the situation but didn't. Every time Charles called a parliament together he was flooded with new requests and complaints about his rule. What absolute ruler needed such insolence? He realised he needed them to raise funds for whatever state opportunities he wanted to do, but they were a burden.

In 1639 Scotland was sliding into war (called the Bishops War) sparked by Charles's attempts to model the Scottish church on Anglican Protestantism, to the fury of many Scots. It had got as bad as full scale raiding and battles as far South as Durham. Charles needed an army and money to solve the problem, so he called for a parliament again. It was never intended to last for long but sat from 1640-48 and was, unsurprisingly, remembered as "The long Parliament". The first order of business was the accusation of treason. I do not want to get too mired in 17th century politics (you may be glad to hear), so let's leave it that Charles had rebellious Scottish armies marching through northern England, the usual uprisings in Ireland and now, an English Parliament with the members at each other's throats. All the stability that had been around for generations was palpably ebbing away.

By 1641 Charles was involved in pretty much any scheme that could stop the edifice of his power from tumbling. He was conspiring with Scottish nobles, he was attempting to raise armies and he was defying parliamentary wishes as often as possible. The whole situation was turning into a mess and he was at the centre of it. Parliament was turning more and more hostile to him, so he chose to leave London and make Oxford his base in 1642. Charles was digging in his heals, refusing to accept the realities that in Britain, things had changed. He had numerous options to avoid conflict, but at almost every turn chose to ignore them or took them, only to renege on them later. The Petition of Right was in tatters (as Magna Carta had been).

The image of the monarch was still powerful and many chose the king over their elected officials. It seems that part of James's and Charles's desire to be seen as divinely anointed absolute rulers had paid off; either that or the alternative was so loathsome that it was a case of "better the devil you know". Charles had support in everywhere except Scotland and the south east of England, with London being the natural Parliamentary capital. By the autumn of 1642 only war could determine which side would win the argument. And so political battles turned into real ones.

Chapter 12 The Last Civil War

Throughout this book I have described eras almost exclusively through the viewpoint of monarchs. This is a valid way of looking at things before the civil war of the 17th century. Earlier monarchs were generals, politicians and statesmen; in essence the country was there for the monarch. What this war was about was making the monarch there for the country.

Some historians have described this conflict with Charles I as the English Revolution and it's a fair description. Prior to this conflict the civil wars of the past were about who would rule England; this one was about how England would be ruled. Contrary to popular belief the Parliamentarians (nicknamed the Roundheads after a type of helmet that was quite prevalent at the time) didn't want to overthrow Charles *per se* they wanted to contain him and Charles had enough support to resist this. That's why this conflict was different, but it shouldn't be remembered by the name "The Civil War" as that almost willingly forgets all the other wars that have been fought on English soil.

The title "The Civil War" also came about because this was the first serious violence to have been experienced in English towns and cities for generations. Medieval civilians lived with regular outbreaks of fighting, but to the average farmer of the 17th century, this was a terrifyingly novel situation to deal with.

The weapons of war had changed, too. It was in the late Tudor period that the longbow was phased out in favour of the musket. At first glance this was a very odd thing to do. A musket has the reload rate of a crossbow; it also had a much shorter effective range than a longbow and couldn't be used in the rain. The modern rifle beats a longbow in every aspect and allows one man to kill many in seconds but there was at least three hundred and fifty years of the gunpowder-based long range weapons lagging behind the key weapon of the British arsenal of the medieval period.

The obvious question is why switch from a superior weapon to an inferior one? A number of reasons combined give the answer. Firstly, there's the factor that it was new technology and as it was new, people naturally assumed it was better. Secondly, the sheer noise of a musket can lead to troops routing and many psychological experiments have shown (I think rather nicely) that humans would rather scare off an enemy than kill them. Finally, longbow men took years to train. At the battle site of Towton it is easy to tell which skeletons were archers because of differences in the back and shoulder bones (sometimes even with vertebrae fused together), showing that years were needed to gain the strength required to pull back the bowstring. The use of a musket required minimal training and anyone could fire it.

However with the invention of the bayonet still a way off, the musketeers needed to be protected while they slowly reloaded. They would stand in lines and then be replaced by the line behind them after the first volley was fired in order to keep up a constant stream of fire. The musketeers as a whole would be protected by pike men who would stand in rows with their sharp-edged pikes sticking out before them like steel hedgehogs. In many ways it was the ancient Greek phalanx or the medieval Scottish Schiltron all over again.

The other major change was artillery. Canons had been used as far back as Crecy but they had improved substantially. Cannon of the 17th century could outrange almost anything that had come before and were now seen in their dozens on battlefields and in naval engagements. They fired three basic types of projectile: first of all, the cannon ball, a solid projectile that would rip through ships' hulls, ranks of men or shatter fortress walls. The second type was called many things like canister or grapeshot, but it was basically a shorter range anti-infantry shot that sprayed dozens of musket balls at the oncoming enemy turning the cannon into a lethal, giant shotgun. The third type was exclusively for naval battles where two smaller balls were connected by a chain. This was fired at the sails and rigging of an enemy ship in order to cripple it. Artillery had become the most feared multipurpose killing machine on the battlefield.

Muskets and cannons made armour less useful than it had been. A musket could puncture all but the thickest armour and cannon would rip through anything, so speed and manoeuvrability returned to the battlefield. Foot soldiers wore almost no armour and the cavalry were no longer encased like steel lobsters but would quite often have a helmet and breastplate to ward off blows in close quarters. Overall, in the space of one hundred years the art of war had changed more than it had in the previous five hundred.

The war of words turned into the real thing with the first major battle being in October 1642 at Edgehill which could be considered a draw and then the Royalist forces (also called the Cavaliers) got as close to the city of London as Turnham Green (which nowadays is comfortably inside London) but a stand-off ensued and Charles returned to Oxford.

Battles were happening all over the country and the clashes varied wildly in size. For example the forgotten (and not very important) Battle of

Hopton Heath saw fewer than 3,000 combatants on the battlefield. The next year at the far more famous Battle of Marston Moor there were around 40,000 men involved.

Marston Moor in 1644 was a key battle. The Roundheads (with the Scots) had been besieging the royalist stronghold of York. The Cavaliers were led by Prince Rupert (one of Charles's cousins) who was every inch the dashing and brave general, a renowned master of the cavalry charge. He also had brought with him the most feared of weapons, his white hunting poodle called "Boye". Rupert and Boye are a good example of something else that was new in the field of war- propaganda.

With the invention of the moveable type printing press and an increase in general literacy, creating pamphlets was a cheap, popular and easy thing to do. One of the reasons the Thirty Year's War is remembered so bitterly is that real massacres were exaggerated and lurid descriptions filled the pages of these uncensored papers. All sides did it and it was now common practice to have propaganda printed and distributed. Then just as now, everyone liked a good gossipy story, so from imaginative drawings of Martin Luther literally breaking wind in the face of the Pope to unsubstantiated tales of cannibalism in the Rhineland, pretty much anything was said about anyone. It makes the modern media look positively coy by comparison.

What has this got to do with Rupert? He was a successful Cavalier general, which meant he won more battles than he lost and his loyal dog would always follow him into battle. So the myth/slander was spread that Rupert was a student of magic and that Boye possessed magical powers as his familiar. Rupert encouraged the idea, seeing this as a psychological advantage on the battlefield. This loyal poodle was turned into a hound of hell which genuinely did scare Roundheads who saw it running alongside Rupert.

Rupert, with his usual vigour rushed to York's aid, gathering troops on the way. On arrival he carefully outmanoeuvred the Roundheads and relieved the city. The next day, despite having the smaller army, he sought to bring the roundheads into a pitched battle. On the day however, the preparations dragged on and it was the Parliamentarians who attacked first towards the end of the day.

The Roundheads were lead by the Earl of Leven, which shows that all the aristocrats did not rally to the king when war broke out and that there was a genuine feeling of grievance that the king was acting tyrannically. Saying that, Parliament wasn't full of the "common man" either, as you still had to have land and a certain level of income to be a member of Parliament.

Earlier in the day there was an attempt to get around one of the Parliamentarian flanks with royalist cavalry, only to be repelled by disciplined musket volleys. This wing of the army was led by

Colonel Oliver Cromwell. Battle commenced at 4.00pm but it was joined in earnest at 7.30pm after a brief thunderstorm, just when the Royalists were preparing to stay in their positions overnight, and started to make dinner, so losing any initiative they once had.

Cromwell's cavalry charged into the Royalist right wing and quickly broke it. Oliver received a wound to the neck in the process. However Rupert brought in his reserves to bolster this wing of his army. The Parliamentarians in return brought in the Scots who tipped the balance in favour of Cromwell, and his cavalry broke through.

This was happening at the same time as the Roundhead centre got past a ditch protecting the Royalist centre and pushed back the main body of troops. Rupert's left wing held and launched a counter charge which routed this part of the Parliamentarian army. As sunlight faded the fierce fighting in the centre was becoming disorganised and the Scots and other Roundhead infantry began to leave the battlefield in poor order. The advantage was seesawing backwards and forwards between the two armies, almost by the minute.

The Scots rallied and returned to the fray, but now, with no generals in close proximity, and with the sun set completely any semblance of order in the centre was deceptive as men desperately fought on. Cromwell had organised his cavalry and with a combination of the parliamentarian reserve, charged into the mass of shadowy figures illuminated by the moon. It was a moment of supreme skill, reorganising cavalry mid-battle and having them charge effectively at night was almost unheard of.

The entire Royalist army was now in full retreat back to York. The Roundheads' casualties were light, but Rupert had lost thousands either killed or captured, and Rupert's loyal dog Boye had also been killed. It was a key victory for Parliament and brought to everyone's attention the middle-aged, puritan cavalry officer, Oliver Cromwell.

The Puritan movement is an important one to understand because it had such a disproportionate effect on British history. Once Henry VIII set up the Church of England, Protestant reform church, some thought he hadn't gone far enough. This new church still had priests and large places of worship full of gold, in many ways resembling the Roman Catholic Church they had just broken from. The Puritans, as the name suggests, wanted to go further. They wanted to strip away all of the symbols of an organised and hierarchical church and take all the sin and debauchery out of society. It's hard not to consider them miserable spoilsports but they were doing it for the greater good of the soul. Surely it was better to go to heaven than to be distracted by something as worldly as bawdy Jacobean plays?

The Pilgrim Fathers, who had gone on to start key colonies in America, had not gone because of religious persecution in the way we assume.

Because they were so puritanical, they received no official backing in England, so they left for a new world where they could do things their way. This complete lack of compromise and religious zeal can be seen in some Christian communities in America to this day.

These Puritan settlers were so concerned with God's work that they brought more Bibles than farming equipment to the new world (and bizarrely, one man brought over one hundred pairs of shoes), believing that God would provide. However it is also in the Bible that God helps those who help themselves, which they had forgotten and had it not been for the pity of the local Native Americans offering them food to get them through the winter, they would have perished. This is the origin story of the American Thanksgiving Holiday. The puritans repaid the kindness of the local natives by declaring them heathens and did their best to steal their land and attack them with the other thing they had brought plenty of- guns.

It didn't take long for the settlers to turn inwards, accusing each other of heresy and witchcraft. This outbreak of paranoia in the 1690s was to be remembered as the Salem Witch Trials where dozens of innocent people were killed. Given their early history, it's a miracle the American colonies didn't all just die out.

As we have already seen Cromwell neither started the war nor was he one of its early leaders; he rose to power by merit, a relatively novel idea in Britain.

He was from a minor house of gentry. The Cromwells in the past had been hugely powerful, with key ancestors major players in the wars with France and a Thomas Cromwell worked as a key advisor to Henry VIII on the dissolution of the monasteries. Oliver's branch of the family wasn't the main one, so they lived in modest surroundings. He wasn't poor but neither had he been born with all the advantages of a major noble household.

Cromwell is one of the most divisive people I will mention, and he's an example of the confusion history can create. Children tend to put people in the "goodies" and "baddies" bracket. Once labelled, they don't change sides; and as the elected officials of the land were fighting a tyrant king, that would make Charles a "baddie" and Cromwell a "goodie". So why did everyone seem to hate him as soon as he was in charge? It maybe that at times of war people tend to want one type of leader, and then as peace arrives, another is required, a situation that Churchill could relate to who lost the 1945 general election.

In 1628 Cromwell was elected as MP for Huntingdon, and had civil war not broken out, he would have been utterly forgotten. The war made him and from out of nowhere, with little or no previous military experience, he turned out to be an exceptional cavalry officer and later, a gifted general.

After the success at Marston Moor he had arrived politically as a major player. In 1645 he built The New Model Army, a fulltime professional army that could fight in Britain, Ireland or abroad if necessary. It was obviously pro-Parliament but also Puritan in its views. Other British armies had performed well, but as soon as the campaign was over, they broke up, The New Model Army was on standby at all times. Cromwell had created the most effective and professional fighting force in Britain since the Romans.

Charles realising the war was being lost, fled to Scotland but was handed over to the Roundheads. There was a lull in fighting as Charles was in captivity. It's interesting to note that at this stage, it wasn't Parliament's plan to kill Charles. However the king still refused to recognise that he was beaten and tried playing the various groups off against each other to create some leverage for himself. It worked, and in the winter of 1647 the Scots invaded northern England, backing Charles. In the spring of 1648 some Roundheads switched sides to back the king (some of this was for the less-than-noble but understandable demand of being unpaid). Revolts for the king broke out all over Britain, culminating in the pitched Battle of Preston.

This battle is quick to write about because Cromwell did such a thorough job of winning. While the Royalists were strung out along the roads and bridges in the area, Cromwell threw everything he had at the Cavaliers before they formed into a coherent fighting force. The Royalists fought bravely but in vain, and were then attacked in the rear by more Roundheads. The end result, one hundred of Oliver's men were dead and almost the entire 9,000 strong Cavalier army, either killed or captured.

All the momentum Charles had tried to build was shattered at Preston, and once again, Cromwell had shown himself an excellent military commander. Cromwell is another figure who has had plenty written about him, but a lot of it tends to be partisan, portraying him either as an early republican and democratic hero or as a genocidal, religious zealot. Antonia Fraser's "Cromwell, Our chief of men" is a reasonably balanced account of his life.

We can go beyond the bare details of Cromwell's life as many of his letters and correspondence still survive, both official and personal. He was obviously a very religious man who increasingly saw his struggles in terms of good and evil, with his side naturally on the side of the righteous. This binary thought process led to him acting as a tyrant and dictator, always perceiving his actions as necessary for the greater good. That is not to let him off the hook. Indeed many people have acted on what they thought was the "greater good" (Hitler and Bin Laden are two examples nobody should aspire to), but to him, power was a tool to be used, not a goal in and of itself.

Cromwell sent one of his trusted officers, Thomas Pride, to purge the House of Commons of anyone not seen as loyal. The remainder was forever known as "The Rump Parliament". They were Oliver's men and would do his bidding. The king had been a tyrant, so he and the Rump Parliament decided to put Charles on trial for treason. The idea was not a bad one. Rather than deposing or killing a king, it was time to take the whole concept of monarchy to court to put it in a legal framework. However, to accuse a king of treason was a bad choice. How could a king be treasonous? Monarchs were the state, so it was a strange accusation.

The court was a fiasco. While it's bias was never in doubt, it could have prepared a better prosecution. It mistreated Charles (in the legal sense) so badly that many of the onlookers, who were not natural royalists, felt that the king did a good job, rising to the situation with dignity and eloquence. Throughout the proceedings Charles refused to recognise the court's jurisdiction, which only infuriated the prosecution even more, leading them to push for a whole week just to get Charles to enter a plea. He refused to do so.

The outcome was never in doubt, but the opportunity to hold a king legally accountable for his actions had been badly mishandled. Charles had not been a good king (although there had been worse), but he made an excellent defendant in court. As he was taken to his execution in January 1649, Charles wore extra clothes to ensure that he didn't shiver from the cold, which he feared could be misconstrued as him trembling with fear. Cromwell was not present and after the beheading allowed Charles's head to be sown back onto the body so his family could pay their respects.

Cromwell was now in power and it's ironic that his statue stands in front of the Houses of Parliament because when the Rump Parliament was deemed not loyal enough, it was whittled down to "The Bare Bones Parliament" of his most devoted followers. In 1653 he became "Lord Protector" and planned for his son to inherit his titles. For a republican he was acting an awful lot like the man he had taken to court for treason.

Cromwell's war machine served him well. After Charles's execution, he went to Ireland to put down rebellion there. He was successful, but in the sieges of Drogheda and Wexford, siege was followed by massacre. Thousands of civilians perished. While Cromwell had a special loathing for the Papist Irish, his actions set in the context of the day, were nothing unusual. He did not carry out a deliberate campaign of genocide, but in comparison to what had gone on during the recently ended Thirty Years War, he perpetrated relatively average attacks on civilian populations. Wexford certainly wasn't deliberate and was a rare example of Cromwell losing control of his troops.

It wasn't just his military actions that were to lead to the demonization of Cromwell in Ireland, but what happened next. He outlawed Catholicism meaning any Catholic priests found would be executed and Catholic-owned lands were given to Protestants. To modern minds this is barbaric, but again, this was common practice at the time, with Protestant or Catholic populations being victimised throughout Europe. Cromwell wasn't especially cruel; he was a warrior of his time.

Cromwell was literally on a mission from God. He banned the theatre as it was seen as licentious and sinful. He had a point. At the time "actress" and "prostitute" were interchangeable terms. He famously banned football but it wasn't like the modern game, more a riot with rules between local towns; he wanted to avoid unnecessary violence and harm. He meant well. He was neither devil nor saint; he was a human trying to do what he thought was best and sometimes getting things wrong, terribly wrong. He was trying to protect the English from themselves and as a Puritan looking on, that meant some very harsh measures to stop the whole country going to Hell (literally). Unfortunately for him his zealous dedication to his countrymen's souls was largely unwanted.

The Scots backed Charles's son, Charles II, and invaded England, only to be soundly defeated at Worcester. To stop rebellion in the overseas empire he set up the Commonwealth and reinvigorated the navy to protect these lands. His planning worked as he went to war with the Netherlands, one of the premiere naval powers of the time, and won. Perhaps most strangely, after seeing how intolerant Cromwell was of Catholics, he actively encouraged the return of Jews to

England, they had been banished for over three hundred and fifty years.

So England was set to be a Republic until the rather sudden death of Cromwell from malaria (no really) in 1658. The hero of this hour was not Oliver's son Richard Cromwell, nor Charles II, but a man you've probably never heard of- General George Monck. Monck had been an officer on both sides of the war so was well placed to see the situation from all viewpoints.

Between the winter of 1658 and the summer of 1660 anything could have happened. The most likely outcome was a third round of civil war. Monck managed to quietly outmanoeuvre everyone who could have vied for power, and without firing a shot, positioned himself as the *de facto* power in the land. Once he was in London with an army, he invited Charles II to come home and restore the monarchy.

The British Isles were exhausted from war and wanted no more. Add to that the crippling cost and even greater uncertainty that war creates, and you can see that Monck did a service to every man, woman and child on these islands and deserved their thanks for rather selflessly handing over the reigns of power to a monarch who could once again unite the country.

Monck disbanded the New Model Army (although his regiment, the Coldstream Guards remain to this day) and was lavishly rewarded after the

Restoration. He was given lands and titles and became a Knight of the Garter with an annual pension of £7,000 (the true value of revenues is notoriously hard to put into a modern context, so let's just say he became a very rich man). General George Monck is a man largely forgotten by history but his name should be remembered, and with gratitude. It's not often that a general stops wars and saves lives.

Chapter 13 Empire

With the return of Charles II we can see that power was no longer held in the fist of the monarch. Charles was "invited" back; he didn't take the crown by force. This echoed James's accession to the throne. The kings weren't the ones running the show anymore. Indeed on Charles's death, his younger brother James VII/II, a Catholic (anathema to Protestant Parliament) was ousted and his daughter Mary and son-in-law (also nephew) William of Orange (from the Netherlands) were "invited" to run the country. Monarchy had become more of a symbol than an actual power. This explains how Britain was able to expand and thrive despite a veritable rogue's gallery of Georges in the 18th century.

However what super-fuelled the rise of a British Empire was the 1690s Darien Scheme. Scottish gentry, businessmen and government all wanted to get on the bandwagon of empire building in the new world. They chose an area of modern day Panama and named it New Caledonia (showing that the Scots were no more original in naming things than the English). It was a reasonable idea, by the time the European powers had finished building overseas empires, even Belgium had a slice of the pie. Why shouldn't Scotland have its own empire?

New Caledonia was a disaster. The area chosen was little more than a malarial swamp. The land was agriculturally poor, meaning the colony was not self-sufficient, let alone profitable. The settlers were ravaged by tropical illnesses, which annihilated the population, turning the flood of new arrivals into a trickle. When the Spanish eventually attacked they needn't have bothered.

Scotland had badly overexposed itself in this venture and the state and most of the gentry faced bankruptcy. It happened for different reasons but it was a similar situation to the near collapse of the global banking system in 2008-9. There simply wasn't enough money in Scotland to allow the economy to recover. The financial institutions had ground to a halt and the country had undone itself economically. More serious than any war, battle or invasion, Scotland had destroyed itself from within.

The crowns of Scotland and England had been unified for about a century, so Queen Anne had a vested interest in using the growing financial power of England to aid Scotland. England paid

Scotland's bills and in return in 1707, the Acts of Union brought together these two old enemies into one unified kingdom.

An emotive way to describe this is a hostile takeover, but Scotland had got itself into its own mess. This new situation, which initially started so cautiously, ended up being a golden opportunity for Scottish entrepreneurs. At a stroke they now had access to all of the colonial markets, with the same rights of trade as the English. From bust, Scotland boomed. The tiny town of Glasgow turned into the largest city in the country, just one example of the benefits of union to the Scots.

The Scottish nationalist poem "Wha's like us?" is still lovingly remembered north of the border. It's a list of some of the finest achievements of Scottish invention and ingenuity, much to the despair of Englishman in the poem. However like all nationalist propaganda, it's a half truth. Every one of the men mentioned in the poem found success either once they had left Scotland or by doing business with the English. The Scottish market simply wasn't big enough to gain global importance. The Scots needed the head start the English Empire could give them. This attempt at racial superiority in a poem is inadvertently an example of why countries need each other. On our own we have potential, but when societies combine and share, they can become great.

Queen Anne tried her best to create an heir for the throne. She was pregnant nineteen times in her life, but none of her children made it to adulthood. The efforts ravaged her body and she died before her time. In a way she needn't have bothered. The country was now run by Parliament, not the monarch, and after her death the government searched for a European Protestant royal vaguely related to previous British monarchs. They came up with George of Hanover. He couldn't speak English and wasn't very British in any other discernible way. While this slim claim to the throne a hundred years earlier may have led to civil war, by the 18th century it was actually a strength. It allowed the government to get on with the productive job of running the country and a burgeoning empire while George got on with living in palaces and proving that his French was almost as poor as his English.

This situation led to Robert Walpole becoming Britain's first Prime Minister in 1721, and for twenty years, Walpole busily got on with the job of governing. Unlike the rest of Europe, Britain now had an effective bureaucracy that could run quite independently of the whims of the monarch. This allowed continuity of effective governance that other countries wouldn't have for a century or so.

With little threat of war in the British Isles and with burgeoning trade routes and colonies overseas, now was the time for Britain to gain momentum in the business of empire.

Britain's empire has an interesting legacy in modern Britain. Ask an Italian about the Roman Empire and he can be very proud and wistful about "the good old days". Ask a Turk about the Ottoman Empire and he will smile as he recounts tales of Suleiman the Magnificent or the Conqueror Mehmet. In some countries the pinnacle of past power is praised, with little thought to the darker side of that history. In Britain the word "empire" is a mess of emotions: it's slavery, trade, colonialism, industrialisation, repression, scientific breakthough, racism and victory.

I have tried my best to steer an interesting and relatively even handed course through the events of this island nation, but I am now at a point where no matter what is said, I know some will disagree. I think this is a good thing. I love historical debate provided it is thoughtful and based on fact rather than emotional, ill-informed mud slinging.

Was the British Empire a force for good or evil? The answer is, of course, both. Again I am sticking to the basic rule of judging events by contemporary views. Nowadays "empire building" has to be considered a bad thing, but as the world opened up to Europe, there was a simple rule: expand or die. Britain was not going to wither on the vine deliberately just because two hundred years later people might feel a bit guilty. Although Britain ultimately won the race, it's nice to note that it was a more responsible imperial power than anyone else.

Let's talk about the gravest mark against the British Empire- slavery. Today slavery is an abhorrent notion, but that is a relatively new concept and that revulsion can be traced back to the abolition movement in Britain. It is a deeply unpleasant fact that slavery has been inherent in all the civilisations of the world. It was not exclusively a white on black crime. African tribes would take opposing tribe members as their slaves. The Aztecs turned captured enemy warriors into their slaves (or sacrifices). The Ottoman Empire needed thousands of white slaves to become soldiers or concubines for the Sultan and black slaves became eunuchs. Slavery is in the Bible and there are quotes in both the Old and New Testament that tell slaves to obey their masters. Slavery was part of global civilisation for thousands of years and no culture thought it was wrong.

There were slaves in Anglo-Saxon England and the British had been turned into slaves both by the Romans and Vikings. What the British Empire did though, was to turn the process into an industrial scale enterprise. Then, while it was still hugely profitable and against the backdrop of a war they were in danger of losing, Britain spent time, effort and resource dismantling it.

The history of finding slavery morally wrong is a legacy of the British Empire. Let's look at how it came about. There is nothing pleasant about this story.

After the Restoration, Britain found peace and prosperity again. New found disposable income could be spent on luxuries such as coffee, tea, sugar and tropical fruit (a middle-class family might buy a pineapple and place it in the window to show the neighbours they had enough money to buy one- it would not be eaten).

These goods fetched huge prices, particularly sugar. The tradesmen of Britain would go to the coast of Africa where they would trade the output of Britain's workshops for slaves. They would then sail to the Caribbean where slaves were needed to work on the sugar cane plantations. Sugar cane was such a tough crop to grow and refine that only slaves were considered to be suitable for the back-breaking work. Here the slaves were traded for sugar which was taken back to Britain.

This triangle of trade made Britain's economy boom and as it grew, so did its merchant navy. To protect these investments Britain's fighting navy also grew, and it was this process that was to make Britain the most powerful country on the planet. All of this was built on the back of slaves and a desire for luxury. This trading pattern lasted for at least one hundred and twenty years. It's estimated that around eleven million Africans were sold into slavery (and that's not including the children who were then born into slavery. Born a slave, what chance does that child have?). Of the eleven million who took the terrifying and dangerous trip across the Atlantic against their will, it's estimated that around 1.4 million lost their lives before they even reached the Caribbean (stats from Wikipedia).

It's easy to use the word genocide and in a way it was, but as always, things were a little more complicated than they first appear. The Europeans (and it wasn't just the English) who took African slaves didn't go into the interior of that continent to find a tribe and round them up. Europeans generally died when they went into the African interior, rarely from native activity but often from tropical disease. Instead, the Europeans set up trading posts where Africans would bring captured enemies to the outposts and sell them. Africa was not a nation but a continent of warring groups, just like Europe and again just like Europe, more than capable of carrying out horrifying acts of violence against each other. So Africans were selling other Africans to the white traders. Nobody walks away from the topic of slavery with clean hands.

However in the late 18th century some Christian organisations in Britain began questioning how, if all men are created in the image of God, what gives us the right to sell some of them like cattle? Humans weren't possessions, no matter what their skin colour. The whole system was morally wrong.

Some tried to defend the indefensible by making outright racist claims that the white man was superior and that the slavers were somehow doing the African slaves a favour by giving them something to do. I will give this offensive argument no more space than it deserves.

By the late 1780s an MP called William Wilberforce had taken it as his goal to end this most distasteful of trades. Josiah Wedgwood (the famous potter) created a mass-produced a brooch with the picture of a slave and the words "Am I not a man and brother" written beneath. It was the first human rights' campaign. Books were discussing the inhuman conditions on slave ships. Some were written by ex-slaves like Olaudah Equiano, describing what slavery was like and became must reads in influential circles.

This was the world's first example of a charity campaign. Events like Band Aid and wearing a badge or wrist band for a cause can all be traced back to the tactics used to heighten the awareness amongst the people who mattered in Britain, to put an end to the trade.

The campaign would have succeeded earlier had it not been for the start of the wars with France that would later become known as the Napoleonic Wars, but were called at the time "The Endless Wars". However to Wilberforce's credit and despite serious threats of invasion and regular news of defeats in Europe, he persevered and kept the momentum going. In 1792 the country of Sierra Leone was created for ex-slaves to settle. It was not a smooth start, but it was a start.

A bill was eventually passed in 1807 (with war still raging). It was not a simple emancipation of all slaves, but stopped the trade by the British. It also brought about naval patrols to stop the use of the trading posts for the import of slaves, and as Britain had the world's largest commercial and military fleet, it made it difficult for everyone else to continue.

Britain was first to do this, ahead even of the Catholic Church or indeed, African cultures. Britain led the way and would shape the world's view of slavery. To put it into context, it would take the rest of Europe decades to catch up; and in America where apparently "all men are created equal", it would take another two generations and a bloody civil war to settle the matter once and for all. Making slavery a dirty word was a British invention.

I have a friend who is a Welsh Nationalist who wants independence for Wales. We have had some interesting debates about this but he came up with an eloquent summary that's worth mentioning in this section: "surely local concerns should be dealt with by local governmental bodies" which is a fair point. I then pointed out that this view is contrary to the fact he's also pro-European Union, to which he added, "And I'm a hypocrite".

The concept of local people solving local problems is at the very heart of what people don't like about empire. Many empires came in and annihilated the local customs while exploiting the local people for as long as they could. I have already mentioned the Spanish in America. They bullied the locals into stripping all the assets they could and shipped them back to Spain. There are many examples of deliberate or inadvertent mismanagement in the story of every empire. There is an overall assumption that when a Western power arrives, it destroys some kind of local nirvana and ruins everything. This is a way too simplistic an approach to world history.

For example the Brits in the American colonies would ally themselves with some Native American tribes because the "friendly" tribe was at war with another tribe. The combined resources would allow the friendly tribe to prevail and the spoils of the defeated tribe could be split between settlers and the "friendlies". In many cases the indigenous population replaced one empire for another. Egypt was under Ottoman rule but had been all but ignored by the Sultans in Istanbul for a century by the time the English arrived. Similarly, India was mainly under Muslim Mughal rule (whose rulers had come from Afghanistan), which was just as foreign to Hindu Indians as were the British. The difference was the Mughals made them build The Taj Mahal (very pretty, but of no use to the locals), the Brits made them build railways, which helped everyone.

Then there's the Britain's scientific explosion. The simple fact is that compared to other countries, Britain's contribution to art and music is slim during the age of empire; (Elgar's good but Beethoven is better), but in the area of science, imagine a world without the following:

- Sir Isaac Newton who explained the laws of gravity that would allow NASA to land Apollo 11 on the moon. He invented calculus, showed that white light could be broken into a spectrum of colours and invented the reflective telescope.

- James Watt who turned early steam engines into the efficient machines that powered the industrial revolution. Robert Louis Stephenson then made early attempts at turning steam engines into the locomotives that would transform transport across the globe.

- Adam Smith who wrote "On the Wealth of Nations" inventing the discipline of economics in the process and improving trade efficiency.

- Edward Jenner who invented inoculation, which would lead to the demise of small pox, amongst other illnesses, so saving untold millions of lives.

- James Hutton who came up with the concept of geology, challenging the literal reading of the Bible and also leading to more efficient mining.

- Michael Faraday who established the laws of electromagnetism, and at the same time, created the electric motor and the power generator. Fancy a steam powered computer? It's safe to say the modern world owes Faraday a huge debt of gratitude.

- James Clark Maxwell who came up with his electromagnetic theory and correctly working out the constant speed of light- how good was he? He was one the physicists that Einstein idolised.

- Darwin who developed the theory of evolution that so eloquently and without the need for high concept equations, explains the massive diversity we see in the natural world.

The list could go on but in the space of one hundred and fifty years or so, there was an explosion of discoveries coming from Britain. This was in part thanks to the foundation of various scientific groups (like the Royal Society) and museums (like the British Museum) that concentrated these great minds and refined some of these ideas.

It can be argued that Victorian missionary zeal did more harm than good to local communities. Take Nigeria- blighted by sectarian violence between Muslims and Christians, both religions imports, one from Arabia the other from Britain. However not all British interventions were bad. The introduction of the English language in India has become a unifying not dividing force. Similarly in India the practice of Suti no longer happens (when a high caste man died, his still living wife was made to burn on his funeral pyre,- a custom we can all agree is a bad one). So while not all well intended plans have left a positive legacy, likewise, not all local customs should have been allowed to thrive.

Britain's jewel in the crown of its imperial assets was India. The first book I read on the history of the subcontinent was John Keay's masterful summary *"India a History"*. What I wanted to know was how a small island race half a world away, could successfully become overlords of the highly sophisticated and populous nation of India. It's a fair question and the answer is basically that the Brits traded them into submission. Sounds a little odd? Then read on.

The British Empire was strangely fixated on the Roman Empire and mirrored it with architecture, art and even the use of Latin for inscriptions. The Roman Empire was seen as a beacon of civilisation in a sea of barbarism, and that's what the Brits were aiming to achieve globally. This inevitably leads to a feeling of superiority to other ethnicities (which is simply racist,) but one area of Roman imperialism that Britain did not imitate was how it grew its empire.

Britain's army was always small by comparison to mainland European ones. However it was tiny at its peak in the early 20th century when the British Empire covered about a quarter of the world's land mass and about quarter of its population. Doing simple maths, Britain should have easily needed the largest army the world has ever seen to conquer and hold this territory. That didn't happen. Where was Britain's version of the Roman legions?

Britain did have a huge navy that from the 1750s to the 1930s had no real match on the globe. Navies are very good at protecting trade routes and dispatching small contingents of troops to faraway lands, but they are very bad at crushing rebellion and capturing territory. Britain's entire imperial plan was based on trade.

Linked to this was the industrial revolution. I have mentioned this in the introduction where I said it was important but dull, and rest assured, I haven't changed my mind. Where it comes into the story of empire is that the factories in cities like Manchester and Glasgow were able to produce cotton in such large quantities that it was cheaper to buy imported British fabrics in Cairo than it was to buy locally made products. Britain in the 19th century was like China in the 21st century.

The other advantage Britain had was that its empire sort of spread by accident. The government rarely set a target on a map and sent a bunch of Brits to capture it. Instead, with private enterprises like the East India Company, businesses with goals for profit and efficiency led to the best men for the job rising to the top. By comparison, the French in India would send well-connected aristocrats, regardless of whether they were capable diplomats, generals or traders. Not since the time of the Mongols was there a more meritocratic empire building system in place.

The fact that the British Empire was different in tone to others can be seen in its monuments, or lack of them. Buckingham Palace was built at the height of British imperial confidence, and while it's a lot bigger than my house, I once heard it described as looking like the back of a much more impressive palace. That image has stuck with me. Nice though Buckingham is, it's no Versailles. Go back just one generation to George III and his main residence at Kew Palace. This is a lovely and intimate residence, but quite frankly as palaces go, it's little more than a large house. The most striking thing about it is it's made of bricks; it's not clad in marble or made from huge slabs of sandstone, but just standard everyday bricks.

The British Empire had more money and resources than the Roman Emperors, the Ottoman Sultans, Russian Czars and Indian Mughals combined. If Britain had wanted to, it could have built Versailles, next to the Taj Mahal on top of the Kremlin in Norfolk if it fancied. Instead, there are a few smallish palaces. The most elaborate British imperial building projects were almost all practical and helped trade. Why waste effort on something as pointless as the L'Arc de Triomphe, when you could build the Clifton Suspension Bridge, St Pancras Station and the SS Great Britain.

The most elaborate building constructed in Britain during the empire was The Houses of Parliament (after a fire burnt down the medieval buildings in 1834), which are of course, a symbol of democracy, not monarchy. It was a sign of the practical nature of the British Empire.

Another good example of how the British Empire differed to others was the Arrow Wars, more commonly known as the Opium Wars with China. By the 19th century China had fallen badly behind the West in terms of learning and technology. The Confucian system may have created one of the world's best bureaucracies, but it also stifled change. However China assumed it was still the centre of the universe (literally as well as figuratively) and superior to all. It was arrogant and frustrating to deal with. The phrase to *kow tow* comes from the Chinese demand of a *kow tow*, a kind of ritual grovelling that Western diplomats had to perform to the emperor and his advisors. Britain (and other Western powers) wanted to trade; China didn't want to play ball.

So the East India Company began exporting opium to the country in the 1830s in an attempt to create a market. It is worth mentioning that opium at the time was not illegal in Britain, and while it's addictive nature was known, some people have rather emotionally compared these actions to the brutal Columbian drug cartels of the 1990s. It's unfair as comparisons go but the trade was cynical, amoral and designed to generate more "customers", i.e. drug addicts.

The Chinese authorities protested and were lured into a diplomatic trap. They destroyed some of the opium, which was against existing agreements, and so the illegal attack allowed the British to respond with force. The results were catastrophic for China. With out-of-date weaponry both on land and on sea, the tiny British force was unstoppable.

Opium may have been the ostensible cause of the war, but the real reason was the aforementioned Chinese refusal to trade, and its continued arrogance about not accepting anyone else as an equal (it wasn't just Europeans who could be racist). The Chinese view was wrong, but importing hundreds of tons of narcotics into a country for the sole purpose of creating demand was worse. Parliament came to its senses and stopped the war and this is the remarkable thing about the Opium Wars. How many times has a country stopped a war it's winning comfortably because it was morally wrong to continue its prosecution?

This is worth pausing for consideration. Certainly it's desirable to stop a war you're losing or end a war that's uneconomical, but who stops a war you're winning easily? Britain could have carved up China with the other Western powers, as it did with Africa. But it didn't, because it recognised that even by the shaky standards of international diplomacy and law in the age of empires, that this was not playing fair; and while it led to concessions by the Chinese, they were not nearly as punitive as they could have been. For example, Britain was loaned the island that would become Hong Kong but had to give it back (and did) in 1997.

When people say that the British Empire was evil, I always want to know "compared to what"? Usually the answer is a modern, liberal democracy, and yes, compared to that, the empire doesn't come out well at all; but that's a naive argument. Those didn't exist in the 17th- early 20th centuries so it's neither a fair nor useful comparison. The simple fact is that life was better in a British colony than a German, French, Spanish, Belgian, Portuguese, Russian, Ottoman, Japanese or American one. It's also worth remembering that the modern concepts of "liberal" and "democracy", and the fact they are seen as good things, are also legacies of the British Empire.

Chapter 14 Britain's First World War (also known as the Seven Years War)

...and that's for Joan of Arc!

What makes a war a "World War"? With the war from 1914-18 there was a lot of conflict in Europe, a huge amount in western Russia, some in the Middle East and minor battles in Eastern Africa and the Pacific. North America and India sent troops, as did Australia and New Zealand, but the whole of South America and most of Asia was unaffected by the war. Yet this war was called a "World War". If many countries and at least three continents are involved in a conflict, then by my reckoning, there have been four.

Three of them are well known, generating huge amounts of films, documentaries, games and literature around them. If you want to know more there are plenty of places to look further and deeper. What I intend to do is give an overview to correct a few misinterpretations about these events and to realigning some of the stories to show once again, how nations can distort past events. What follows is not a blow-by-blow account of topics such as the rise and fall of the Third Reich, but I will challenge some traditional summaries and established views.

I shall start with the earliest and least well known of these world wars, the conflict which in Europe is known as the Seven Years War, and in America referred to as The French and Indian War.

In Europe it was a showdown of the main military powers to reposition themselves. Overseas, it was the battle to see who would become the premiere imperial power. There was fighting in Canada and the American Colonies, battles all over Europe, invasions in the Caribbean, naval engagements against fleets of ships and war raged in India. Britain even faced the first real threat of invasion since the Spanish Armada nearly two hundred years earlier. So saying all this, it surprises me that earlier and later conflicts have sparked the popular imagination, but this one hasn't.

The war lasted from 1756-1763, although most of the fighting was really done by 1762. It didn't have a single defining cause (unlike the assassination of Franz Ferdinand in 1914) but was the culmination of continuing Darwinian diplomacy of supremacy that had been rumbling on for at least a century. There were the Wars of Spanish Succession, then Austrian Succession; earlier there had been the already mentioned Thirty Years War. There had also been an Eighty Years War in the Netherlands. It was war without end and for every generation there was an inexorable descent into European-wide carnage and with these countries now backed by overseas empires, each conflict was becoming bloodier. In the 1750s Britain feared the loss of their Hanoverian lands in mainland Europe, the ancestral homeland of the Georges who were now the Kings of England. These lands were not worth fighting a war over on their own, but the British and French territories in America had just started to meet each other in Ohio. Therefore if this conflict could involve potential gains to the overseas lands of the empire, then Hanover had its value in the diplomacy leading up to war.

In this particular war, the Prussians led by Frederick II, were Britain's main allies, with other German states and Portugal coming in and out of the alliance too. The enemy was France and Austria (later joined by Spain, Russia and Sweden). Britain's way of fighting wars in mainland Europe had changed considerably since the time of Henry V. Now Britain's power was projected through its navy, with the army little more than an expeditionary force that could fight in conjunction with other European armies.

The distances covered in this first global conflict were so vast that co-ordination for the most part was impossible. It was hard enough to keep communication with Frederick in Prussia (known to history as Frederick the Great), let alone ensure that the campaigns in India and Canada were happening at the same time.

Frederick definitely deserves the title "Great". He was a fascinating man shaped by the age of enlightenment. Likely to have been gay, his militaristic father (whom he loathed) had Frederick's close friend and probable lover shot while Frederick was in the same prison and could watch the whole ghastly thing. He wrote books and was an accomplished musician, composing music still played on the flute today. One of his quotes on ruling shows an interesting attitude: "A crown is merely a hat that lets the rain in". He had a slight build and in every possible way was not suited to being a military leader.

However looks can be deceiving and he turned out to be one of the most efficient military commanders in history, talent that served him well as he had to fight a war on three fronts. Austria, Russia and France were all closing in on him, each one with larger armies than Frederick's. He didn't win all his battles, but he won the ones he needed to win and was almost constantly outnumbered.

Frederick pinned down huge armies and won battles completely against the odds in mainland Europe which in turn protected Britain's minor interests on the mainland. While Frederick fought like a lion in Europe, Britain got on with the task of taking on France everywhere else on the globe.

Robert Clive in India (remembered by history as Clive of India) got the ball rolling for the British with the key victory of the Battle of Plassey where his 3,000 men, a mixture of both European and Indian troops, faced a Bengali force of over 50,000. The numbers make Agincourt look like an even fight. There is no way an army could realistically take on such an overwhelming force in open battle and prevail. However Clive had already sown dissent in the Bengali ranks and some of the key Indian units did not join battle. Losses were light on both sides but the Bengali army crumbled, so giving The East India Company command of large areas of eastern India.

It was the year 1759 that would be crucial to Britain. In the summer British troops were in Germany, having linked up with some German principalities against the French. On August 1st they fought the Battle of Minden, a huge engagement by British standards with just over 40,000 troops on the British Hanoverian side and a little more than 50,000 on the French side. The battle was won due to a misunderstanding of orders when British and Hanoverian infantries attacked the French cavalry, an action never intended by the allied leadership and a highly dangerous move. Infantry hardly ever attacked cavalry head on because it was so likely to fail against the superior manoeuvrability of the cavalry; however it was such an astonishing gambit that it caught the French by surprise and broke the potent French cavalry as an effective fighting force. For a loss of around 3,000 men, the British had inflicted a major defeat on a larger French army which lost 10,000 of its own men.

Then in September, General James Wolfe, a suicidal and vicious man, attacked Quebec intending to capture France's main base of support in Canada. After a three month siege he decided on a daring night manoeuvre which involved his troops scaling steep river slopes onto the flat Plains of Abraham in front of the city gates.

Against the odds he managed to get his troops in position and in good order before the French could react. There was a brief and decisive battle in front of these gates, which led to Wolfe being mortally wounded (which more than a few historians think he was quite happy about, knowing he would be immortalised by dying at his greatest victory). With Britain now in control of the largest French town in Canada, massive areas of North America fell to the British crown.

All these victories had been impressive and severely hampered the French, but the biggest setback was in November of 1759 at Quiberon Bay on the west coast of France. As already stated, armies won wars but navies protected trade. It was on the sea where the biggest damage could be done to any imperial power. The British, understanding this, had carried out a tactic of naval blockade to keep the French from breaking out their formidable navy to assist their overseas lands and to stop an invasion of England.

The blockade had worked and resupplies to the Royal Navy had been thorough enough to ensure that even after months at sea, the ships were still seaworthy and the crews hadn't succumbed to scurvy or other debilitating illnesses. It had already been a victory of organisation and logistics on a scale never attempted before.

It was the job of Admiral Hawke to patrol the Bay of Biscay and to stop any French attempt to invade England. Hawke had all the motivation he needed as he had succeeded Admiral Byng who three years earlier had failed to relieve Minorca, which led to him being relieved of his own office. Byng was then tried "for failing to do his utmost" and was executed by firing squad (an extremely rare punishment). Hawke was therefore determined to "do his utmost".

Hawke was up against Marshal Conflans who was bottled up in Brest Harbour with over twenty warships. In November however, the winter weather was becoming rough and a storm blew up. Hawke not wanting to risk his own fleet, was forced to retreat to safer waters. This allowed Conflans to make a break for it, however Hawke had posted a fast ship to keep an eye on things. Once the French were on the move Hawke quickly returned to the French shore.

Conflans, knowing that the weather could only to get worse, moved his fleet into Quiberon bay, an area with treacherous submerged rocks and shoals that could easily destroy a ship. It was a safe defensive move that should have ensured a stalemate. But Hawke was not going to be accused of over-cautious tactics and even though he was in gale force winds, ordered his fleet to chase and close on the enemy, despite the dangerous weather and shoals. The Royal Navy was faster and more disciplined than that of the French and started to overtake the French stragglers.

The French formation was in disarray and Hawke made the most of it, attacking what ships he could and causing panic amongst the remainder. Some French vessels threw their guns overboard to escape and at least four ran themselves aground. Hawke had literally scared some of the ships out of the water. It was a complete fiasco for the French with over a quarter of the fleet destroyed and one ship captured. The remainder of the fleet was bottled up harmlessly, now even further away from Britain than it had been a week earlier. It was one of Britain's greatest and most technically difficult victories over the French. Fighting an engagement in a gale by the enemy coast near unknown submerged obstacles was extremely dangerous, but Hawke's aggressive tactics had paid off handsomely and the French stayed in port for the rest of the war.

There was further fighting in all the theatres, including the American colonies. Roger's Rangers heroic (if in the greater scheme of things, minor) assault on Fort Ticonderoga would become the stuff of legends and form the U.S. Rangers, an elite unit still in existence in the modern American

Army. There was even a young colonial major called George Washington who acquitted himself well in the name of the British monarchy, although at one point he did lose control of his Native American allies who massacred a French garrison. This would always, be a black mark against his name.

By 1763 Europe was exhausted from war. Prussia and Britain created separate peace treaties. Frederick enlarged Prussia's European lands (mainly Silesia on the borders with Austria) but it was Britain that gained the most. The conquest of Canada was ratified, as was their capture of Florida. French interests in India waned to virtually nothing and British gains in the Caribbean were also solidified. Even Minorca, the island that had cost Admiral Byng's life, was restored to the British crown. The Treaty of Paris made France the junior imperial power to Britain and paved the way for further British expansion on two vast continents.

None of this was inevitable. There was no reason to assume that Prussia, while always a formidable military force, would be led by one of the most gifted military leaders in history, one who could hold his own against the odds. Britain had not dominated India with its armies before this time and there was no reason to expect that they would when war broke out.

Looking at the great victories of 1759, Hawke could just as easily have destroyed his fleet in an overzealous attack as win the victory he did, so leaving the way open for France to invade. Minden was won on the miscommunication of orders and the subsequent bravery of the infantry at the heart of the battle. Wolfe was unlikely to capture Quebec without his bold move, meaning that had the siege lingered until winter set in, he would have had to retreat or face his army freezing to death.

Britain and Prussia had ridden their luck, but sometimes that is enough. On this occasion both powers rose considerably, while the main loser was France. From 1763 onwards the French, while still a feared force in Europe, never again caught up with Britain's expansion overseas.

By the end of the war George III was king and he was given a coach covered in gold leaf. This gilded carriage weighs tons and can only be pulled by horses on flat ground. It is still used by the royal family on very special occasions, a golden reminder of the power of the British Empire.

Just a dozen years or so later in 1776, the American colonies exploded into revolution. The American War of Independence can't really be treated in isolation. It may have happened on another continent, but it was a very European war. While Britain lost the legitimacy of its rule and the moral high ground with the first shots of the war, the reality was that in some ways the whole war was payback from France after the defeat of the Seven Years War.

Britain's main mistake had nothing to do with red coats in green forests or Washington being able to evacuate in the fog. It was simply failing to secure an ally in Europe. This allowed the American rebels to use the French navy and French made rifles and cannons to wage war. The American Revolution is another area where there is a glut of books (try "Fusiliers" by Mark Urban), but in essence, with no counterbalance in Europe, Britain was forced to fight an unpopular war far away where a small rebel army was constantly bolstered by hostile nations.

It's also worth remembering that this war was not "Americans" versus the "British" (the famous tale of Paul Revere riding through the streets shouting, "The British are coming" would have made no sense to settlers at this time. They were all "British"). Many of the engagements were between continental settlers, with almost no British involvement. Many Native American tribes, and even slaves, sided with the British. (Their lot definitely worsened after independence from the crown.) The most loathed troops on the American continent were not the British army regulars, but the German mercenaries hired by the British and nicknamed "Hessians". The ghostly headless rider from the early American gothic story "Sleepy Hollow" is one of them, a fantastical echo of the hatred towards these mercenaries.

As always nation building mythology oversimplifies and debates about tax are turned into patriots fighting a tyrannical overseas dictatorship. Tales of the brave "Minute Men" ambushing red-coated lines of dopey English troops has some accuracy, but it's worth remembering that in most of the pitched battles of the war, the British actually won.

However after seven years of costly war, the prize was seen as not worth it. In the 1780s Jamaica generated more revenues to Britain then all the thirteen colonies combined. In 1781 Yorktown was surrendered, marking the end for Britain. Here it's worth pausing to consider the impact of the French on the American Revolution. Some 9,000 British troops had been under siege in Yorktown by about 8,000 American soldiers and another 20,000 French marines and sailors. There's no way Washington could have won without that sort of assistance.

After Cornwallis surrendered, the Americans were bemused to see a dinner organised between the British and French officers. This was not an unusual thing to happen in Europe, but to the colonists, to see these enemies eating together when days before they would have been shooting at each other was very odd.

France had won the American War of Independence for the Americans and when everything was ratified in 1783, tens of thousands of royalist Americans moved to British-held Canada in disgust at the break from the crown. Despite modern celebrations pretending otherwise, not everyone was proud to end the association with the motherland. The French had their revenge for the humiliation of the Seven Years War. The gloating would be short-lived.

The loss of the American colonies was not a setback in terms of a major loss of resources. The defeat was keenly felt because it was settlers who had rebelled, not a native culture. It was this failure that was to haunt imperial philosophy from that point and led to a desire to rule fairly, with good governance. It didn't always work, and there were still stains of blood to be spilled on the Union Flag, but the fact was that Britain wanted to be a productive and fair ruler, not a smash-and-grab enterprise like other European empires.

Chapter 15 Britain's Second World War (also known as The Napoleonic Wars)

Louis XVI had backed the Americans in their War of Independence and while he could initially bask in the glory of winning a proxy war with Britain, it was to be his undoing. There were three contributing factors that led to Louis's downfall.

Firstly, while England/Britain had evolved a form of government where power transferred from the central point of the monarch to Parliament, France was still an absolute monarchy. Louis was smart enough to realise that this way of ruling was becoming a liability and wanted to change it. However it was a case of too little too late, and as a weak ruler in his own right, he could not force through the changes and make them stick.

Secondly, Louis was always a little uneasy about backing the Americans who did not want a

"Kingdom" of America, but a "Republic". Worse still, he allowed American ambassadors to regularly stay at his court. People like Benjamin Franklin and Thomas Jefferson were anti-monarchist republicans allowed to stay in the largest royal court in Europe. They should have been treated like cancers and cut out of the body of the court altogether. Instead, these men were allowed to pour out their anti-monarchist views right under the nose of Louis.

Additional to the American diplomats, there was now a whole generation of French officers and men who had fought with the Americans to overthrow a king's authority. They were all allowed to meet up and even communicate with the Americans, all without regulation or concern.

Thirdly, Britain had revolutionised its finances with the introduction of a stock exchange, currency markets and the raising of revenues from government bonds, so becoming the world's first modern economy. This would be later shown as European alliance after European alliance was paid for by Britain, showing the ease at which Britain could re-finance itself compared to any of the other major European powers. The French government by contrast, still generally raised money via taxation. The war in America had been long and costly and had come shortly after the defeats of the Seven Years War meaning they had fewer resources to pay for the revolutionary war, not more. Louis was broke and the only way he knew how to get more money was to raise the taxes.

Therefore it should have come as little surprise that the French export of republican revolution was imported back to France, and in 1789, the French Revolution exploded across the urban populations. Cutting a very long and complicated story very short, the country descended into complete anarchy. The initial good intentions of the revolutionaries were corrupted into a blood bath of executions. Louis, and later his Austrian wife Marie-Antoinette, were executed along with thousands of nobles, military officers and common people. Numbers are hard to establish because the administration was in a mess, too; but a death toll of around 20,000 just from execution would be a reasonable guess.

Just as Cromwell horrified Europe with the execution of a king, so France became "public enemy number one" due to its murder of the king and queen. One of Europe's most "civilised" nations had collapsed into bloody chaos. From the ashes came a huge but poorly supplied army that started to take on all the neighbouring countries. Initially it was led by a number of generals and politicians but one man, with the support of the key diplomat Talleyrand, was to rise to the top, a Corsican called Napoleon Bonaparte.

Napoleon, for a man of average height, is truly one of the giants of history. He's known globally, reviled and admired in equal measure. A good biography of the man is Vincent Cronin's "Napoleon". For a summary of the era there is the very readable "The War of Wars" by Robert Harvey. Even though Harvey's book is an excellent summary, it's still a thousand pages. But lets' put that into context- this conflict was to last nearly twenty five years and affect almost every continent. You can also buy entire books on just one campaign or even one battle.

Napoleon is an industry in and of himself; he's one of the few historical figures whose name alone guarantees to sell extra copies. There are simply thousands of books on this period, so what is there new to say about? The answer, to be honest, is not a lot. What I will do instead is use the period as another opportunity to show how history itself is used.

Napoleon has been so thoroughly discussed that opinions come in like waves. There is a period where he is a master military man, then that becomes unfashionable and he's portrayed as a chancer who rode his luck, which ultimately ran out. Others argue that he was better with smaller armies than large ones (his massive invasion of Russia being little more than a battering ram). Of course there is truth to all these points, but they are often exaggerated to add a bit of controversy and to sell a few more books. The real person gets lost in a storm of opinion.

Napoleon was a man, which means he sometimes showed the best of humanity with ingenuity, humour and intelligence as well as the worst with temper tantrums, hubris and ego. To those who try to diminish his military record (it's true some battle strategies were cleverer than others), I would like to say, "Go on, you do it." It's very easy in hindsight to unpick a battle or campaign, but try getting it right in the heat of the moment, with smoke swirling across your field of vision. If what Napoleon did was easily explainable, then why haven't dozens of other men done it and done it better?

Whenever an army marches into a country, it is likely to be remembered in a bad way. Occasionally the occupying force does such a good job of integration which ends up being remembered fondly. William the Conqueror is seen that way, but this is very rare. Usually the invaders are reviled as alien. Sometimes they perpetrate horrific crimes of pacification. Even if they don't, rumours of such horrors will circulate anyway. A large part of Europe's population reviles Napoleon today. His troops invaded their country and destroyed the *status quo.* How does this explain his burial site in Paris at Les Invalides?

I have paid my respects to the great man and it amused me that his tomb is so much larger than those of the men who beat him. Please don't misunderstand, Arthur Wellesley's resting place in St Paul's Cathedral is more grandiose than mine will ever be, but he doesn't get his own pantheon dressed in marble.

Images of Napoleon are largely defined by which side is doing the portraying, and sadly Napoleon is the last great person of history before the invention of the camera. The epic French paintings make him look every inch the virile general, rather than the physically average (and later plump) man he actually was. The English throughout the war, in their own papers and magazines showed him as a grotesque, curved nosed, bony and invariably short to the point of being a midget.

However, not even the men who painted him while he was alive dared to show him as he appears on his tomb, draped in a Roman toga, with slabs of pectoral muscle and bulging arms. He is physical perfection and has become Hercules himself. He masterfully points to lists of achievements and there is of course of all his key battles. Actually, the better way to describe it is a list of his victories because Waterloo was a pretty key battle, but it fails to get a mention anywhere in the vicinity of his remains.

In some ways I feel sorry for Napoleon. At age twenty seven after begging Josephine to marry him, she eventually acquiesced. He was a rising star in the revolutionary army but had yet to build his reputation to its later heights. He was then sent to the Italian border with France with orders to secure it. He disobeyed those orders, and in the space of a year, he struck like lightning down into the Italian peninsular and conquered it all. In just one campaigning season he had unified Italy, something every ruler had failed to do since the end of the Roman Empire. He was applauded wherever he went. He was a military genius to be sure, so he sent for his wife and gave her a palace. She wouldn't come as she was too busy having an affair with a dashing cavalry officer. Honestly, after conquering a country and giving the woman a palace, she was still not impressed. What's a guy got to do?

Sometimes it seems almost every time Napoleon wins there's some bad news ringing in his ears. His finest victory is considered to be Austerlitz in 1805, also called the battle of the Three Emperors because by then Napoleon was one and he fought against the Austrian and Russian emperors. He won the day thanks to clever manoeuvring and timing his attacks to perfection. It was a text book example of how to split an enemy force and defeat them as two separate armies in one battle. And yet, sadly for Napoleon, no matter how well he won that battle just a few weeks earlier his entire French fleet had been smashed at the Battle of Trafalgar, which reduced his strategic options far more than winning or losing at Austerlitz.

In 1812 Napoleon invaded Russia but unlike Hitler 130 years later, without the advantage of mechanised divisions. His march to Moscow is a major achievement. He attacked Russia because the rest of Europe had been beaten. Indeed, except for rebels in Spain and the annoying fact that he couldn't invade Britain due to the lack of a navy, his only option left for war was Russia. He'd done the impossible. Nobody, not the Romans, not the

Mongols, not anyone else in history has had control of Rome, Paris, Berlin and Moscow at the same time.

Victory complete, he settled down for the winter with his *grande armée* (at that point the largest army ever assembled in Western Europe, and likely the world. at its height it had about 675,000 men. Although not all units entered Russia, it was likely to have been the largest army every put into the field before the 20th century). However the Russians, possibly the hardiest and most pragmatic people in the world, burnt down their own capital city to force the invaders away; the winter did the rest. Of the estimated 500,000 strong army that marched into Russia only about 100,000 made it back again. Once again, just as Napoleon had everything under control and the outlook was great, something had to ruin it for him.

But my sympathies are limited. While he may have been a great general, he wasn't a great leader. Quite simply, he didn't know when to quit. This is a common issue with "great" military leaders. Napoleon had a number of occasions to stop the war (and at one point there was peace), but he would always return to try and gain more territory and more titles. Eventually everyone's luck runs out. But when this involves the control of all of mainland Europe, the consequences are terrible for everyone.

Napoleon made some strange choices. The weirdest one in 1798 was his desire before settling the power balance in Europe, to attack Britain's most vital colony India, via Egypt. If Napoleon could capture India it would be a crippling blow for Britain. In principal he could land in Egypt from the Mediterranean and then cross the country, taking ships direct to India. But the scheme was pretty insane and he didn't have enough men to realistically take on large swathes of the Indian subcontinent (although he did bring plenty of scientists).

This campaign created two epic moments in the story of the Napoleonic Wars. The first occurred during the romantic sounding Battle of the Pyramids where Napoleon's army of about 40,000 met the Mameluke army of 80,000, complete with their famous cavalry, resplendent in their silks, their muskets with mother of pearl handles and their curved scimitars. All fought with the ancient pyramids looking on.

It was however an example of western imperial technology versus native bravery, and unfortunately, technology tends to win. Napoleon formed his army into anti-cavalry squares so there was no way for the cavalry to outflank them. The Mamelukes then faced walls of muskets and bayonets no matter which way they charged. A handful of French died compared to the thousands of brave Muslim warriors.

The second moment occurred just two weeks later (here's Napoleon's bad luck again), Admiral Nelson found the French fleet in Aboukir Bay; and in one of his greatest victories, captured three quarters of it and destroyed most of the rest, including the French flagship L'Orient. This massive warship took a direct hit to its powder store and exploded. The noise was heard over twenty miles away. It was so shocking that for about half an hour both sides stopped fighting to pick up survivors. Nelson was badly wounded in the battle and part of the mast of L'Orient was recovered to be used as his coffin. He survived but seven years later with his death at the Battle of Trafalgar, it was found and used.

Napoleon was now cut off from France, and while he fought his way into Palestine, adding to the whole romantic notion of the expedition, it really was a fool's mission. Eventually he slipped back to France having deserted his forces in Egypt, most of whom never saw France again.

Another example of Napoleon not knowing when to quit was failing to heed Talleyrand's objections. Talleyrand was an astute diplomat and politician who, on a number of occasions, pointed out that Napoleon's peace terms were often humiliating so that rather than bringing allies to his cause, he was polarising opinion against him and storing up resentment that would be paid back in the future.

Napoleon tried to blockade British goods from the continent (why make his enemy richer?), but Britain was by now industrialising rapidly and well ahead of mainland Europe. Inevitably there were shortfalls of resources that he could afford but refused to allow the business transactions.

Napoleon had inadvertently created sanctions against his own regime.

Another serious error was the 1808 invasion of Spain, an ally. Despite the pros and cons over the merits of invasion, there is a cold logic to "getting them before they get me". Revolutionary France had a lot of enemies that Napoleon did very well against. However to invade an ally is just dumb. No matter how well it goes (and on this occasion it didn't go well at all), more is going to be spent garrisoning an area where previously there was no need.

The reason for the invasion seems to be as basic as Napoleon thinking he could get away with it. Once it turned sour, he left the peninsula never to return. Instead he made his brother Joseph King of Spain and hoped he could sort out the whole mess. If not, Napoleon could always blame him.

Then the British finally made their decisive move into Europe. Britain did not suffer as the rest of Europe did from invasion. Unlike many other counties they were never humiliated as French armies marched through their capital city. Britain didn't even have as many fighting men as some of these other countries.

Britain became Napoleon's nemesis because he couldn't beat it. The navy and the narrow straights of Dover were just enough to stop him from sweeping across the Channel. It meant that Britain was a thorn in the side of revolutionary France from start to finish. At the time, the King was George III, who was frequently in the grips of delirium and madness. Had the British government rested solely on his shoulders it would have been in big trouble, but the Napoleonic Wars were testament to the fact that by now the monarch was little more than a figure head, allowing far more gifted statesmen like Pitt the Younger to get on with running an empire and fighting a war.

Early British contributions to the war involved landing small armies in the Low Countries and allowing them to wander around a bit, being largely ineffectual at everything and then going home before they were destroyed. This changed with Napoleon's folly of invading Spain when Britain's string of naval victories turned into a string of land based ones.

Arthur Wellesley, later immortalised as The Duke of Wellington (and even later, Prime Minister), may have cut his teeth in some impressive engagements in India, but he made his name on the Iberian Peninsular. One of the reasons why The Napoleonic War is so much better remembered than others is because of a satisfying narrative. Napoleon is the winner through most of this time, a time when the ruler is still the man in charge on the battlefield. But Wellington arrived in Portugal, and this new enemy of France rises in Spain beating Napoleon by proxy. However the two giants had yet to face-off, until the final battle that neither can afford to lose. It's the story arc that fits so well into a film or book.

Wellington started by taking a huge risk. Realising he was outnumbered and likely to be outmanoeuvred in Portugal, he went quiet for months. Apparently his army was inactive. He did not advance and his reports back to Britain were perfunctory and bland. Public opinion turned against him. It was only his family connections in the cabinet that stopped him being pulled back to Britain in disgrace. When the French finally attacked, he sprung his daring trap.

For months he had been creating a line of defences at Torres Vedras. He retreated to them, destroying any food or resources the French could use as he went. By not telling the higher command about it, he had ensured complete surprise and when the French arrived at the fortifications the French general declared-

"The devil cannot surely have built these mountains"

An assault was easily repelled and led to a standoff where the French army slowly wasted away due to lack of food. If the French invasion had been an incoming tide, it broke on the walls of Torres Vedras and after that ebbed away with Wellington pushing into Spain. In 1813 when things were going badly wrong for Napoleon and he was eventually defeated, Wellington had the first army in France, beating the Prussians, Austrians and Russians.

It's interesting to note how much Wellington fought in Spain and Portugal because, while he sometimes worked with very brave (and often very brutal) Spanish irregular forces, these are the ones who get the plaudits in modern day Spain, not Wellington. He's a passing figure in the history of their war with France. Maybe this is unfair but later, we do the same with Waterloo.

I have two American uncles and as I was sitting with one of them in his home in West Virginia, watching a news report, I asked what I thought was an innocent question:

"How old is the White House?"

"No older than 1812," came the reply.

"Why?" I enquired.

"Because you Brits burnt it down."

This was the first reference I had to what the Americans call the War of 1812 (it actually lasted until 1815). Earlier I said a world war has to involve at least three continents; and so far I have mentioned Egypt and the Middle East and Europe. But Britain started to get heavy-handed with trade regulations that so inflamed America, it briefly sided with Napoleon. It was a senseless war. Britain didn't want a fight with America and had the US government waited just weeks, the main reason for war was abolished by the British government anyway.

America has turned this war into either a stalemate or some sort of defensive victory. In reality if you accept the backdrop of the serious situation in Europe, this was a sideshow. Britain never gave it much attention or put its full resources or into it. America should be a little embarrassed about siding with a dictator who was waging war across Europe. The most pointless battle of all was the final siege when a British task force assaulted a heavily defended New Orleans. The British were repulsed but the whole battle happened after a peace treaty had been signed. It just took a little too long for the armies to know about it.

As for the White House, the British invaded via Canada and wanted to get America out of the war as quickly as possible. As luck would have it, Napoleon was busy in Russia, and as we know, that ended in a debacle. Most of this conflict involved a British blockade of US ports, with raids into the mainland. It was the raid into the capital (which Britain held for a time) that led to the accidental burning of the White House. Ironically the remainder of the structure was painted white to hide the smoke stains and became known as the White House after this period.

While that was one distraction, it wasn't the only one. In 1806 with Spain allied to France, the British government planned to attack Spain's vulnerable South American colonies. It was a good plan in theory and a sizeable force was landed in modern day Argentina. While the Spanish sent little help, they didn't need to as the locals fought bravely and valiantly to repel the Brits. This is the rare occasion where an invading force is remembered quite fondly. The fact that the South American colonies had acquitted themselves so well led to a growing feeling that Spain was superfluous as an imperial overlord. The catalyst of South American independence is often marked as starting with this invasion.

So the British had been fighting in Europe, South America, Egypt, North America and on the high seas. It truly was another world war that stretched resources to the brink. It all came to a bloody finale on June 18th 1815 near a small Belgian town called Waterloo.

Napoleon had been sent into exile and had returned, catching almost the whole of Europe off guard. Had he won Waterloo, it was inevitable that he would have run out of luck at some point; he had made too many enemies to expect any realistic support. However European wars were becoming profoundly bloody and if further carnage could be avoided, then so much the better.

The Brits did not win the Battle of Waterloo; they were part of a coalition. Wellington had under him German troops from Hanover and other principalities, and Dutch troops, too. This is where Britain is guilty of national myth making. In British minds it's all red-coated, tough cockneys and kilt-wearing highlanders doing the fighting, and while they were there, there were other nations doing their bit, too.

The battle boils down to the fact that Wellington kept most of his troops safe behind the crest of a hill, while Napoleon was oddly distracted and ill that day (he may have been suffering from a recent overdose of medicine; and his piles might have been playing up too, making it hard to stay in the saddle and respond quickly to the developments on the battlefield).

The battle didn't get underway until midday and by evening, and Napoleon was anxiously awaiting for the arrival of another French army. Late in the day troops could be seen in the distance. They were however not French reserves, but tens of thousands of angry Prussians aching to get revenge. They were led by General Blucher a seventy two year old war horse, who was nicknamed "Marshall Vorwarts" (forwards) because that tended to be his order whenever he saw the enemy. His soldiers joined at the end of the day, tipping the battle in favour of the allies. It was a close-run battle and it was the Prussians who saved the day. Napoleon's cloak, taken from his coach at the end of the battle because he had to flee with such indecent haste, is displayed today in Windsor Castle. The fact that Napoleon felt the need to flee so rapidly shows what a decisive victory it was.

By the end of the day more than 40,000 men were either dead or wounded, the huge loss of life lead Wellington to declare:

"Second only to a battle lost, the saddest thing you'll ever see is a battle won."

And so ended nearly a quarter of a century of bloodshed that had cast its shadow across the globe.

Chapter 16 Britain's Third World War (also known as The Great War)

You know what lads, this might work!

After its defeat in the American Revolution, Britain was now a decisive victor at Waterloo, creating a springboard for further imperial gains. The Victorian Era was the golden age of Britain. It was the centre of the world for economics, trade, science and of course, power.

It is often seen as a time of peace, but it wasn't. None of the conflicts were an existential threat to Britain and spread over the whole globe, they were hardly a massive spasm of violence, but lives were still lost. A few have remained lodged in the mind. The Crimean War is seen as a pointless war, but in reality, it was the usual European game of war as a form of diplomacy, warning Russia to curb its aggression; and the warning worked. It also introduced the then novel concept of Britain and France working together.

The Boer War is remembered as a dirty war that we had no right to start, and it's true. An entire empire bullied some farmers because they were living on top of massive mineral reserves. Slightly sensationally, it's also remembered as the birth of the concentration camp, which it was, but it's disingenuous to compare those camps to the later Nazi ones. The book "Commando" is an autobiography by Deneys Reitz, a young Boer who fought in the war and held no special hatred of the Brits, nor did he think it a "dirty" war; he had no reason to be magnanimous unless he felt that way. It is therefore an interesting comparison to general British perceptions.

During the 19th century there was the Ghurkha War, the Sikh Wars, The Persian War, the Kandy War (Sri Lanka) and the Flagstaff War (New Zealand), to name a few. By my count (and there could be more) from 1800 - 1900 there were at least twenty nine wars or conflicts involving Britain but many of these were very small. What is interesting is how often the Brits co-opted these cultures into their own colonial armies. The Ghurkhas are still part of British forces today, and over their length of service have accrued a disproportion number of Victoria Crosses. There are similar situations with the Sikhs and Maori colonial armies. In short, it was nice to have them on our side. While all this is part of the imperial story, it all seems a little exotic and distant. It's hard to relate to.

Then there was the war that started in 1914 with the shooting of the Austro-Hungarian heir to the throne. Once again I am veering into well trodden territory, the Great War or World War I (if you must) similarly has a plethora of books, documentaries and movies to choose from. Some of the books seem to have been printed purely because they know someone will buy them. I've read a few where I have no idea how they got through quality control- staggering dull works, which on a lesser topic, would never have made it past the editor's desk. I will be kind and not mention them here.

Mention the war of 1914-1918 and what comes to mind? I would put a bet on trenches, mud, brave men callously ordered to walk towards enemy machine gun posts and massacred in their thousands. There's the constant bombardment of artillery raining down, high explosive destruction, barbed wire, the pervasive mists of deadly gases- and all of this summarised in powerful, heart-breaking, achingly honest poetry.

It is my firmly held opinion that this war is the most misunderstood event in history. There's a keen race to be the most politicised event in history, but this war is a strong contender. All that I have mentioned above are distortions of the reality.

Firstly a modest example is, the humble word "trench", now forever associated with stalemate and a war of attrition. A trench is a standard military defensive work; it's been used for thousands of years and have saved innumerable lives. They are in and of themselves completely neutral, but the associations that have been forced on us since school fills our minds with mud, rats and the futility of war.

John Keegan is a master of the popular history book and he has written definitive one-volume editions on both world wars. They are amazing reads. His chapter on how close war came to not breaking out in 1914 is paced like a thriller. He and other writers like Gary Sheffield (who wrote the excellent "Forgotten Victory") have spent considerable time and effort trying to readjust the misconceptions that swirl around this war.

One of the main accusations levelled at this conflict is a lack of problem solving by the high command. The common view is that British and French generals happily sent troops to their death, hoping the same old strategy might work this time. This is wrong. The Great War was a veritable laboratory of new ideas and technology. For about five thousand years prior to this war, a nation had two defence forces: the army on land and the navy on the sea. This didn't change, until on December 17th 1903, Orville Wright successfully launched a heavier-than-air flying vehicle.

The era of flight had arrived just in time for the war and all sides embraced this cutting-edge technology. First it was used for reconnaissance and later air-to-ground attacks and even air-to-air fights which earned the name dog fights. It was all very new and while it can criticised in hindsight for not making enough impact, to have gone from brand new invention to military application in the space of ten years will mean there's going to be some teething problems. Had the generals really been set in their ways, they would have dismissed the novelty of aircraft and not used them at all. Instead, they were used in their thousands; anything to lead to a break in the stalemate.

Then there was JFC Fuller and his invention of the tank. Critics point out that the early tanks could only grind along at four-six miles an hour, hardly the beasts of *blitzkrieg* of World War II. This is not a realistic assessment. The tanks were slow, but they weren't slower than soldiers moving over rough terrain, so it allowed infantry to use them as cover and move along with them. The initial German reaction was to run a mile when they saw these terrifying metal castles roaring towards them, their rifle fire harmlessly bouncing off. True, many broke down, but that's what happens with new technology.

Another new technology was poison gas which turned out to be a waste of time. It needed perfect weather conditions and a guaranteed wind that moved it away from your own soldiers for it to work effectively. War is rarely fought in perfect conditions. Rapidly improving gasmasks meant that the memory of gas being used and its actual impact as a weapon are entirely out of proportion. John Keegan points to just 0.5% of Western Front casualties were caused by poison gas. That's not to diminish the horror of hearing the bell to warn of an incoming gas attack, but as an effective weapon, the simple rifle was better by far. However it's another example of generals trying something new, something that has been exaggerated by poetry and films.

The fact that the Western Front solidified at all is another sign of new technology. Why hadn't this situation ever happened before? The answer is because of food. Even during Napoleon's time he had to keep moving to feed his troops which involved either a massive baggage train of supplies or living off the land. Tens of thousands of troops will strip an agricultural area bare in no time at all. The invention of canned food and railways meant that thousands of tons of preserved food were available to a mass of troops, without them needing to go anywhere.

Because the trenches are just about the only things discussed in history lessons and poetry, I made the assumption (as many people do) that the troops lived most of their lives in the trenches. They didn't. The trenches were the front line, and with any front line, the troops were regularly rotated to re-equip them and allow them to rest. So in reality, a unit would be on the lines for about seven to ten days before moving behind the lines for retraining and recuperation.

Similarly, the poems are about the moments of attack. When they came they were bloody indeed. Prior to this war, casualties were in the thousands; in some of these Great War battles, the numbers are in the hundreds of thousands. It is estimated ten million lost their lives by the end of the war, which makes it one of the bloodiest wars in world history. However, battles were not daily occurrences, and likewise, to preserve ammunition, the trenches were not under constant shelling. Most of the time troops on the front line were cold, wet, tense and complaining about rations, but they weren't constantly being shot at, and after ten days of that they went behind the lines. It was not the four year constant Armageddon of war that I thought it was when I was at school.

Then there was the level of technology at the front line, which at this point favoured defence. The premiere reason was thanks to Sir Hiram Maxim who, in 1884, invented the machine gun. This tubular gun was mounted on a tripod and had a belt of ammunition feeding into the side. Without getting too technical, the difference between a machine gun and a "normal" gun is that the machine gun uses some of the bullet's energy to push out the empty casing and pull in the next bullet. In short, you pull the trigger and the gun keeps firing as fast as it can until it runs out of bullets. The Maxim could pour out about six hundred rounds a minute, ten a second, and it used a rifle calibre bullet that was effective for hundreds of yards. Two men could do the damage of several companies of troops armed with now obsolete muskets.

As the poem "The Modern Traveller" succinctly put it:

"Whatever happens we have got
The Maximum gun, and they have not."

When it came to colonial troops being outnumbered, this wasn't a problem if they had a Maxim.

The issue was that in 1914, all imperial nations had their variant of the Maxim (referred to by the British as a Vickers named after the company that made them). They were cumbersome to move around, but set up in a defensive position with a clear field of fire, and any infantry didn't have much chance against them, particularly when the way was obstructed with barbed wire (another recent invention- light to carry, quick to put up, but as effective as a stone wall in stopping infantry or cavalry).

Because Germany made the first move and had captured most of Belgium and areas of eastern France, it had the advantage; and throughout the war in the West, tended to take a defensive stance, forcing France and Britain to attack these effectively defended positions. Hence the invention of the tank and the creeping barrage.

You could view the Western Front as the largest siege in history, and in the way of sieges as soon as one side had a new weapon, the other side created a counter measure. The Brits created the rolling or creeping barrage where artillery would pound the front, tearing up all the barbed wire, then it would edge forwards and settle on the German lines forcing them to keep their heads down and give precious minutes to the infantry to move from their trenches nearer to the German positions.

Once the barrage lifted there was a frantic rush on both sides- for the Germans to get up out of their concrete reinforced bunkers (a counter-measure to artillery) and set up their machine guns, for the French and Brits to get to the German lines before they could do it (unlike the famous footage of training, nobody walked slowly towards the enemy lines). There were other complications. Not all fired shells detonated, meaning the barbed wire could still be there; and because radios had yet to be used extensively, the whole offensive had to be executed to a pre-arranged timetable. Alterations were made by telephone, which were then relayed up the chain of command. There could be long delays as plans were changed, leading to assaults faltering and territorial gains being lost by German counter assaults.

Had the war happened ten years earlier, there wouldn't have been as many modern weapons on the field, had it happened ten years later, radios and aircraft would have changed the strategic options beyond all recognition. Looking at what actually happened then all sides did the best they could with the technology available to them.

To those who claim the generals showed a lack of initiative or no strategic imagination, it's worth remembering this war saw the first mass use of machine guns and the first large- scale use of modern hydraulic artillery. This clash of empires witnessed the first air war, and on the oceans, the submarine was the new terror of the seas. Tanks were invented to overcome the problems of barbed wire and to bring movement back onto the battlefield. There was more innovation in this war than there had been in the previous one thousand years of conflict. How much more initiative could the generals have shown?

1914 saw a lot of movement. The Germans exploded out in every direction and it was the Anglo-French rapid response to defend what they could that helped set up the trenches but they were not there from the start. There was the "Miracle of the Marne" where a handful of British divisions (all regulars, not the later volunteers) kept a much larger German army at bay. But the Schlieffen plan (the German imperial war plan to win the war in a matter of weeks) meant that the central armies also attacked Russia simultaneously. In all sectors, initial major gains were made before the digging of trenches.

In 1915 knowing that stalemate had occurred in the West, Winston Churchill, the First Lord of the

Admiralty, came up with a plan to knock out the Ottoman Empire (an ally of Germany's) and break the deadlock. The plan to land in the Dardanelles, just a few dozen miles from the Ottoman capital of Istanbul, was a good one and enough men and naval vessels were used to ensure a reasonable chance of success. Unfortunately, the rivalry between the army and navy and the tenacious Turkish defence led to a bloody mess. It should be remembered that the plan itself was a decent one. Worse plans had worked and better plans had failed but it should not be judged as folly because, in hindsight, it didn't work. Churchill, appalled by the debacle, heaped the blame on himself, resigned his post and joined the front lines. More politicians should be made to do that.

In 1916 the Germans attacked, taking Verdun and bringing France to near collapse as it poured almost everything it had into the Verdun area. To relieve this pressure, General Haig had no option but to start his own offensive earlier than he had planned. Had he not, it was likely the Germans would have broken through. As it was, he had to do the best he could to get the German's attention. The area where he launched his offensive was believed to be a relatively lightly defended one near the Somme River.

Now we come to one of the great nation-building legends of Britain: The Somme, the bloody, costly Somme, the battle that claimed more British lives than any other in history. Failed by the leadership and dying in their tens of thousands everyday, soldiers were callously ordered to their graves. The Somme is Britain's biggest military failure. That is the way it is portrayed in the popular subconscious- and it's wrong.

Sixty thousand died on the first day so how can I say this is wrong? The answer is that while the first day was the bloodiest in British history, the strategic reason for the attack was to relieve the dangerous pressure on Verdun- and it worked. France did not collapse. Worse still for the Germans, 1916 cost them 1.3 million casualties. They may have inflicted larger casualties in the Somme than the Anglo-French armies inflicted on them, but it had been a battle the Germans did not want. The Somme had been costly to the central powers, too. It was no German victory, so how could it have been a British defeat? This strategic disaster for Germany meant that in 1917 they were forced to retreat behind the Hindenburg line and start unrestricted submarine warfare to try and knock Britain out of the war, but in the meantime, this desperate and illegal act helped to portray Germany as the international pariah it so desperately didn't want to be seen as.

1917 saw some novel ways to end the war. Germany had been fighting against Russia and slowly winning, but it was running out of men and needed to end the war in the east, so it sent Lenin in a sealed train to Finland where he crossed over into Russia. The Czar had already been deposed and there was a new fledgling democracy. Had Lenin made his way to Russia after all hostilities had finished it was likely he would have ended his days as some kind of socialist intellectual on the fringes of power. Instead, with the new government still getting to grips with power, Lenin started the Russian Revolution, the founding of a communist state. He was so busy fighting his own people, he did what the Germans had hoped for, making peace with the central powers and conceding large amounts of land and resources, so enabling the Kaiser to use all this released potential on the west in 1918.

The Germans also backed Irish nationalists, even landing Roger Casement in Ireland with a u-boat in an attempt to open up a second front for Britain. It worked for a time, with the Easter Uprising and other rebellions requiring the attention of the British government, but it was never big enough to really dent the British war effort.

In terms of creating a "fifth column", the Germans had done very well in Russia and quite well in Ireland; therefore, they decided to go for the hatrick and tried to entice Mexico into invading America. The idea was that the central powers would back Mexico's claims to Texas and New Mexico as a ploy to keep the USA from sending troops to Europe. Mexico at the time was at civil war, so the whole idea was ridiculous, however, it proved to be a pivotal moment in the war. Britain had cracked the German codes and found a bizarre telegram which broke all terms of neutrality with America. America however did not want to be drawn into a European war and despite provocation (the sinking of the civilian cruise liner Lusitania by a German u-boat), had still not gone to war.

The message to Mexico (called the Zimmerman telegram after the German foreign minister) was such a naked act of aggression that when the British brought it before the US government, the Americans assumed it had to be a clever British fake. However, in what has to be one the worst diplomatic mistakes in history, Zimmerman confirmed its authenticity, leaving America no option but to go to war.

It happened not a moment too soon because in 1918, Germany threw all its eastern troops at the western front. This so-called *Kaiserschlact* pushed back the Allies by miles, in some cases taking them past their lines in 1914. It was the last point where the Germans could have won the war. However this offensive, although very dangerous initially, ran out of steam. The allies absorbed the losses and because the Germans had used their crack storm troopers to fight this campaign, their best troops were now dead, wounded or captured.

The Battle of Amiens, which commenced on the 8th August 1918, was the Allied strike back. It achieved total surprise and in one day, thanks to careful coordination of artillery, infantry, air force and five hundred tanks, pushed the Germans back fifteen miles. This is the bit of the war that's forgotten by Britain. It's referred to as The Hundred Days, in hindsight because from August to the German surrender in November, the Allies went from one victory to another, constantly pushing back the German forces. By the end of this three months the Germans had lost more than a million men, killed or captured. This was no stalemate, this was no "draw". This is what victory looks like.

It's strange to think that the 1960s peace movement has something in common with the Nazis, but in just one respect, it does. They have both distorted how the war ended and turned a clear Allied victory into a stalemate. The poetry doesn't help either, because while Siegfried Sassoon and co. may have been great poets, they couldn't know the future; so while they were peerless in bringing the immediacy of the trenches to the reader, they never survived them. Therefore, in our minds, those men are always in trenches, always fighting; but the war did end and it ended to Britain's advantage. While I won't go on and on about the Versailles Treaty, it's worth noting that the war reparations Germany had to pay were similar to the amounts (with inflation) France had to pay Germany after the Franco-Prussian War of the 1870's. So while the terms were punitive, they weren't designed to push Germany into a financial crisis.

The end of the war was not some sort of grand stalemate guaranteeing a future repeat of the war, nor was it seen at the time as futile. If you look at press clippings and diaries from the day, people thought it was a bloody war, a terrible war, but a war worth fighting, with a clear victory at the end.

Indeed Britain came out of it stronger, having inherited most of Germany's overseas colonial possessions. Some areas in the Pacific were now being administered by Australia, so the colonies now had colonies. Britain was not on her knees after this war (you're confusing that with the next one); instead, this was the zenith of empire.

I have talked mainly about "The Western Front" and that is the popular reference of the war, but it was a world war. The Japanese were the first Asian nation to appear as a major force in a world war, and it is surprising to know they fought with the French and British against German territories in the Pacific. Hundreds of thousands of troops were involved in this, but it gets forgotten. Similarly, Britain didn't just fight the Ottomans at Gallipoli. There were years of campaigning in the Middle East; Jerusalem was captured by the British and absorbed into the Empire until 1948.

Russia has done a very good job of rewriting major chunks of its history in the first half of the 20th century. Russia was involved in the war from the very first days; it was Russia's support of Serbia that escalated the conflict in the first place. Millions of Russians died. Poorly equipped farmers were forced to charge against German machine guns, with none of the attempts to support them that the West was trying out. It led to the collapse of Imperial Russia, which is why it's largely forgotten, but for three years, the Russians fought and lost men.

Africa was also involved. A German general called Von Lettow-Vorbeck has the distinction of being the only German general still active and fighting by the end of the war, his force diminished but undefeated. The fighting in Africa was tiny compared to Europe, but it shaped entire African nations (Namibia and Uganda to name two). While there were never any trenches or mud, the land itself was the main enemy, with its disease, monsoon rains and vicious local fauna (one British assault had to retreat due to the amount of wasp stings troops were receiving, rather than through enemy attacks). This is all part of the more rounded view of what happened in the war and once again shows that the overwhelming view of the Tommy sitting in his trench is only part of the story.

Another part involves u-boats and the battle to keep merchant shipping going in the Atlantic. In 1916 when the German fleet tried to break out into the Atlantic, it was stopped by the Royal Navy at the Battle of Jutland. This was the first major sea battle the Royal Navy had to engage in since Trafalgar in 1805 and it was not a pleasing victory. Strategically it did its job and the Germans remained bottled up in port but during the battle the Royal Navy lost more vessels than the Germans, so the Kaiser's navy could claim a tactical victory. This is just one example, but overall, tens of thousands more found their graves in the oceans of the world, and not in Flanders.

The Austrians spent most of the war fighting the Italians in the Alps and it didn't take both sides long to work out they could kill more enemy soldiers by firing at the snow drifts above the trenches to cause avalanches. Thousands were crushed under hundreds of tons of snow.

I have use the term "Germans" for simplicity. The reality was that three empires were on the "Central Powers" side: The German Empire, the Austro-Hungarian Empire and the Ottoman Empire. Bulgaria also sided with the Central Powers too. At the start of the war the Czars of Russia, the Kaiser's of Prussia and Germany, the Austro-Hungarian Emperor and the Ottoman Sultans had all been ruling for centuries, in the case of the Ottomans, since the 1300s and yet, just a few years after this war, all this history, all these outdated absolute monarchs, had been deposed. The only emperor left was George V of England and he was merely a figurehead.

So the war had been the one of the bloodiest in history and yet the death was not over. Soldiers coming in from America were sick with something that initially doesn't sound as scary as The Plague, it was influenza- flu. Influenza often gets confused with a cold. They aren't the same thing, flu is a serious illness and this flu strain was the most virulent and deadly in history. The close contact of thousands of troops in transit across the globe guaranteed the virus spread like wild fire. By the end of 1920 the global pandemic killed between 50-100 million people. This outbreak killed far more people than any war in history and all in the space of just over one year.

Chapter 17 Britain's Fourth World War (also known as World War II)

And so we come to the "big one". This fourth occasion of Britain going to war on a global scale is big in every sense. I have mentioned peaks of interest in historical eras. There is a glut of books and documentaries about the Romans; there is an unhealthy interest in the Tudors; The Napoleonic Wars get a flood of books, but none of these compare to World War II. TV series, major films, video games, documentaries, battlefield tours, and board games- the list is endless. No topic in all of global history gets more coverage than the war of 1939-45. It makes all other areas of history seem untouched by comparison.

I am not going to tackle the war as a narrative; it has been covered too many times by people a lot smarter than I am. John Keegan is again a great place to start and anything by Anthony Beevor is well written and thought provoking; "*Europe at War*" by Norman Davies is also a masterful piece of non-fiction. Instead, I want to use this best known of wars to ask a few uncomfortable questions.

Firstly, why is the Great War the "bad" war and World War II the "good" one? Rough estimates of casualties from 1914-18 are around ten million. In 1939-45, it's sixty million. The first one lasted 4 years the latter 6 years. So why is it that the generals of one war are dolts who didn't care about casualties, and yet the one with six times the amount of death is full of genius generals?

The gut reaction is there was more manoeuvre in World War II (or World War 4 by my count). That may make the maps of the progress of this war far more exciting than the earlier ones, but as a soldier, does it matter how you die? Dead is dead, whether it's from machine gun fire in no man's land or a mortar shell on some Pacific island. If mortality is something to avoid, then that makes World War 4 the worst war, not one to somehow be cherished. By 1939 war had become so industrialised that killing had become staggeringly easy.

Secondly for once in history, everyone can agree that the Nazi regime was an evil one that had to be dismantled. You get no argument from me.

America and the British Empire tried to maintain their humanity in the face of a terrifyingly evil dictatorial machine they were more successful at sometimes than others, but always held the moral high ground. However Britain and America had the Soviet Union as an ally; and while the Nazis were the number one evil in the war, had Hitler not been around, it would be hard not to come to the conclusion that Stalin's dictatorship was anything other than evil itself.

The conundrum was best summarised by that great man of quotes Winston Churchill:

"If Hitler invaded hell I would make at least a favourable reference to the devil."

Why so harsh on Stalin? Undeniably the Soviet effort was key to winning the war, but it didn't start that way.

Germany is remembered as starting the war by invading Poland in 1939, however Germany split Poland with Stalin. It was a cynical land grab where two natural enemies put aside their differences to carve up a helpless neutral country. There follows an event in 1940 that is little known in the West. Stalin ordered Polish nationalist officers to be rounded up and taken to Katyn forest where they were massacred. 22,000 men lost their lives. Later, the Soviets tried to cover it up and claimed the Germans did it (they did far worse), but forensic evidence and NKVD records proved that the Soviets perpetrated this crime, despite what some communist apologists say. This is what Britain's soon-to-be ally was doing before formally joining hostilities.

If killing people is bad and government orders leading to the loss of life of a country's own people is worse, then both Germany and Russia need to hang their heads in shame. Nowadays Germany does. Its citizens are well versed in the horrors the Nazis perpetrated; in Russia it is forgotten. The Holocaust is estimated to have killed six million, however Stalin's Gulags and man-made grain famine in the Ukraine is thought to have killed 5 million. The only thing in Stalin's defence is that he never explicitly set about annihilating specific people, and forced labour camps in Siberia weren't quite the guaranteed death sentence of Auschwitz, but the differences were at times paper thin.

Stalin created two fronts where the first front line fought the Germans; however if they retreated without orders, he had a second line of commissars and NKVD agents who were ordered to shoot anyone who retreated. This second line of troops was usually better armed than the ones shooting at the Germans. This utterly callous arrangement eventually worked, stiffening the resolve of the woefully underequipped Soviet infantry.

There are some who will say I'm being hard on the Soviet Union. Without the killing fields of eastern Europe, the Nazi war machine may well have won. When the USSR became the enemy of the West immediately after the war, its contribution was diminished in western history books- quite unfairly. Therefore 1939-45 is perhaps the best example in this whole book of how complicated history is and how this complexity is reflected in patriotic half memories where uncomfortable truths are hidden beneath flag waving and exciting dramatisations.

So one more uncomfortable truth for Russia before I dish out the credit. The Great Patriotic War (that's what the war is called in Russia) was not fought and won by Russia. There is a huge difference between The Soviet Union and Russia. Most of the fighting took place in the regions of Belorussia and Ukraine, neither of which are part of Russia. While Leningrad and Stalingrad were truly epic moments in history, the Axis powers never penetrated further than 4% into "Russia". It's been estimated that 51% of the Soviet forces were Russian, so there were millions of brave Ukrainian, Tajik, Uzbek, Azerbaijani and Mongol soldiers who have been scrubbed from the Russian memory of the war. While I have used the word Britain, rather than the British Empire, the imbalance in numbers of colonial troops to motherland troops was far lower in the west than in the east.

What I find encouraging despite all the horrors of war, is looking at the war the three main allies, they needed each other to win. Britain was the only one to fight from '39 to '45 (America and Russia both use the years 1941-45, as if all the battles that happened prior to their entry somehow didn't happen). Had it collapsed or been invaded in 1940, America would never have been able to land troops in Europe, and Russia would have had to fight more than a million more Axis soldiers, backed by thousands more tanks and planes that were tied down in the west due to Britain being a clear and present danger. Britain kept shipping lanes open to Russia and was the nation which cracked the German enigma codes. While Britain could never match its two partners in men and resources, in the long run, it was of vital strategic importance.

The Soviet Union was the charnel house of the war in terms of casualties. Stalingrad was the biggest battle in world history. In the months of hard fighting in 1942-3, in and around this city on the Volga, an estimated 1.5 million people lost their lives. It's not unusual that human remains are found when road or building works go on in the city to this day.

Then there was the nine hundred day siege of Leningrad, along with the Battle of Kursk (the largest tank battle in history), the Battle of Narva in Estonia, and the capture of Berlin. All these engagements dwarf Allied efforts like the invasion of Normandy, and yet, hardly any of them get the popular attention of much more minor but western campaigns like El Alamein or the Battle of the Bulge. It could be summarised that the war was won with British intelligence, American money and Soviet blood.

The Eastern Front was as close to the Apocalypse as we have so far had in history. Initially the

German divisions smashed through Eastern Europe, catching Stalin completely by surprise (mainly because he ordered the imprisonment or execution of any agents who told him that the Germans were about to launch an attack, he stopped getting the reports). Stalin lost millions of men, thousands of tanks and aircraft and thousands of miles of territory. It remains the single biggest string of defeats in history, and yet, through ice cold logic, he managed to bully his commanders and soldiers into finally stopping the Germans near Moscow. The Soviet Union fought on to victory despite Stalin, not because of him.

The Eastern front absorbed more than two thirds of the German army. Imagine if that many more troops were waiting for the Allies on D-day. It's not an exaggeration to say that because of the combat deaths, deaths from air raids and artillery, and the rounding up of Jews (either to be machine gunned on the edge of towns or transported like cattle in trains to certain death at places like Dachau), this one front saw more death than the whole of the previous world war.

The Soviet people suffered like no other in history. So when their troops marched west and eventually surrounded Berlin, it was time for revenge. Most conquering armies have lapses in discipline, but it was obviously on the Soviet agenda to make everyone in Berlin pay. This was revenge on a national scale, there were combat casualties but also summary executions and rapes on an industrial scale.

And what of Britain? Britain has an interesting relationship with the war of 1939-45. This was its fourth world war, but unlike the others, while they were undeniably victorious, it felt very much like a defeat. Its original trigger for war was to guarantee Poland's neutrality and independence which was made a mockery when it was absorbed into the Soviet Union against its will. After all that fighting, Poland swapped a Fascist dictatorship for a Communist one.

Hitler had even offered Britain a deal in 1940: as long as Britain left him alone, he would leave Britain alone. Britain would keep its global empire and Hitler would enjoy the fruits of a continental one. To Britain's eternal credit, Churchill turned him down. Britain's policy of enlightened empire was leading to its own self destruction; once a people could show they could self govern, what right did the Brits to be there anymore? The war was a catalyst to this view point, and as India sent hundreds of thousands of men to fight both overseas and against the Japanese on their own borders, it was inevitable that India would become independent once hostilities ceased.

Britain was brave and resolute throughout the war. Its soldiers had performed well in the jungles of Asia, the deserts of North Africa, through the fields and towns of Europe, on the high seas and in the wide open air, but the war exhausted all of its resources. It gained no fruits of victory, no more colonies, no war reparations from its enemies.

Britain had become a spent force fighting its greatest ever threat.

This war had been so destructive that it changed society. This was the point where "empire building" became a dirty word and greater accountability was forced on politicians and generals to reduce the carnage modern war could unleash. Living post-Nuremburg Trials we have become far harsher about any actions of wars. For example in the past it was common practice to surround strongly defended towns and starve them into submission, if an assault was likely to fail. It worked and nobody saw this as an outrage. Nowadays by targeting all occupants, both combatants and non-combatants in a living area, it would be considered a war crime.

This war was the first war that made the whole world pause and think about our destructive tendencies and how to mitigate them to ensure we never have such a devastating war again. It's one problem is now people second guess military actions before this era with the point of view and laws created afterwards. I have already highlighted the folly of this reasoning.

Britain didn't win the war, it was on the winning side, but unlike previous world wars, by the end it was very much the junior partner. It could hold its head up as a moral victor but morality doesn't pay the bills. Britain was broke. America found it so unfathomable that an empire could be financially ruined that it required the great British economist, John Maynard Keynes, to go to Washington and explain it to them. The loan he managed to negotiate saved Britain from starving. Things were literally that bad in Britain. Keynes may be remembered as a great economist, but he may be the only economist who saved lives, and we should remember him for that, too.

Conclusion

So why end in 1945? Mao Zedong was once asked what he thought the impact of the French Revolution was. "Too soon to tell" was his pithy response. He makes a fair point. It feels safer talking about the Vikings than the British Empire. The Vikings did many terrible things, but enough distance exists between us and these past events that there is a grudging respect (even admiration) for their bloodthirsty ways. However with a recent war, it's likely for people to know of ancestors who fought in them, or to have photos of them or even to have met them. Therefore it's not "history", it's still alive, it's still part of "now".

I remember getting up early at a friend's house, going downstairs and bumping into her grandmother. She sat there and told me, out of the blue, that she was informed of her parent's death during the Blitz on her 21st birthday. The horrors of total war were being discussed over a cup of tea and toast while I was still a little bleary eyed. To me, the war was history; to her, it was being replayed in her head on a daily basis.

"When does history start?" Is a complicated question because some early moments of history can become quite politicised (Biblical archaeology being an example), while other events from just fifty years ago are completely forgotten. I have tried to be fair and also tried to unpick some of the neat assumptions that have arisen around certain events.

This has been a brief but, hopefully, interesting journey through British history, from its origins to the 1940s. So what big lessons can be learned?

Firstly there's an issue of nuance. Too often we tend to pigeonhole people into "good" or "bad". Some of the people mentioned did amazing things, but that tells us nothing about their own personal moral fibre. Should we admire these people? Maybe, but beware national heroes because usually it doesn't take much digging to find another, more human and flawed side to them. At the same time, though, we should judge these people in the ethical frame work of their time, not ours.

Secondly, I have mentioned scores of people in this book, but it's interesting how few of them are outright villains. Bad guys are really a myth of storytelling and drama. The reality is far more interesting because, looking at things the other way around, while there are few pure villains in this book, there are absolutely no flawless heroes.

The final conclusion is that nothing is preordained. Almost all of the events mentioned could have played out another way, irrevocably altering the path of history. I don't believe in fate, but I do believe in luck and this random element is more important than any leader, plan or invention.

Printed in Great Britain
by Amazon